Public Relations, Activism Social Change

Why are some voices louder in public debates than others? And why can't all voices be equally heard? This book draws significant new meaning to the inter-relationships of public relations and social change through a number of activist case studies, and rebuilds knowledge around alternative communicative practices that are ethical, sustainable, and effective. Demetrious offers a powerful critical description of the dominant model of public relations used in the twentieth century, showing that 'PR' was arrogant, unethical and politically offensive in ways that have severely weakened democratic process and its public standing and professional credibility. The book argues that change within the field of public relations is imminent and urgent—for us all. As the effects of climate change intensify, and are magnified by high carbon dioxide emitting industries, vigorous public debate is vital in the exploration of new ideas and action and if alternative futures are to be imagined. In these conditions, articulate and persistent publics will appear in the form of grassroots activists, asking contentious questions about risks and tabling them for public discussion in bold, inventive, and effective ways. Yet the entrenched power relations in and through public relations in contemporary industrialized society provide no certainty these voices will be heard. Following this path, Demetrious theorises an alternative set of social relations to those used in the twentieth century: public communication. Constructed from communicative practices of grassroots activists and synthesis of diverse theoretical positions, public communication is a principled approach that avoids the deep contradictions and flawed coherences of essentialist public relations and instead represents an important ethical reorientation in the communicative fields. Lastly, she brings original new perspectives to understand current and emergent developments in activism and public relations brought about through the proliferation of Internet and digital cultures.

Kristin Demetrious Ph.D. Deakin University, Australia.

Routledge Research in Public Relations

1 **Classical Rhetoric and Modern Public Relations**
   An Isocratean Model
   Charles Marsh

2 **Public Relations, Activism, and Social Change**
   Speaking Up
   Kristin Demetrious

Public Relations, Activism, and Social Change
Speaking Up

Kristin Demetrious

NEW YORK   LONDON

First published 2013
by Routledge
711 Third Avenue, New York, NY 10017

Simultaneously published in the UK
by Routledge
2 Park Square, Milton Park, Abingdon, Oxfordshire OX14 4RN

First issued in paperback 2014

*Routledge is an imprint of the Taylor and Francis Group,
an informa business*

© 2013 Taylor & Francis

The right of Kristin Demetrious to be identified as author of this work
has been asserted by her in accordance with sections 77 and 78 of the
Copyright, Designs and Patents Act 1988.

All rights reserved. No part of this book may be reprinted or reproduced or
utilised in any form or by any electronic, mechanical, or other means, now
known or hereafter invented, including photocopying and recording, or in
any information storage or retrieval system, without permission in writing
from the publishers.

Trademark Notice: Product or corporate names may be trademarks or
registered trademarks, and are used only for identification and explanation
without intent to infringe.

Library of Congress Cataloging-in-Publication Data
Demetrious, Kristin, 1958–
  Public relations, activism, and social change speaking up / by Kristin
Demetrious.
    p. cm.— (Routledge research in public relations ; 2)
  Includes bibliographical references and index.
  1. Public relations.   2 Social movements.   3. Social
change.   I. Title.
  HM1221.D46 2012
  659.2—dc23
                               2012033454

ISBN 978-0-415-89706-8 (hbk)
ISBN 978-1-138-92186-3 (pbk)
ISBN 978-0-203-07844-0 (ebk)

Typeset in Sabon
by IBT Global.

For my mother Marjorie Julienne Huntley

Contents

	Acknowledgments	ix
	Introduction	1
1	What Is Public Relations, Where Is Public Relations?	7
2	Agents of Social Change and the Dispersal of Ideas	33
3	"No Protest Zone": Public Relations and the Management of Activism	55
4	Worlds Collide: Public Relations, Activism and Late Modernity	78
5	New Social Realities: Grassroots Activism and Public Relations	102
6	Not Public Relations: Sustainable Communication	129
	Notes	159
	References	161
	Index	173

Acknowledgements

The forces which coalesce to bring a book in to being are complex—something to say, the means to say it, the time to say it. At times each one of these has been a struggle, nonetheless, here it is. I am often gratified by the good hearts and generosity of my colleagues and friends who over the years have helped me with this project which began in 2001, with the conceptualisation of my PhD thesis.

So a special thank you to Dr Patrick Hughes, my principal PhD supervisor. In an office across the corridor, Patrick and I had many long and animated conversations about the thesis and its central ideas, contextualised within my own real life activist campaigns, which served, I believe, to deepen my understanding of the public relations/activism nexus.

Thanks also to Professor David Birch, for his prodigious energy and belief that an understanding of discourse is central to meaningful reform in business practice.

I also owe a debt of gratitude to Associate Professor Christine Daymon. Inevitably Christine's intelligent, strategic and incisive advice got me out of many a flat spot when the complexities of life seemed at times overwhelming.

In researching activist campaigns, many other people have shown kindness and willingness to engage with ideas. In particular, thanks go to Matt Peacock, Thomas Shevory, Harry van Moorst, Simon Birrell, Rue Lees, Stuart McCallum and Iain Lygo.

Warm words of appreciation to colleagues who assisted with drafts: Kay Weaver, Christine Daymon, Phil Connors, Rhonda Breit, Patrick Hughes and Ruth Lee. Their insightful comments greatly improved the work and helped to develop coherence and readability. In preparing the work I thank Deakin University's Elizabeth Braithwaite and Wendy Owen, and Routledge's Liz Levine.

Many of life's other offerings were put on hold while the book was in progress. Special thanks to dear family and friends, to my partner Jim for discussing ideas and encouraging me, and to our children Jannes, Alexis and Eugene, and to Georgia and Annie, Ginny and Caroline for sustaining me with good humour, patience and belief.

Colleagues at Deakin University have been particularly supportive and encouraging over the years, especially in the public relations discipline in the School of Communication and Creative Arts. The Centre for Memory, Imagination and Innovation provided much needed funds to keep the momentum going.

Special thanks go to the School of Journalism and Communication and the Centre for Communication and Social Change at the University of Queensland, for hosting me over a period of academic study leave in 2011.

Finally, to the many grassroots activists that I have worked with over the years, thanks. With your practical wisdom, good character and a commitment to create a better world, working together has taught me so much.

Introduction

Public relations can be highly effective in the promotion of large business interests, but also narrowly self-serving and at times socially autocratic, particularly towards activists who challenge expansionary or protectionist activities. In this book I survey the complex interplay between public relations and activism, within and through the dynamic of social change, which despite its centrality to the powerful political and economic currents determining thought and action in media daily, is one of the least understood domains of communicative culture. Broadly adopting a sociocultural and communicative approach to understanding social change, I analyse the agency of activist groups to act independently of social constraints and the correlation of this to public relations. Thus, public relations and its relationship to activism will be described in terms of their role and characteristics in three stages: in the twentieth century, at a point of transition on the cusp of the new millennium, and those emerging so far in the twenty-first century.

In the main, I concentrate on case studies of public relations and grassroots activism between 1995 and 2003 in the southwest region of Victoria, Australia. Unifying elements in the case studies are that all opposed industries with wasteful, high-risk unsustainable practices and that all campaigns were situated in a severe, extended period of drought. At this time, gardens dried up, water restrictions were imposed and the greater awareness of the consequences, socially and politically, repositioned people's relationship to nature. Each case study offers a different standpoint—but together they are a prism through which to view cultural change when environmental issues are given greater credibility, when there are many political voices, and when the community as a whole experiencing was these uncertainties. Also of interest is the changing political climate over the period of the case studies. In the early campaigns, a rigid, pro-development state government intolerant of dissent dominated the media and political landscape. With this culture came lack of opportunity to engage, but spurred the mobilisation of voices as a collective means of expressing a political end. The instances of activism added up, and contributed to an unexpected change of government. The left-wing opposition party, taken unawares, formed a minority government with independents, which in turn refocused the political agenda on issues raised by activists.

Grassroots activism is a strand characterised by a community-based response, and holistic, strategic campaigns conducted with the minimum of resources. Bold, inventive and effective, these campaigns show that new communication practices and approaches are emerging, seemingly undescribed in public relations literature. Not only this, but in generating support for their ideas, the grassroots activists are also enhancing community understandings of complex issues in deeper and creative ways that are influencing empowerment and participation. For this reason the three case studies I analyse centre on the power, chemical and timber industries in detail within a socio-political theoretical framework.

In general public relations as an occupational and intellectual domain has guarded and protected its authority and terrain, through both its ideologically invested theories and tightly bound professional associations. Regarding activists as hostile intruders, it has sought to keep their perspectives at bay. But some of the most dynamic, creative and effective organisational communication is happening now as activism. Analysing the logic driving grassroots activism and focusing on its unconventional campaigns in action provides for innovative new analytical perspectives. Similarly, the "letting in" of other forms of knowledge and acknowledging their legitimacy, rather than blocking such forms, could potentially change the way public relations and its activities are viewed, and practised in the coming years.

WHEN WORDS FAIL

The public relations industry produces powerful "words." However, contextualised by its dominant position in modernity, at times this is a dangerous product, one that has obscured and impeded the public's ability to engage with processes of social change. Public relations agents working to further the interests of powerful companies, oriented around maximising profits, market share and influence, have confidently been able to approach media outlets to adopt their narratives over others. Their aim is to produce a discursive environment which promotes favourable, even biased, commentary furthering their self-interest. They also are active in the reframing or suppression of relevant facts, such as the strength of community opposition to their activities. In this process activist groups—an important element of civil society—may be singled out and discredited. These political circumstances are exacerbated by journalists failing to take reasonable steps to verify the accuracy of the proffered opinion and promulgating further one-sided support for business. Published time and time again, and often accompanied by visuals imbued with subtle symbolic meanings and metaphoric exchanges, the claims are represented as "truth," and the process goes unnoticed by many of the public lacking in media literacy.

In gaining social traction "truth" travels at high-speed through the many channels of discourses—social media, television, newspapers—to claim a further measure of credibility. In part this is because the "media" in society has unusual potency, as it is a constant and intense point of cultural intersection in modern lives. Media "authors" such as journalists, by extension have the social privileges of "authority" that, by association, link to the special qualities of "authenticity" and "valour" (Foucault 1969, 1). However, for public relations, a schism exists in this relationship because while public relations is involved in the media authorship, many of the public do not know what it "does"—let alone how to find traces of its textual artefacts. Who are the "authors" in public relations and why is it that the only time they do become visible is at moments of shame? Arguably, reluctance to accept public relations as a legitimate profession and an activity that benefits society is in part due to its opacity—both in authorship and artefact—because it fails to demonstrate adequately the coupling of "truth" with courage and wisdom and thus should not have the privileges of "authority."

Our planet is hot and getting hotter: the temperature is .8C higher than at preindustrial levels. As the effects of carbon pollution become more obvious, a mood for change will gather strength and in its wake will be a shift in thinking, ideas and action. And unlike what much of the popular rhetoric suggests, there is no substantive or credible debate within scientific communities disputing that human activity caused the increases in carbon dioxide. There is, however, scholarly debate about the extent to which specific parts of the climate system and the social world will be affected. An example is how increased moisture in the atmosphere will affect rainfall patterns across the planet. Will this mean more droughts, more floods, and for whom? There is also intense speculation about how changes, such as the rising sea levels, will affect managed eco-systems, farms and agriculture and human habitats, our cities and towns. Moreover, what are the consequences of this for social relations, between citizens, governments, and industries (Climate Commission Secretariat 2011worldview 60). But debates like these have been long contested and resisted in modern society. Instead, self-interest and misinformation have confused public discussions, causing potential contributors to dismiss and disconnect from these important issues, or despair, that climate action will not be sufficient or in time to mitigate the manageable effects.

In contemporary society sectional interests have influence, control and powerful agendas working through media and culture. The case I present is simple. The manufacturing of "words" by public relations practitioners and the effects of these words need to be understood beyond marketplace imperatives. I will argue that there are alternative approaches to communicative activities, seen at work in the grassroots activists' case studies at the cusp of the new millennium, which conceptualise knowledge and practice in innovative, holistic and fair-minded ways. And the challenge to mitigate the effects of carbon pollution provides a compelling case for change.

NEW IDEAS, NEW WAYS OF SEEING

Public relations is an object which manufactures appearances, at the same time it is designed to be unseen—as such it is a most singular discursive manifestation requiring special attention (Habermas 1984; 1989; 1995). In order to understand public relations activities better, I use the notion of discourse as a foundation concept to analyse how language is socially constructed (Foucault 1972; Fairclough 1999). Rules of discourse, if applied, can establish a deeper understanding of public relations. For example, public relations and its status and privilege can be understood in relation to the rise of modernity, the changed social and economic conditions associated with advanced trade and capitalism, democracy and class based social structures; and as a corollary to the rapid rise of public opinion. Its legitimacy to "speak" is gained from the gravitas of its industry associations, its admittance to universities, and proximity to powerful communicative, economic, administrative and political spheres. Through these dynamic interactions, the unity of public relations strengthens. In turn it positions subjects, such as activist groups, further on the political fringe. As well as analysing the status, prestige and relationships of public relations as a discourse, I also canvass normative cultural currents in modernity which determine relationships and propel ideas to gain acceptance (Beck 1992; 2002; Beck and Willms 2004; Giddens 1995). Many of the categories in modernity's latter stages are fluid, morphing and hybridising, providing new avenues for business, government and civil activities. Thus to understand public relations and activism differently and with a contemporary focus, I develop a synthetic, inter-disciplinary approach, drawing from communication and media studies, sociology and politics.

To explore ways to develop more accountable and more empowering communicative practices, I apply a citizenship framework to public relations and activist activity (Hudson and Kane 2000a; 2000b; Marshall and Bottomore 1996; Turner 1994). In particular, it is used to clarify the conditions and influences that affect participation and belonging in late modern democratic society. Citizenship theory's intellectual scaffolding is fundamentally robust, standing the test as adaptive and responsive to changing social conditions. The theory in its multifarious forms also assists by shedding light on the politicisation process for individuals and groups and the formation of public opinion. Therefore this framework is pivotal, not just as a lens to view the activities of public relations, but also to evaluate how activists use communication and whether it is anchored to ethically normative structural and cultural frameworks. This is important because the integrity and responsibility in communicative activities apply equally to activists and to public relations practitioners.

Public relations practices shape people's understandings of political issues; for example, policy reforms, or support for interventionist business activities. Inherently political, public relations should thus be viewed and evaluated from a social justice perspective. Underpinning my critical discussion of public relations is the understanding that language is powerful and influences individuals' social development. In large-scale societies, our actions depend on the quality of the information received. To be denied this is to undermine agency and the ability to make informed choices. Language should be treated with the utmost respect; therefore the ways public relations uses language should be scrutinised for its social effects (Christians 1997, 13). Equally, "when things go right" in public relations, as they sometimes do, it is important to have a deeper understanding of the meaning of this and how it can be replicated. To understand approaches in communication and aim for a more inclusive and dialogical mode, I argue that a deeper understanding of the properties of language and communication ethics is essential. Thus it is hoped that this investigation will have benefits for all forms of public relations and its practices by providing new ideas and opening up alternative directions in ethical practice.

CHANGING CONTEXTS FOR UNDERSTANDING

For some readers, focusing on the contentious and fractious intersection between public relations and activism—often with its extreme political consequences—may eclipse, unfairly, the fact that there is other worthy work produced under the rubric of "public relations." Therefore, let me be clear, there are many politically benign and responsible forms of public relations that perform socially legitimate and constructive activities, especially in the areas of preventative health and wellbeing. However, I leave any documentation, description and analysis of such work to other scholars engaged in this research. The remit of this book is particular. It is to focus on and analyse public relations, and investigate its social relations with activist groups opposing high carbon emitting industries. Rather than demonise public relations and/or canonise activists, this book attempts to rebuild knowledge around alternative communicative practices and relations that are sustainable, fair and rational within the uncertain and transforming social conditions of the twenty-first century. The aim is to show that there are other effective forms of organisational communication occurring within dynamic politicised conditions, and, importantly, that within the unity of public relations these are largely unnamed, undescribed and unacknowledged. Broadening the analysis of public relations activities beyond narrow scope of professional practices and institutional sites allows for a more lateral and creative understanding of communicative practices. In addition, the book develops a set of guidelines that underpin an alternative form of social relations, called "public communication."

Perhaps for other readers, the idea of finding an alternative way of social relations other than public relations is idealistic—well-intentioned but not of the "real world." I believe it is realistic to aim for a higher standard of political debate, of citizen engagement and of ideas. Without realistic ideals we would still be bemired in the slave industry, feudalism, and accepting without reflecting. Effecting social change is difficult, and entrenched relations of power should never be underestimated, but language and communicative processes are known ways that can transform meaning. Moreover, social conditions are changing and opening up new possibilities. The twentieth century constituted a dynamic and turbulent period: the insatiable rise of the corporation and the gluttony of consumerism, the rapid uptake of technology and pervasiveness of media cultures. Many of the directions taken were unknown, and sometimes characterised by impunity; people and organisations avoided blame and punishment because they could. In these conditions public relations was a new industry, a new conception of communicative practice, which was powerful and played, sometimes dangerously, with that power. Today, there is a sense that society can do better than this. If we do not aim for more intelligent, thoughtful and fair-minded ways to communicate about complex political issues that affect us and future generations, we all lose.

Lastly, for some readers it will not matter whether communicative activity is called "public relations" or "public communication"; it will be always problematic and always be just "spin." However, a change of name is not what I propose. I concede that communicative practice is a complex area that presents significant challenges, but taking a new trajectory, looking through the lens of the activists, shows it in a different light. In particular, it shows it is important to understand *the practices* occurring under these rubrics. If there is a shift of focus to the communicative practices, away from institutional sites, and a desire to understand them at a new level then it is possible to begin the debate in earnest. The idea of "public communication" emerged from the case studies of grassroots activism and the frameworks and thinkers of my doctoral thesis. However, in this volume, I begin the development of theory around public communication that could be generalised more broadly.

In summary, this investigation of communicative activities aims to comprehend public relations and activism as discourses, how they interact and are entwined, and their effects. Next, it aims to understand and evaluate the social benefit of this activity. Underpinning this analysis is the premise that people need to be able to think, question and organise collectives to take action not only to rein in the excesses of growth and nourish the state, but vital if society is to respond effectively to the unfolding effects of carbon pollution.

1 What Is Public Relations, Where Is Public Relations?

> Public relations activities are often equated with spin, stonewalling, distortion, manipulation, or lying. The media tend to use the term "public relations" in ways that impugn the motives of the organisation or person. When was the last time you heard public relations referred to in a way that did not imply something negative? (Coombs and Holladay 2007, 1)

Activism is a critical social site for interpreting the cultural complexity and power relations of public relations. This chapter argues that within the domain of public relations there has not been enough reflexivity or deliberation of activism and its relationship to social change. The valorisation of public relations within its ranks, coupled with its failure to consider the complexities and role of activism in bringing unsolvable social contradictions to light, has led to insuperable problems in theory and practice, particularly with ethics and, as a corollary, its professionalisation project. This failure to consider activism from alternative, interdisciplinary and imaginative perspectives has led to deep and interrelated problems in society both difficult to identify and difficult to resolve. The chapter argues that a complex understanding of activism is central to unlocking meaningful occupational reform in public relations. In scoping this argument, it attempts to move understanding of public relations beyond the marketplace to its relations towards society as whole. This exclusion of activism, and the inflated belief that public relations "knows best" about what is in the public interest, is deeply embedded in powerful driving ideologies that have been discursively embedded and hence difficult to shift. While there are a few scholars who are trying to reposition public relations' relationship with activism, in the main there are deep structural factors at play, which inhibit any real development in this area. In arguing the case for greater reflexivity and consideration of activism in public relations, this chapter looks at critiques of public relations as a starting point to understand the idea of "PR". Following this, public relations history and roots will be reviewed, in particular, early encounters with social activism. Social theories to contextualise the place of public relations in modern society, including its political ideologies, will be canvassed, as will discursive structures on which its activities can be understood to be constructed. The chapter concludes that these questions are not radical, but central if public relations is to understand its impact, social reality and potential for meaningful reform.

A core criticism of public relations is that it abuses its power in modern media focused societies, in particular this affects the agency of activists to challenge business activities (Dutta 2011; Beder 1997; Demetrious and Hughes 2004). But in public relations it is not just a cavalier practitioner "expert in the art of vague PR" who is subject to the criticism or even nests of corruption that spring up in certain circumstances—rather it is the unity of "public relations" per se that struggles to convince society it has intrinsic worth. This chapter seeks to understand what public relations "is," and why it de-legitimises activism, as a starting point for reform. It argues that existing definitions of public relations, fixed to a functionalist worldview of society, describe only an ideal of what is desirable. They ignore public relations' potent role in relation to discourse and to identity formation, and to agency. At a broad social level, this failure to understand or describe what "PR" is and does, has meant that the extent of its power and the consequences for social life, environment and the development of ideas—have either not been realised or addressed. Acting within these limited constraints, public relations activity and behaviour have been self-serving, overconfident, unscrupulous and ideologically invasive. Hence it has failed to obtain the acknowledgments and privileges that society confers when an occupation is recognised as a specialized professional authority. This is significant, not for status or respectability, but because the establishment of professional credibility in society indicates, more broadly, that the values and ethical standards promoted by an occupational domain's theorists, institutions and practitioners are working and being monitored and renourished. In a study of professionalism in British and American public relations, Pieczka and L'Etang argue that:

> If research interest has been expounded on the study of public relations at the level of career and role (i.e., think individual and institutional levels), then the larger scale interests (i.e., looking at public relations in terms of its engagement with the state and the big social structures of society) has remained a fairly marginal interest. Typically, this has meant that when we engage with knowledge and discourse (rhetoric) in public relations, we link them to improved effectiveness of public relations or, more critically, to the issue of image and presentation. We have not, however, been very bold in looking at the type of "social realities" that professional communication experts construct in their efforts to communicate more effectively. (2006, 271)

Breit and Demetrious discuss the idea that claims to professional status engage with various intersecting elements: discrete knowledge and expertise; ongoing education; a social benefit beyond profits, professional structures; and rules and conventions. (Shudson and Anderson 2009, 89). They found in a study of the international public relations umbrella institution Global Alliance, as well as the Public Relations Institute of Australia and Public Relations Institute of New Zealand, that: "As an instrument of trade and industry, it seems to have developed a weak ethical culture where high standards are espoused but few breaches are brought to light and sanctions for wrong-doing are rare, with only a few complaints being dealt with each year" (2010, 21). Therefore, the movement from "occupation" to "profession" represents an external validation demonstrating that the knowledge, understandings and values that support the public relations work, normatively articulate to wider social contexts.

In unpacking the argument, the chapter begins with a discussion of the history of public relations and then moves into an analysis of public relations effects and relations to power in modern society. The research trajectory, in an attempt to say new things, will draw on a two-pronged analysis: first an investigation of the surface effects or normative activity of public relations, and second: a deeper investigation of communicative structures on which public relations is founded.

A MONSTROUS INDUSTRY

Despite the fact that it is a growing and highly profitable industry sector—the public relations industry grew by just over 8 percent in 2010 (The Holmes Report 2011)—the reputation of public relations as an unscrupulous practice peddling lies, deceit and "spin" is promulgated frequently in the media. Remarking on this is Darryl Siry, CEO of a software service for PRs and journalists wrote an article called "why is Such a Valuable Industry so Frequently Maligned?" in which he comments:

> Nary a week passes without some journalist or blogger writing a screed lambasting PR people or the PR industry as a whole. There are even entire blogs dedicated to bad pitches or embarrassing exchanges between journos and PR. Generally, satisfaction levels among companies using PR agencies is not great either. Yet the PR industry remains a thriving industry, estimated at $6 billion in the US alone ($7.5 billion if you include media relations services). It is also growing . . . and profitable. What gives? (Siry 2010)

The schism between the dubious standing of public relations and its clear profitability as a business sector is brought into relief by social theorist Noam Chomsky who in the 2003 Canadian documentary film *The Corporation* refers to public relations as a "monstrous industry," lending support to powerful corporations' intent on reducing citizens to "mindless consumers":

> We have huge industries, public relations industry, monstrous industry, advertising and so on, which are designed from infancy to mould people into this desired pattern. (Achbar and Abbott, 2003)

This criticism is severe and is anchored to an understanding of the importance of civil society and citizenship in democratic society. Civil society broadly refers to the promotion of citizens' political engagement and development and "a lively, vibrant space, full of argument and disputation about matter of greatest import to its citizens" (Lyons 2001, 207). It follows then that the more robust the civil society, the more cooperative, fair and productive the society. Thus, civil society, sometimes called the third sector, is integral to the concept of democracy. It centrally positions the social importance of individuals and organised groups acting outside the state and business realms, such as trade unions, charitable groups, associations and activists in nourishing ideas and building the common good. According to Verrall (2000, 191) civil society should be characterised by "openness, overlapping memberships, voluntarism, and democratic internal organisational structures." Citizenship as a broader concept is concerned with political inclusion, the distribution of resources and participation in democratic society. The sub-concepts of active and passive citizenship are useful to understand individuals' responses to participation in civil society and its institutions. "Passive citizenship" describes the right or entitlement to be a member of society, without the extended role of making a contribution in public life or creating the capacity to participate or defending the rights of others. "Active citizenship" is the idea of involvement or participation in the public life of a community that nurtures a sense of belonging which in itself is seen as a civic virtue. Examples are environmental or corporate citizenship where citizens have a sense of moral obligation to issues that are important to their global communities and act as bearers of responsibilities, rather than bearers of rights (Kane 2000, 223–224). Thus for Chomsky, public relations transmogrifies the "citizen" into the "consumer" and by deeply offending these democratic ideals, is dangerous on a number of social levels.

However, Chomsky's view of audiences as passive receivers of mass manipulation engages with the transmission model of communication, which in turn is "closely linked to the popular use of propaganda techniques in the United States and Europe in the early decades of the 20th century. Indeed according to Weaver, Motion and Roper "there is a direct relationship between stimulus-response transmission theories of communication and the beliefs espoused by Lippman, Lasswell, and Bernays" (2006, 10). Moreover, underpinning these early communication research and institutional practices was a strong belief in positivism. For Lindlof and Taylor (2002, 8) positivism as it was used in communication sought to explain behaviour and provide the means for its predication and control, for example in media effects research. Deeply entrenched, positivism is a paradigm which claims that the social world is a mirror of the natural world and that a testable hypothesis will produce a social fact (Deacon et al. 1999, 4). It is associated with structural functionalism, a model of society that views it as equivalent to an organism in the natural world, in which each element, for example, church, business, state, performs a function which ultimately produces a 'healthy' or 'well' society to one degree or another (Deacon et al. 1999). However, by the second half of the twentieth century, critiques of positivism challenged its "core premises and practices" and as a result, communication researchers looked for other methods (Lindlof and Taylor 2002, 9). For Daymon and Holloway qualitative methods offer the means "To study complexity, power relations and the co-construction of meaning in a holistic or critical sense" (2011, 5). Thus for Weaver, Motion and Roper, critiques such as Chomsky's are "surprising" given "the discrediting of transmission stimulus-response models and their replacement by transactions models in which there is "acknowledgement of the active receiver, the obstinate and recalcitrant audience" (2006, 11).

Given views like these circulate widely, recent years have seen public relations theorists attempt to "rethink," "reconceptualise," "reconfigure" the reputation public relations (Moloney 2006; Macnamara and Crawford 2010; McKie and Munshi 2007). Although these lengthy justifications may lead to theoretical discussion and even a narrow refashioning of ideas, they do not fix the problems in any substantive way and go largely unheard by an impervious and sceptical public. Public relations theorists Timothy Coombs and Sherry Holladay discuss why the disparaging views associated with the practices of public relations are so difficult to sway:

> People tend to regard anything labelled as "public relations" with great suspicion. Colloquial usage reflects a lack of understanding of the nature and practice of public relations. We have focused on the media's (mis)use of the term because most people do not have direct experience of the actual practice, and are dependent on the media in forming their ideas about it. The negative impression given may lead people to wonder if society would be better off entirely without public relations. (2007, 1)

These statements, from within the domain of public relations, are significant in a range of ways. Firstly they imply that the very idea of "public relations" as an entity or a thing in the public's mind is not formed: what it is, what it does, what it looks, feels and sounds like, and why it is of benefit to society. Secondly, they suggest that any ideas that have formed are more akin to doubts, tinged with mistrust. Lastly they suggest that the public has very few direct experiences of public relations, hence the media, largely negative, is the "authority" speaking to uninformed audiences. However, Coombs and Holladay suggest that, structurally, public relations is plainly unable to address this criticism either theoretically or in practice:

> There is no magical code of conduct that will solve all ethical concerns experienced by public relations professionals. Anyone who offers the one-size-fits-all ethical solution is viewing the context of public

relations too simplistically. . . . The best advice is that public relations practitioners must listen and utilize two-way communication to be ethical. Two-way communication sets the stage for mutual influence. You cannot be influenced by a group if you never hear it. . . . Ethics ultimately reside with the individual. People can choose to abuse any public communication, and public relations is no exception. The ethical outcomes of public relations actions are governed in large part by the ethics of the practitioner, not the structure of the public relations practice or well meaning codes. (Coombs and Holladay 2007, 48)

Kevin Moloney's book "Rethinking Public Relations" (2006) is another critical assessment of the practice of public relations and its relationship to democracy and with a plea that the domain be rethought. Moloney defines all public relations as propaganda—one sided, selective and manipulative but inevitable because it is "rooted in the pluralist, self-advantaging promotional culture associated with liberal democracy (2006, 168). Moloney challenges as idealistic, the assumptions that underpin the "Grunigian paradigm" (139). His argument reads that rather than try and fit a square peg (public relations) in a round hole (the common good) via such constructions as the two-way symmetric model of balanced communication, it is better to admit its self-serving flaws because "We cannot wish PR away" (176).

Having mapped out this territory—that is public relations is all propaganda but we have to learn to live with it—Moloney argues that with the right approach it should work, on balance, to society's benefit. This is achieved by people's greater capacity to practice and the development of their critical abilities to deconstruct public relations in all its forms, in other words, media literacy. These are laudable sentiments, but more work is to be done to achieve any meaningful capacity to deconstruct public relations. For example in relation to unethical public relations Moloney discusses that an antidote is in the form of an individual's vigilance, likening this to 'caveat emptor' in "neutralising the negative effects" (96). But it is not clear how these 'negative effects' manifest and what precisely "neutralising" means, especially in relation to unequal power relations for different groups in society. Nor is it clear just how corporate monopolies or collusion between state and business interests augment these negative effects. Underpinning this strategy is also an assumption that individuals and groups have the desire, time and resources—to analyse, understand and address unethical and concealed public relations, and its myriad changing forms.

Critics from within and outside public relations agree that change is necessary, and while there is a group of scholars within public relations bringing new voices, perspectives and understandings to questions of power, ethics and influence, there is still more work to be done in bringing a viable alternative that can overcome the seemingly intractable elements described so far.

"PUBLIC RELATIONS COUNSEL": A CONTRADICTION OF TERMS

Going to the heart of the uneasy relationship between public relations and society is the contested idea of the "public" in modernity. This is very evident in 1920s United States landmark writings about public relations. Edward Bernays intellectualised the field by hybridising management theory, with journalism, advertising, political science and social psychology. He also progressed the idea and professional status of public relations in *Crystallizing Public Opinion* (1923) and *Propaganda* (1928). As such he is still retains high standing as the "father of modern PR" especially in the US (Tench and Yeomans 2009, 10). Underpinning Bernays ideas is that, democratic organisation works on two levels: seen and unseen. Therefore while there may be an *appearance* of a democracy, in reality this does *not actually* perform the function of government; rather that role is performed by unseen manipulators that control the public's "organised habits and opinion." In fact Bernays weakens and hence destabilises the notion of "democracy" in *Propaganda's* first lines when he promotes the idea of legitimately manipulating the "masses" for the common good:

> The conscious and intelligent manipulation of the organised habits and opinions of the masses is an important element in democratic society. Those who manipulate this unseen mechanism of society constitute an invisible government which is the true ruling power of our country. (Bernays 2005, 37)

Invoking the metaphor of society as a human body, Bernays describes this elite group as belonging to a "natural order" and thus having superior capacity to act in the masses' best interests by pulling "the wires which control the public mind" (2005, 38). Typical of social Dawinism theories in the nineteenth century, Bernays creates an intellectual alliance between these functionalist ideas and evolutionary theories of natural selection that legitimised social progression of some groups over others.

The grey area of democratic political theory in Bernays' argument is the conflict between an assumption of tolerance and an expectation of diversity. Around the time that Bernays was writing, this conflict of oppositional elements in democratic theory was also the subject of the book *Public Opinion* by Walter Lippmann published in 1922. Miller argues that Lippmann was the source of Bernays' "vision" and his "intellectual hero" (2005, 16). In *Public Opinion* Lippmann argued that it was an "intolerable and unworkable fiction" to imagine that every citizen could capably proffer opinions about policy debates; rather "public opinions must be organized for the press if they are to be sound" (2010, 22). Accepting this point Bernays took it a step further: "it remains a fact that in almost every act of our daily lives, whether in the sphere of politics or business, in our social conduct or our ethical thinking, we are dominated by the relatively small number of persons—a trifling fraction of our hundred and twenty million—who understand the mental processes and social patterns of the masses" (2005, 37–38). Bernays' writings (2005, 39) show he was aware that persuasive communicative practices had their critics both as the "manipulation of the news" and "the inflation of personality." Despite the knowledge that complex relations of power were embedded in the communicative process, in Bernays' mind, the disconnect between the ideal of democracy and the "unworkable" reality overrode these criticisms and public relations was, quite justifiably, essential in maintaining orderly life.

Nonetheless, the questions raised by Bernays and Lippmann about how the ideals of democracy are actually applied in practice were also raised by others. Noted political theorist John Rawls also asked "how is it possible for there to exist over time a just and stable society of free and equal citizens, who remain profoundly divided by reasonable religious, philosophical, and moral doctrines?" (1993, 4). To resolve this Rawls goes deeper into the principles of equity and fairness in democratic theory. However, Bernays does the opposite. He seeks to theoretically reconcile this contradiction by transmogrifying the principles on which democratic culture is founded. Indeed, Bernays does more than "bend" the concept of democracy to fit with his views, he opens the schism wider. Thus from the outset, public relations was conceptually weak and was anchored to a flawed logic that affected its credibility and suitability in democratic society. So while *Propaganda* discusses the role of the "citizen" in democratic society, it "is primarily a sales pitch, not an exercise in society theory" (Miller 2005, 17).

Propaganda exposes other reifications that provide valuable insight into the ideas, beliefs and values to which public relations activity is anchored. One of these, as Miller points out, is a gendered understanding of the "crowd" as female "in its feverish responsiveness" and the propagandist's power as "cool and manly" (2005, 21). He argues that this idea stemmed from nineteenth century positivism and was commonplace around the time Bernays was writing. Indeed, Bernays' writings depict the public as vulnerable, bewildered, and yielding to the wise counsel of men "who govern, mould minds, form tastes and suggest ideas" (2005, 37). The wise male counsel steers the unsteady public through the confusing array of choices; they are able to excavate people's deepest desires and deliver pleasure to them: "The new propaganda, having regard to the constitution of society as a whole, not infrequently serves to focus and realize the desires of the masses" (2005, 57). So while the crowd has agency, it is disorganised, and therefore must be directed and controlled for its own good. On the other hand, the category of individual citizens, denoted as male, appears stable in its characteristics.

Bernays' intent in *Propaganda* was to establish the new profession of public relations counsel. In doing so he established the idea of an institution identifying a grouping or association for the purpose of social control.

Linking this to a workable form of social equality, Bernays argues that "This invisible, intertwining structure of groups and associations is the mechanism by which democracy has organized its group mind and simplified its mass thinking" (2005, 44). More generally, Bernays' ideas about groupings and associations that can be organised to influence thinking and action equates to the widespread institutional strategy and practice of targeting "publics" in public relations that gained traction in subsequent years (Grunig and Hunt, 1984; McElreath 1997, Coombs and Holladay 2007). Bernays, in discussing the many different types of "groupings and associations" and their intersections, includes a political reference to a member of a "league for or against prohibition or of a society for or against lowering the tariff" (2005, 44). While not using the term "activist", Bernays referred to the individual's engagement with political processes and civil society and thus founded public relations on an irreconcilable contradiction leading to insuperable problems.

The two reifications discussed so far: the reworking of democratic principles to fit with public relations practices, and the gendered view of the public as needing guidance, provide insight into public relations relationship to activism and social change. For example, in public relations a problem is defined when groups resist or refuse to yield or consent to the "special pleader who seeks to create public acceptance for a particular idea or commodity" (Bernays 2005, 45). This is compounded when they are openly hostile and fight back as activists do. From a public relations perspective this transgression and unfettered agency represents a threat of the most fundamental kind to the smooth conduct of society and its social order. The righteousness of reigning in social unrest was coupled with another functionalist view in early modernity, that of social friction and resistance as useful in keeping the constitutional system vigorous. Thus Bernays states with confidence: "Small groups of persons can, and do make the rest of us think what they please about a given subject. But there are usually proponents and opponents of every propaganda, both of whom are equally eager to convince the majority" (2005, 57). These convictions suggest that in public relations the "intelligent few" know better than the "ineffective and disorganised masses" and "self-interested proselytizing minorities". It suggests that early and later iterations of public relations were permeated by a self assured belief in their natural dominance in order to achieve the "smooth functioning of society". These convictions constituted a particular type of "Other"—that of marginal "publics" or activists—that needed but resisted guidance and had the potential to intervene in normative structures and upset power relations.

"TRUE PUBLIC RELATIONS": EARLY AND EMERGENT DIRECTIONS

Critical to a deeper understanding is the triangulation of news as commodity, the idea of a mass audience, and public opinion as a corollary of democracy. First published in 1962 and written by Jürgen Habermas, *The Structural Transformation of the Public Sphere: An Inquiry into a Category of Bourgeois Society* is a socio-historic discussion of the public sphere. This is a conceptual space, separate from the state, where citizens, in a free and open way, engage in dialogue and debate focused around issues for the common good. Its genesis can be traced to early Greek and Roman democracies within the social patterns of the *polis* or city and the idea of *lexis* or discussion. In this context, issues of social importance were clarified by citizen discussion because: "only in the light of the public sphere did that which existed become revealed, did everything become visible to all. In the discussion among citizens, issues were made topical and took on shape" (Habermas 1995, 4). The idea of the public sphere, as a centre of self-interpretation that promotes the good of its members, gained acceptance in succeeding societies and periods, including modernity (Habermas 1995, 3–5). In tandem, the rise of European trade and capitalism created a new middle class with substantial power. It was these conditions that had empowering effects on who developed a distinct communicative activity, one where the legitimacy to take on a political, civil or commercial role in society was linked, not just to law, but to the collective opinion of the people. Thus the public sphere was the realm of communicative activity "now casting itself loose as a forum in which the private people come together to form a public, readied themselves to compel public authority to legitimate itself before public opinion" (Habermas 1995, 25). By the eighteenth century, Habermas claims that people were using communication "without historical precedent" as the organising point and the process by which to critique their lives using reason (1995, 27).

The idea of the public sphere is important to understand how public discussions that shape understanding and meaning develop within Western media focussed society. However before we proceed, it is important to acknowledge that there are many challenges and criticisms to Habermas' concept of the public sphere. For example Andersen (1997, 314–315) argued that the concept is flawed as the "public sphere" is bound by socio-economic and socio-sexual structures that prevent citizens from equal participation, for example women. She also argues that it is idealistic as it never was "public" in an open and equal way. Instead its early formation reflected the privileges of emerging bourgeois class. Therefore the idea should always be considered in relation to normative conditions.

Public relations is quite singular to other media industries and Habermas is one of the few prominent social theorists to pay it special attention. He argues that for public relations to be successful consumers develop a false consciousness and believe that they are actually making a decision based on their own judgement about what is good for society. Indeed for Habermas, public relations is an insidious and controlling instrument used by specialised commercial interests to create consent and acceptance. In particular, he thinks it is more subversive, politically oriented and powerful than advertising because it exploits and invades the processes involved with the formation of public opinion. In a double blind, people "think" they are thinking for themselves but are actually being controlled to "think" in this manner. In this way the presence of public relations in the socio-democratic processes negatively affects the development of rational agreement arising from exchanges of different opinion (Habermas 1995, 195). For Habermas, this form of publicity in modernity is dangerous for democracy because it strengthens prestige and position, without drawing attention to unwanted discussion. Organisations and functionaries become interested in representation, not just from the outside, but as a form of legitimisation (Habermas 1995, 201). Of concern for Habermas is that, for some people, this relationship between business, politics and the media is formless and its effects on society difficult to understand and see.

In a later work, Habermas (1989) builds on these ideas, arguing that communicative action is the structural basis for social theory because language is the mechanism used to coordinate activities in modern societies. He explains that, when communicative action such as rational argument and debate is applied to a goal-oriented or teleological outcome, it leads to agreement and understanding of the human world (Habermas 1989, 397). For Habermas (1984) the term 'rationality' presupposes an association with knowledge. But herein lies a fine distinction: for Habermas rationality does not imply knowledge but how the "speaking and acting subjects acquire and use knowledge" (1984, 8). This means that if the speaking and acting subjects express knowledge in ways that are congruent with notions of reliability, objectivity and in goal-directed actions, then knowledge is deemed rational in relation to the norms and conditions of the time. Thus being seen as "rational" is crucial to the success or failure of public relations and of activists.

Habermas' (1984, 1989) refinement of the concept of rationality leads to his premise that in modern societies an individual subject may respond to two aspects of reason to coordinate action. The first form of rationality is instrumental, which implies a teleological outlook, used to create systems that appear to be totally rational, for example engineering. Again, the appearance of rationality is an important point, because Habermas argues that there is sometimes confusion between this "system rationality" and what he calls "action rationality" which leads to an inability by participants to separate the two (Habermas 1989, 333). System rationality refers to instrumental reasoning that is successful to the extent that people integrated in its maintenance assume it has higher order of rationality, and lose sight of its original purpose. This is a case that might be argued in relation to public relations when campaigns that are designed around a narrow instrumental goal prevail and lose sight of broader collective goals or the common good. The second form of rationality for coordinating action is communicative; this implies an interpretative consensus of understanding and mutual agreement, for example that is reached in church and community centres on issues such as morality and law (Habermas 1984). However, the situation according to Habermas (1984, 397), is that in the modern world "religious-metaphysical world views lose their credibility" and, together with an "instrumental reason that has gone wild", converge to override the conditions that support communicative action. Another essential element of the conditions in which communicative action takes place is the self-structuring of its symbols by the interpretative accomplishments of its members. Therefore, for Habermas (1984) a society saturated by media images and symbols gives the appearance of communicative action but not in authentic ways that contribute to communicative rationality and morality. These theories are useful for understanding how public relations interacts with activists who publicly contest the legitimacy of risk-producing industries in late modernity. In particular, they show how public relations, as the instrument of the system rationality, can be presented to the public in the guise of communicative action, to gain a higher order of credibility in society and undermine the activists' claim to rationality and interpretative consensus as well as losing sight of what's important socially. Being both instrumental and teleological, public relations is indeed successful within financial terms and because of this, confers upon itself misplaced legitimacy.

Industrialist capitalist societies favour the growth of technology over moral progress. For Habermas instrumental and communicative reason corresponds to two dimensions in modern society: the system (technological progress) and the lifeworld (moral progress) (1989, 118). He defines the lifeworld as an encompassing concept of the everyday and the lay that is "intuitively accessible" and implicitly bound up with the notion of communicative action and "the totality of sociocultural facts" (136). As discussed Habermas argues that the problem with rationality in modern society is the imbalance between economic and technological progress, on the one hand, fuelled by ideas about growth and capitalism, and on the other moral progress which is conferred lower status. These conditions lead to many social pathologies or ills in modern societies. However, he argues that an extension of communicative reason and by getting the balance right between technological and moral progress can overcome these problems. He says that, when this is achieved, there will be a fairer, more mature society where progress is measured in more complex ways than just scientific advancement. Public relations has found its place in modern society as a form of system rationality and instrumental reason, that invokes the lifeworld through its use of symbols and signs to give an appearance of communicative action while all the while reinforcing system rationality. This explains its opacity and how this contributes, not just to its singularity, but to the general suspicion of its practices and motives.

Historically, Habermas (1995, 193) locates the political practice of public relations as an activity first in nineteenth century North America, when practitioner Ivy Lee worked for the President of Standard Oil Company, John D. Rockefeller Senior, and with the Pennsylvania Railroad to develop counter-attacks targeting social reformers and promote his public image. At that time the U.S. was increasingly "[a] nation dominated by laissez faire, dedicated to the status quo and paying homage to the dollar as a symbol of success." However social reformers or so called "muckrakers" "shocked" the newly literate public "into awareness that this was not the best of all possible worlds" (Weinberg 2001, xvii).

> The nation was one of contrasts. Millions of immigrants who had come to the United States were ghettoed into tenements in growing cities, working in factories, doing the rough and menial work; millions of others moved westward to close the frontier. Americans of older stock, second and third-generation Americans, made up the middle class, the white-collar workers, the owners of small businesses, and the professionals. At the top, the business tycoons—the speculators who directed the beef, iron, railroad and oil industries—lived in grandeur and luxury in palaces and on the Gold Coasts of cities. (Weinberg 2001, xvii)

Ida M. Tarbell, one of the social activist writers, described the events of "The Oil War of 1872" in her powerful 1903 essay. She wrote about the ruthless tactics of the expanding Standard Oil Company, and in particular how it conspired with the "railroad kings" to force rival independent oil producers out of business. She argued that Standard Oil did this by creating the South Improvement Company, which, over time, was revealed as their proxy. Her lucid and detailed account ended with a stinging personal observation of its Baptist leader. She catalogued his respectability, clean living, and good works all the while showing the seamless way he was able to rework the notion of "justice" and "rights" to sit comfortably with the effects of his ruthless business behaviour:

> There was no more faithful Baptist in Cleveland than he. Every enterprise of that church he had supported liberally from his youth. . . . He gave unostentatiously to many outside charities of whose worthiness he was satisfied. . . . Yet he was willing to strain every nerve to obtain for himself special and illegal privileges from the railroads which were bound to ruin every man in the oil business not sharing them with him. Religious emotion and sentiments of charity, propriety and self-denial seem to have taken the place in him of notions of justice and regard for the rights of others. (Tarbell 2001, 38)

Tarbell's description of Rockefeller's contradictory morality is typical of some public relations activity. On the one hand public relations can be ruthless and manipulative: for example conducting detailed investigations into the histories and identities of their critics and developing dossiers for possible legal challenges as well as stymieing public concerns by suppressing important information which could affect public policy and practices, or by flooding the media with diversion statements. Or it can be benevolent and generous with high profile members chairing boards of management, acting as patrons of the arts, serving on valued government committees, raising funds for non-profit organisations, or sponsoring the needy thorough scholarships and gifts. However Dutta (2011, 260–261) explains how philanthropic practices directed at disadvantaged communities can paradoxically serve the organisation's interests. Labelling this process "co-optation" as distinct from "social change," he says this occurs when participation is "constituted within the politics and economic agendas of the mainstream" (2011, 260). Therefore, philanthropy, which directs resources and prestige to favour particular organisations over others has a social agenda and thus political characteristics. In this way charitable practices that seem compassionate and generous can be a platform for hegemonic control that "often ends up serving the agendas of the status quo" (Dutta 2011, 260).

The "muckraker era" rose in tandem with a wider reading public who were able to access "cheap mass-circulation periodicals" and public education (Weinberg 2001, xiv). A precursor to investigative journalism, the movement sought to expose the deepening social inequity and excessive concentrations of wealth and power in the young American republic. Significantly the muckrakers' efforts saw the "court of public opinion," to a greater extent, being harnessed to challenge the authority of corporations which in turn set into motion the passage of laws and regulations that could affect their actions in the marketplace. However, it also legitimised the crusading outsider as an enduring and powerful social actor in democratic organisation. On the one hand this development stands between the somewhat bleak prospect of degraded democratic and communicative processes in the modern society discussed by Habermas (1995), and on the other, the cavalier optimism about its enhancement through the practices of public relations discussed by Bernays (2005). The intersections between Tarbell, Rockefeller and the Standard Oil case are noteworthy, firstly to show how modes of communication expressed the contradictory morality of a large and aggressive business, and secondly as a cultural marker where public relations activities collided with a social actor seeking to intervene in the status quo through social critique.

PUBLIC RELATIONS THEORY: RETURN ON INVESTMENT

By the twentieth century mainstream public relations were concerned, almost exclusively, with the use of communication by large corporations and governments (Wilcox et al. 2000; Hendrix 2001; Cutlip, Center and Broom 2000). Indeed, according to McElreath, public relations' goal-oriented programs of management began "as a way for an organisation to generate positive publicity that might offset public pressures to regulate big business" (1997, 6). According to Coombs and Holladay this "corporate-centric view" of public relations is entrenched and they advocate for greater attention to be paid to "the role of activists in public relations" (2012, 347–353). Arguing that activists are using communication in strategic and planned ways, Coombs and Holladay believe that including their activities in public relations "holds promise for re-imagining the field and legitimizing the works of activists as an important component in public theory and research" (2012, 347). There is merit in these ideas which in turn could promote greater tolerance and breadth of views within public relations companies, educational institutions and public relations' professional associations. However, annexing activism to public relations, and focussing internally on institutions and occupational practices has limitations. Supporting these sites is a narrow focus on consumption and production, and hence functionalism and the associated positivist paradigm. I argue that a more tangential and original understanding of communicative practices, and the problems associated with activism will be achieved, only when they are disarticulated from productive forces, and instead focus on the *variables* of organisational communicative practices (Baudrillard 1990, 105). In order to delve further into why the discourse of mainstream public relations excludes activism this section examines the ideas, the attitudes and the beliefs that are absorbed in its theory.

While the dominant worldview in public relations was functionalist, it was linked to a range of intellectually allied ideas, including the political philosophy of pluralism. Frequently referred to in its literature (Cutlip, Center and Broom 2000; Hendrix 2001; Wilcox et al. 2000), under this model of society, all participants—including activists—have access to various forms of power, with the State as an umpire adjudicating on problems and conflicts that are difficult to resolve. These ideas tend towards a free market view, where generally business activity is not held back by government. Indeed Galston argues that liberal pluralists want to limit the extent that law and authority restrict the individual and "endorse the minimum conditions of public order" (2005, 3). But, he also claims that liberal pluralists endorse the governmental frameworks that organise society's morals and values. He says that this is to protect its social decency and the common good, in areas such as tyranny, disease and humiliation (Galston 2005, 3). He argues that from this position "liberal pluralist government is paradoxically both limited and robust" (Galston 2005, 4). Thus to maintain "harmony" in society, pluralists emphasise the importance of alternative or countervailing groups, like activists, in their role of limiting the influence of powerful groups such as business in creating the so-called "level playing field" (Smith 1993, 16–17).

In particular, the evidence of the association between public relations and pluralism is quite apparent in this definition from the World Assembly of Public Relations that constructs an "organisation" and the "public" as two separate domains of self-interest whereby the soothing influence of public relations can be applied. Therefore, for the authors this does not imply conflict or strike a discordant note precisely because this interplay between competing groups is legitimately part of the social framework (Galston 2005). Indeed, they state that social analysis and the management of programs of action through the "art and social science" of communication management can serve both organisations' and the public's interest in a harmonious balance:

> Public relations practice is the art and social science of analysing trends, predicting their consequences, counselling organization leaders, and implementing planned programs of action which serve both the organization's and public's interest. (World Assembly of Public Relations in Mexico City, 1978, cited in Wilcox et al. 2000, 5)

Echoing this theme is the Official Statement of Public Relations from the Public Relations Society of America (PRSA). Clearly functionalist, it defines society as "pluralistic" and cites the existence of competing groups and institutions as evidence. Used in public relations education and widely known, this "Official Statement of Public Relations" appears in key public relations education texts, such as Wilcox et al. (2000), Hendrix (2001) and Cutlip, Center and Broom (2000), and promotes public relations as a socially useful, necessary and important part of society:

> Public relations helps our complex, pluralistic society to reach decisions and function more effectively by contributing to mutual understanding among groups and institutions. It serves to bring private and public policies into harmony. (Horton, 2007)

Therefore while this "Official Statement" could apply equally to activist or corporate organisations, it actually excludes activism. This is because the general thrust of public relations literature is oriented around a belief in the promotion of business interests, through which greater social good or benefit will be achieved. When not-for-profit organisations are discussed in positive terms, they are usually politically benign and have the organisational features of a large business. The association between public relations and pluralist political philosophy is found also in Grunig and Hunt's definition of public relations as "the management of communication between an organization and its publics" (1984, 6). Theoretically it can apply equally to activism as to any other sector of society but in this work Grunig and Hunt (1984, 320) generally discuss a politicised form of activism in the context of challenges to organisations. For example they write: "More-activist groups, such as the Sierra Club or Clamshell Alliance, use confrontational techniques to pressure organizations to change or to secure government regulation" (Grunig and Hunt 1984, 321). Indeed the notion of "harmony" more aptly a euphemism for "conquest" is evident in this quote that relates to a planned and systematic gauging the popular reach of "environmental publics".

> A great deal of research was done in the 1970s to determine how much concern people have for the environment. This research showed concern for the environment was—to use a cliché—"a mile wide and an inch deep." Many people say they care, but only a young, liberal group of activists do much about their concern (321)

A central flaw in one of Grunig and Hunt's four models of public relations that purports to describe "balanced communication" between groups, sheds further light on the schism. The four models are: publicity/press agentry, public information, two-way asymmetric and two-way symmetric models (1984, 27–43). However a problem is that Grunig's and Hunt's two-way symmetric model assumes that power and influence is evenly distributed in society and that to some extent balance and symmetry can be achieved between organisations and publics (Smith 1993, 27). For example, pluralists would regard an activist group as a counterweight to a corporation's power because the activist group may also have links to other relationships that wield power, such as the church or political parties. This might seem reasonable but Smith argues pluralists pay "insufficient attention to the structural and ideological context and the interests and activities of bureaucracy and the government" (1993, 25). Thus rather than promote fairness, the "two-way symmetric" model promotes pluralistic ideals that advantage business, and at the same time works to marginalise activism further. The failure to integrate social and political contexts and/or acknowledge privilege and disadvantage in public relations extends deeply into frameworks used to produce and reproduce knowledge. So while at first cut pluralism may appear to offer tolerance and inclusion for activists, closer examination reveals that it oversimplifies questions of power and access and also promotes an attitude towards activism that enables business to dismiss the consequences of its activities and marginalise it almost completely.

A model of society where power is distributed and exercised between several participants was an attractive one for public relations theorists, as it reconciled a contradiction and negated the need to worry about those that did not have power. In a similar way for public relations practitioners, the idea of media power fitted with a pluralistic view as it was theoretically reconciled by the idea of "gatekeepers" who were "controlling the information that flows to other publics in a social system" (Grunig and Hunt 1984, 223). Widely used in the U.S. for media analysis, Ryan (1991) argues that gatekeeper/organisational theories, "gravitate toward a pluralist approach" that avoid questions of power relations and "overrates the ability of individuals, or even individual institutions, to create change" (1991, 12). This point is aptly demonstrated by Grunig and Hunt who argue that the power of the self-serving public relations practitioner was counter balanced by the cynical, watchful journalist who drew on wider considerations.

> Journalists feel besieged by hordes of press agents and publicists—"flacks", as they call PR people—who dump unwanted press releases on their desks and push self-serving stories that have little news value. Public relations practitioners, on the other hand, feel they are at the mercy of reporters and editors who are biased against their organization, who would rather expose than explain, and who know little about the complexities of their organisation. (1984, 223–224)

Over the twentieth century, mainstream U.S. public relations theory, with an over-reliance on pluralism, lacks reference to and/or frames political activists adversarially, which buttresses a view of activists as undermining legitimate corporate activity. As further evidence, the work of public relations analyst Larissa Grunig (1992) contains a specific reference to activism but only as something to be "managed." She says studying activism helps "practitioners deal in more than an ad hoc way with the opposition their organisations face from activist groups" (503).This argument is oriented around the view that rather than a negative event, activism applies a level pressure which provides the impetus for organisations to be alert and excel. However, there are deep and enduring connotations associated with these views about activists by public relations that are brought to light in more recent works. In *Managing Activism* (2001), a book endorsed by the Institute of Public Relations, Denise Deegan discusses that few business organisations are prepared for "the growing threat" of an "activist attack," and advises a proactive, rather than reactive, approach in learning how to control and direct them. In particular, Deegan discusses "risk communications" (2001, 94) as a specialist area in the management of public backlash or outrage, if for example "there is a temptation to gloss over" an "accidental toxic spillage" . . . "when communicating with key audiences" (2001, 93). This explanation of "risk" is quite unlike Ulrich Beck's sociological and holistic definition of it as the "hazardous side effect" of the modernisation process that presents global dangers for humanity (1992, 20–21). For Deegan, finding solutions in risk communication is largely a matter of managing perceptions, because "[A]ctivists often exaggerate the risks associated with an organisation" (Deegan 2001, 94).

Despite acknowledging the valid role of political advocacy in the U.S., Heath and Nelson's (1986, 95) advice for public relations practitioners dealing with special interest groups or agitators is laced with words such as "enemy," "marshalled," "force," "polarize" and "adversary" invoking strong military orders of discourse which set the tenor of relations.

> The social movement is ready to confront its enemy it believes it has obtained and marshalled the requisite power resources. After focusing on the advantages and disadvantages of believing two competing points of view, confrontation occurs when the special interest group

polarizes society by trying to force a choice between its position and that of its corporate adversaries. (Heath and Nelson 1986, 213)

A strong fear that somehow activists will gain the "upper hand" is evident also in public relations institutions. In 2005, the Victorian branch of the Public Relations Institute of Australia (PRIA Victoria) advertised a workshop for practitioners conducted by "Controversial Canadian PR consultant Ross Irvine" entitled "ACTIVISTS: How to beat them at their own game." Defining activists as "special interest groups, lobby groups or NGOs (non-government organisations)" Irvine stated that "they know what is best for us—they have assumed moral leadership on many issues globally and they pressure businesses, governments and society to embrace their ideology. They often recruit high-profile supporters to their causes, such as academics, media personalities and stars from the entertainment world." (Public Relations Institute of Australia 2005).

More recently, (in 2008), the PRSA published a discussion on the merits of Chrysler Corporation aligning public relations with the human resources department. This movement of "PR to HR" elicited an unusually vigorous discussion of the differences between the two areas that articulated the "real" role of public relations. If public relations did operate under the auspices of human resources, Cobb posited: "Can it react quickly enough to crises? Can public relations under human resources support lobbying efforts? Can it deal with activists on things such as environmental matters? Later in the article, under the title "They don't know what PR is" Cobb interviewed Janine Turner "a veteran recruiter who leads the PR and corporate communications sector for Mandrake Executive Search Consultants in Toronto [who] says she has counseled numerous companies against lodging public relations under human resources, marketing departments or elsewhere. She argues that moves of this type are not "smart" and a "mistake".

> If public relations is to control a company's external communications effectively, reasons Turner, it must be in a position to caution and advise the decision-makers. "They know what slings and arrows are being fired at the company, and they know that because they monitor blogs, newspapers and other news media," she says. "This is all part of reputation management, and neither human resources nor marketing can control a company's external reputation." (Cobb, 2008)

These defensive sentiments reveal that a complex and continuing role and antagonism between public relations and the civil society exists in contemporary society. However, challenging these views are other recent critical works from within the domain of public relations, which are more intellectually mature and acknowledge the weaknesses of "PR". In particular, they commonly include statements that refer to "civil sectors" and show a preparedness to critically analyse and reform the field (Daymon and Holloway

2011; Breit 2007; Weaver, Motion and Roper 2006; Motion and Leitch 2009; Rakow and Nastasia 2009; Leitch and Motion 2010; Surma 2006; L'Etang 2008; Edwards 2011; Coombs and Holladay 2012; Pieczka and L' E'tang 2006; Cheney and Christensen 2001; Dozier and Lauzen 2000; Holtzhausen and Voto 2002; Moss, Verčič and Warnaby 2000; Moloney 2006; Smith and Ferguson 2001; Tilson and Alozie 2004). Nonetheless, the deep and enduring hostility to activists and the legitimate role they play in civil society show these issues are not yet adequately addressed. This suggests it is time for the legitimacy of the unity of "public relations" to be contested and arguments for its reform to move beyond a "classical pluralist" framework (Moloney 2006, 6).

Thus while mainstream definitions of public relations discussed so far could apply equally to activist or business organisations, in fact they define public relations as a professional offshoot of business (Cutlip, Center and Broom 2000; Grunig 1984, 2000; Wilcox et al. 2000). Some literature suggests how activism can be marginalised or seen as the enemy by business organisations (Cutlip, Center and Broom 2000; Grunig 2000; Grunig 1992; Heath and Nelson 1986; Hendrix 2001; Kitchen 2000; Public Relations Institute of Australia 2005; Seitel 1998; Wilcox et al. 2000). Therefore, while some critical reflection in the literature in this field is apparent, overall, entrenched views about the promotion of business self-interest and its place in late modern society have not changed radically. Making the case quite explicit is this advice from Deegan:

> Activist groups represent a growing threat to organisations around the globe. In an increasingly pluralistic society, more and more people are uniting to make their voices heard. Whether this is through community groups objecting to the siting of an offensive project in their neighbourhoods or through the ever-increasing number of special interest groups, the effect is the same—to disrupt organisations. (2001, 7)

THE PRODUCTION LINE—SYSTEMS OF KNOWLEDGE

Public relations theory—narrowly constrained by liberal pluralism and functionalism—has had a historical animosity to activism. This is because the unity was established by business as their instrument in early modernity and within the spirit of scientific rationalism (Habermas 1995, 193). Public relations was a pragmatic response to the public's resistance to business expansion activities. At this time, business saw resources such as water, forests, air and soil as available for exploitation precisely because the pursuit of technological progress or advancement was regarded as an innate, good and defining human characteristic (Habermas 1995, 9). Public relations theorists constructed and validated knowledge about communication to promote organisations' self-interest, scientifically. Hence, they designed systematic goal-oriented programs of action to measure public opinion and to classify publics, markets or audiences, and often used the press and other information technologies to reach large groups. However, as discussed in the latter stages of the twentieth century communication researchers looked for other methods, notably qualitative (Daymon and Holloway 2011). Nonetheless in public relations, positivist quantitative style research was to become the mainstream approach.

Significantly, public relations and its problems for society have been hard for publics to analyse precisely because it is an unusual form of "system rationality" or instrumental reason that publicly represents itself as communicative action—the form of rationality that links to the lifeworld and its notions of interpretative consensus and mutual agreement (Habermas 1989, 118). To engineer consent in a climate of consensus (Habermas 1995, 194) public relations is saturated with symbols and images of communicative action rationality and of the lifeworld. Imbued thus, it is difficult for people to understand public relations as system rationality because it seems to contradict ideas about what that is and how it should look and behave. This subtle fusion is evident in public relations texts like promotional brochures, for example when a toxic waste facility is depicted, not in reality as it is, but in terms of a future vision of green, lush parkland.

Public relations theory thus collides with key tenets of citizenship. In particular, the active/passive dichotomy shows how public relations is not just averse to a concept of an active citizen but actively works against the development of both the individual and conditions which give rise to this. Influencing the public's adoption of a *passive* mode of reception works against citizenship's doctrines of social participation and commitment, but links back to Bernays' ideas about "moulding minds, forming tastes, suggesting ideas" "largely by men we have never heard of" (2005, 37). This suggests that in the course of achieving organisational objectives public relations practitioners create thin communities and submissive individuals that are directed towards an institutional rather than a common goal. So instead of using communicative practice to empower citizens to work in groups and to build up the social conditions that nurture capacities to meet communal responsibilities, public relations does the opposite. It encourages passive mode in citizens. The disempowerment is evident in Grunig and Hunt's theory of managing "publics." This theory posits that "latent' publics, unlike "aware" publics, do not detect or recognise the public relations problem (1984, 145). They advise, "If public relations managers can determine the category into which each of their publics fall, they can develop an appropriate public relations strategy for each public" (1984, 146). James Grunig went on to develop "Excellence Theory" in 1992 which Coombs and Holladay argue "is the closest the field of public relations has to a dominant paradigm" (2012, 3). Hence while Bernays frequently refers to "citizens" in his *Propaganda*, it is misleading because he is not interested in action that promotes fully participating citizens per se, rather control and manipulation of the masses; and in particular how to "contrive new ways to bind and guide the world" (2005, 38).

As discussed at the beginning of this Chapter, one of the long-term effects of these foundational contradictions between public relations and democratic theory has been to undermine its acceptance as a legitimate professional domain. According to L'Etang (2008, 41) professional status in UK public relations is still an "elusive goal" for practitioners "since entry to the occupation is not controlled by qualification or membership to a professional body". Similarly Breit and Demetrious (2010, 21) argue that "difficulties in scoping public relations' professional project emerge on a number of levels including defining its unique knowledge and expertise; what it does for the domain and how it relates more broadly to modern society." However, despite this, public relations does have considerable status in society. For example, it is taught in most Western universities, there are thick networks of professional societies and legions of practitioners over the globe. And yet this discordant note about its legitimacy of public relations is heard from outside and within the domain and debated without resolution. The contradictions in public relations are thus deep and multi-layered.

STRUCTURAL DIMENSIONS: 'PR' AND THE ANCHORING OF THE OBJECT

As we have seen, public relations manufactures discourse to control and manipulate the meaning making process. However it is more subversive than other forms of consumer communicative cultures such as advertising because the intent is political and the process goes largely undetected by the targeted public. To explain the significance of public relations activity at structural level, this section looks at the communicative scaffolding on which it is fixed, how knowledge is constructed, modes of communication and speaking positions determined, and rules. Underpinning this analysis is the concept of discourse; a term often used loosely and inaccurately, but which is important to define and explore.

Discourse is more than just a cluster of related words; it has a unity of logic and association that relates to normative power, position and legitimacy in society. Fairclough argues that "discourse" is a relationship between language and social change that constructs and reproduces the ways people are positioned in society. A central theme of his work is how the text interacts with the processes of discursive practice—that is the text's production, distribution and interpretation using the resources of a particular social space—to embed social practices in on-going social life (1999, 73). But he discusses also the constraints on consumers for the production and interpretation of texts in ways that raise subjects' agency or capacity for change (80). For Fairclough these constraints are a result of members' relationships to resources such as social structures, institutions, norms, conventions and how these resources determine their beliefs, ideology, social practices and therefore ways of living. According to Parker, a "good working definition" of discourse is that "it is a system of statements which constructs an object" (1992, 5). He argues that discourses, or rather "pieces of discourse", are found in both spoken interaction and written forms (Parker 1992, 6). Similarly, Macdonell (1986, 4) and Deacon et al. (1999, 310) argue that the concept of discourse, as the social production of meaning, is found in speech and written forms of communication.

For Michel Foucault, an investigation of an individual discourse, such as medicine and law, only reveals a narrow and specific understanding. First published in 1969, his book *The Archaeology of Knowledge* explores discourse as central to power, knowledge and historical development. Foucault argues that a discourse is shaped by the mix of social conditions and creates expectations of subjects to produce it. In other words, the subject responds to objects and statements from the discourse he or she interacts with, creating the expectations of what is already linguistically and socially embedded to form concepts that order them into a coherent whole. Foucault says that this is an underlying principle to account for the regular emergence of concepts within different times and places. He argues that unities or groupings and their discourses, such as medicine or political economy, should only be accepted if they are subject to "interrogation; to break them up and then to see whether they can be legitimately reformed; or whether other groupings should be made" (1972, 26). Once ideas about unities are questioned, "an entire field is set free" (26). I draw on Foucault's ideas as the intent of this book is to question the unity of public relations by subjecting its central tenets and ideas, especially around activism, to scrutiny in order to liberate ideas that can regenerate the field.

In understanding the movement of social change and how it gains traction, Foucault pays particular attention to contradictions which have potential to transform discourses and lead to new strategies and concepts. Indeed, they are objects in themselves; and sometimes gather intense momentum through activism and therefore their passage and progression can come under the scrutiny of public relations for its potential threat and other consequences. Some contradictions operate at an *intrinsic* or surface level from the same discursive formation, under the same conditions of operation of the enunciative function "without in any way affecting the body of enunciative rules that makes them possible" (Foucault 1972, 153). On the other hand some "are *extrinsic contradictions* that reflect the opposition between distinct formations" (Foucault 1972, 153).

If Foucault's structural ideas about contradictions and discourse are overlayed onto the popular public relations conceptualisation of practitioners as "boundary riders" functioning at "the edge of the organization, serving as a liaison between the organization and the external groups and individuals" (Grunig and Hunt 1984, 9), some interesting insights into ethics emerge. Seen through this Foucaldian lens, boundary riders in public relations are on the lookout for breaks and tears in the border, or for Foucaldian contradictions, which need to be restored. One way practitioners do this is to construct dichotomies to map out the coherence and limit thought, for example, the polarisations such as "silent majority" versus "vocal minority". The effect of the dichotomy is to limit the permeation of ideas into debate because thought is constrained within discursive boundaries that lead to the formation of particular concepts (Foucault 1972, 59). On the other hand, activists focus on social contradictions—the breaks and tears—and seek to construct them as objects of legitimacy. By this I mean breaks in logic by institutions in modern society "whose connections and factures (neglected on the level of the system) continually produce frictions, disharmonies and contradictions within and among individual biographies" (Beck 1992, 137). Therefore, the role of public relations as boundary riders is to assemble and police a fence around the dominant discourse, the business or the corporation, both to keep in the subject and to keep out new statements that might lead them to an alternative views (Foucault 1972; Fairclough 1999, Threadgold 1993, Chandler 2002). Public relations' role intervening in this process of change and renewal thus is evident in much anti-public relations literature (Beder, 1997; Nelson 1989; Stauber and Rampton 1995).

Structurally, and within the normative conditions of the twentieth century, there are two distinct ways in which public relations responds to contradictions. Firstly, public relations responds to what it believes are surface or intrinsic contradictions, that is, ones occurring inside a discursive formation, by seeking to adjust these through promotion, also known as "spin" and "fluff," but in ways intended not "in any way affecting the body of enunciative rules that makes them possible" (Foucault 1972, 153). Indeed, in order to confuse the public, dense and technical information is produced and dichotomies constructed to stop alternative statements from emerging, so that thought would be funnelled back into the bureaucratic and instrumental systems dominant to this point. Secondly, public relations responds to activist groups differently if it believes that their statements represent deep extrinsic contradictions outside the boundaries of the particular discursive formation (Foucault 1972, 153). In this case it acts aggressively to suppress and/or discredit the activists so that their statements are not distributed and will instead lead the subject back into the dominant discourse. This could include the public disparagement of activists, threats of legal action, spying and other forms of intimidation. In this way, public relations management of extrinsic contradictions can be seen to damage and undermine the agency of individuals to participate fully as active citizens within a democratic society.

Furthermore, public relations deals with extrinsic contradictions to asphyxiate the activists' new or counter-discursive forms and relationships in order to maintain the dominant discourse and "restore[s] to it its hidden unity" (Foucault 1972, 149). However, the engineered harmonising of intrinsic contradictions by public relations is no less socially damaging than the aggressive asphyxiation of extrinsic contradictions. Indeed, Habermas (1995, 195) has shown how the invisible seepage of commercial and political discourses into the public sphere causes its slow, subtle junking that puts at risk critical public opinion shaped by "rational agreement between publicly competing opinions" in a society. Public relations' intervention in the passage of contradictions which has the ability to transform discourses traverses a fine ethical line in democratic society.

Therefore the questions, "what is public relations, where is public relations" are not simple or frivolous, nor just a theoretical problem of concern to those within its ranks. Rather it is an important point that should be scrutinised from all sides of society. Despite a number of recent scholars who have engaged with the reform of public relations, for example, in its relations of power (L'Etang 2008; Motion and Leitch 2009, Rakow and Nastasia 2009, Coombs and Holladay 2012), in challenging paradigmatic assumptions (Edwards 2011) and in applying a range of social theoretical positions to the field (Ihlen, Fredriksson and van Ruler 2009), the analysis of the social apparatus of public relations and its effects, in particular towards activists engaged with social change needs greater attention. The question remains that if the domain of public relations has encountered resistance to the displacement of ideas to the extent that it is unable to address the criticisms around its ethics—should it exist at all? Moreover if the object of public relations is flawed (Demetrious 2008), are not also propositions flowing from this? Justifiably, it is pertinent to ask whether the claim of public relations to theorise and speak for the unity of organisational communication is legitimate, particularly if activism is considered, because it is ideologically invested to include some sectors and exclude others.

Taking account of all of these positions, an alternative and more reflexive definition of public relations is: an organisational social practice within the normative conditions of the twentieth century drawing on the functionalist notion of "harmony" to justify the control of *contradictions* between and through public and private discourses in order to maintain a dominant position of privilege and influence.

In summary, public relations as a domain is paradigmatically constrained by the dominant worldviews driving early modernity, and has not only actively shut down new entry points for knowledge but overdrawn on narrow ideas, concepts and theories of knowledge and relationships. Public relations' strategies, concepts and coherences are steeped in the logic of early modernity, functionalism and pluralism. Using tools such as media releases and advertising, public relations artificially creates and disperses statements, objects and concepts in concentrations that overwhelm others, giving rise to conditions that produce a discursive social monoculture. Its practices can range from the politically benign to the socially divisive, antagonistic and politically offensive, that in some cases are counter-productive. This is significant, because if businesses continue to apply simple approaches in their public relations when dealing with resistance from activist groups, they will not only contribute to significant social havoc through the suppression of ideas, conflict and antagonism but they will waste the collective resources of the state and risk their long-term business viability. Moreover, drawing on Foucault's ideas, there is no reason to accept that public relations has an intrinsic right to exist. Instead we must search to find how it was socially constructed and how it gained normative traction as "legitimate" in modern society and we must ask, if or under which circumstances, public relations can be accepted or justified.

2 Agents of Social Change and the Dispersal of Ideas

> Some of us had the fire of activism lit under us by directly experiencing destruction and oppression. Some of us are motivated by our compassion for others. Some of us react intellectually to the senseless and needless waste of life and human potential. Many are motivated by witnessing the positive and creative actions of others who are fighting for their beliefs. And some are just scared to death of what will happen if they *don't* do something. (Erickson 1990, 7)

A current of ideas and action starts to move, to form, to morph, gathering pace, permeating, confronting, and resisting other movements, other currents of ideas and action. Whether the patenting of a controversial industrial chemical, understanding the extent of a poisonous oil spill or taking a position on whether to tax big fossil fuel users, contested issues of public importance are often far outside people's immediate reference points. Therefore how do individuals scanning through mobile and digital technologies, listening to radio or reading a newspaper, develop a considered political position? With their locus in civil society, social movements provide a level of agency to articulate and respond, collectively. Sometimes called activist, protest, pressure, sub-political or extra-parliamentary groups; social movements play an important role in forming alternative positions through the provision of a social space and cultural resources. But what does activism really mean for its participants and for society, and what changes have taken place; and what is the effect and relationship of this to public relations? In questioning the assumptions embedded in public relations and its relationship to activist groups seeking social change, this chapter develops an understanding of varying forms of activism, and explores the provenance of ideas that have shaped social action and representation. Engaging with the theories of Karl Marx and Friedrich Engels, and of Émile Durkheim, it seeks to give a deeper insight into activism's social role, positioning and relationship to the state and democratic principles. It draws particular attention to development of grassroots activism, a form that the book focuses on, and which is discussed in more detail in later chapters. Finally the media's social representation of activism is examined as a key institutional site for meaning making. Analysing this helps to understand how public relations affects the agency of activists to act independently of social constraints and the ways civil society can be strengthened in order to generate the development of rational critical debate. This study of activism serves an important purpose in setting the groundwork for reform in public relations as it assists to identify social boundaries that delegitimises certain types of public relations activity, but which have been accepted normatively as part of the persuasive process.

WORTH FIGHTING FOR: FORMS OF ACTIVISM

Activists ask questions, demand replies and galvanise others to do the same. Their questions sometimes tear at accepted social and political unities and expose: "gaps, its discontinuities, its entanglements, its incompatibilities, its replacements, and its substitutions" (Foucault 2005, 80). Operating outside the business and government sectors, social movements can be defined as purposeful collective action which advocates with socio-political intent. External to business and the state, its social positioning from the bottom up as "people power" is central. For Burgmann, "A social movement is not a static group, but an enduring process of confrontation characterised by capacity for protest. Unlike a purely political movement, it operates at the level of civil society, whether national or transnational" (2003, 4). Engaging in activism can be enriching for society and individuals. Yeatman argues (1998, 33) that activism is a category of participatory political action which is a "publicly declared and open contribution to political life." Similarly, Raymond (in John and Thomson 2003, 208) argues that collectively, activists effect insightful and important social change and individually "are society's most active, committed citizens."

Despite this, much public relations activity is preoccupied with monitoring, guarding against, or mending "damage" involving activism. In particular, programmes such as "issues management," "crisis communication" and "risk communications" are strategically deployed in such "emergencies." Proactively designed, these strategies have anticipated a range of scenarios that potentially cause a disruption to embedded power relations. Thus when problems arise, such as an accident or disaster, a pre-arranged plan of action is launched targeting key publics and media in order to consolidate authority and optimise positioning, influence and counter. However, with sometimes opposing views, activist groups can dynamically work against organisations that seek to control them and frustrate their public relations plans by garnering public opinion through media coverage, boycotts, rallies, and picket lines. Significantly and for society as a whole, the processes of political participation in which activist groups engage—progressing ideas and alternative positions from outside business and the state—underpin core democratic principles. Therefore the countering or suppression of this activity by public relations has consequences beyond the issues at hand and moreover has been an ongoing source of tension, not only between public relations and activists, but also between public relations and society.

Forms of protest respond to the social conditions in which they are situated. When social conditions transform, political dissatisfaction is expressed in different ways. Broadly, four areas affect the shape of social movements: the issues identified as significant; organisational form adopted; the style of protest or "repertoires of action"; and constituencies (Giddens 2009, 1017–1018). New social movements (NSMs) with a focus on particularity, appear categorically different from earlier ones. Old social movements, for example, were organised around notions of class and trade unions progressed issues such as workers' rights and the eight hour day. However from the 1960s onward, NSMs were organised around individualised social divisions, such as sexuality, gender, and race. In respect of this Burgmann argues: "The most common arguments advanced for their distinctiveness are: their challenge to the form and content of contemporary political organisation; their lack of interest in attaining state power; their 'non-productivist' analysis of power relations; and their over-whelmingly middle-class support base" (1993, 3).

The dichotomy of "old" versus "new" social movements has, of course, limitations and risks oversimplifying complex social conditions. Burgmann argues: "There is a strong implication in discussions of the old that they represent an inferior, even obsolete, form of political mobilisation, that their concerns were too narrowly focused on economic deprivation, that they overlooked other important issues" (1993, 2). Making no judgements about their conduct or character, Castells views social movements broadly, as sociological data, seeing their purposeful behaviour as evidence to track social transformations in values and institutions. Thus there are "no 'good' and 'bad,' progressive and regressive social movements" rather they are "symptoms of who we are, and avenues of our transformation, since transformation may equally lead to a whole range of heavens, hells, or heavenly hells" (Castells 1997, 3). In a similar way, Salmon argues that activism is a socially constructed value laden activity that promotes a particular view for society and should be scrutinised for their "dysfunctional as well as their functional consequences" (Salmon 1989, 47). Pro- and anti- abortion groups that claim "activist" status are an example. The views of Burgmann, Castells and Salmon suggest that activism, operating from fringe positions and representing alternatives, is also part of powerful narratives articulated in social discourses that should not be accepted unquestioningly. Value-laden assumptions around activist groups, for example as "fighting the good fight" and "championing the underdog", draw attention to the complex discursive and social processes at play in the social construction of activism and should be scrutinised.

There are a range of categorical sub-divisions in activism. Burgmann describes two as interest-based and issue-based, "Some social movements are clearly interest-based movements in that they represent the self-interest, whether collective or individual, of those involved in them" (1993, 17). She describes issue-based activism as concerned with matters that do not represent participants' immediate interests, an example are animal liberationists. Of these two types, she argues that interest-based movements are more likely to sustain momentum over time because of the participants' personal commitment to the issue. The sub-divisions of "interest-based" and "issue-based" activism loosely correspond to public relations notions of "organisational self-interest" and "issues management." A related approach to these activist styles is also reflected through the design and intent of different public relations plans. For example, standard public relations plans determine objectives to be achieved in terms of organisational self-interest, then identify "publics" to be targeted, and the various strategies and tactics to be deployed over the short to medium term. On the other hand, issues management plans identify, monitor and prioritise risks over the longer term, and use this information to develop analysis and response. It could be argued however, that these sub-divisions of activism and public relations have limited value in late modern society as ideas and identities are continually being reconstituted and redefined.

At the close of the millennium a new "universalist" form of activism emerged, including peace and green movements, "purporting to act on behalf of all in the planetary community" (Burgmann 1993, 17). Other forms are politically targeted anti-war movements opposed to nation states' involvement in conflicts such as Vietnam, the Gulf and most recently Iraq. In tandem with these global orientations has been the rise and proliferation of non-governmental organisations (NGOs). Emerging over the last fifty years, NGOs have grown and developed into highly skilled and responsive organisations capable of intervening in debates and actioning campaigns in unconventional ways. With borderless charters, NGOs such as Médecins Sans Frontieres (MSF), Amnesty International, Greenpeace and Oxfam collectively draw global attention to environmental, social and political issues such as species extinction and the toxic effects of nuclear testing, the plight of child soldiers and victims of repressive regimes.

Expressions of activism are not random and only occur under certain social conditions. Pakulski (1991, 52–59) discusses this in relation to mass social movements (MSMs) or large-scale mass mobilisations, such as civil rights and feminist movements that challenge social institutions and cause social change. Broadly, he argues that these conditions occur when rapid social changes, together with cultures of exclusion within government—relative to the expectations of the society—exist in tandem with opportunities for social action. For Pakulski, these opportunities depend on the extent to which the MSMs can facilitate social bonds, communication and the political conditions that allow the movement to form and persist (1991, 52–9).

GREEN ACTIVISM

The social and political awakenings of the 1960s and 1970s provided citizens with a social space that accommodated new and experimental ways of thinking and doing, underpinned by a powerful critique of the multifarious excesses of capitalism in modernity and a moral urgency to act. While conservation and nature movements had existed during the twentieth century (and earlier) in various forms, for example field naturalists and bird watching societies, green activism and environmentalism, as a loose grouping, gained considerable social traction in the latter part of the twentieth century.

According to Doyle, in Australia, there are three distinct periods in the movement of environmentalism characterised by different approaches to protest and communication. In the first period activists acted as radical outsiders and protest was "based on direct, oppositional dissent to unrestrained environmental use (Doyle 2001, xxiv). He argues that this revolutionary movement is associated with mass mobilisation protest forms and as it can be construed as structuralist. In tandem, Doyle argues a pluralist strand focussing on influencing the state was in carriage. He says that while still politically positioned as outsiders, these "reformist environmentalists ... demanded legislative change to enable the state to manage the environment more effectively" successfully using techniques like lobbying (Doyle 2001, xxiv). A second period emerged over the mid 1980s when environmental groups, government and business collaborated for change. As a result of this corporatist approach: "Dominant mainstream green NGOs became incorporated into Labor government's policy-making processes and agendas" (Doyle 2001, xxiv). Nonetheless, radical environmentalism continued to agitate on the political fringes. A third period saw a distinct move by government and its relations with the environment movement, away from collaboration, to opposition. Doyle says that in Australia, this was particularly evident from the late 1990s onward, and over a long period of conservative government led by Prime Minister John Howard. At this time, the Coalition government had little appetite to expand its role as an environmental regulator and "In reaction, the movement has often been forced to bypass the state and to deal with other sectors more directly" (Doyle 2001, xxiv). Arguably this seemingly contradictory alliance between activists and business could be fruitful, as Lyons argues "Over the last 20 years, business has clearly become the most powerful force that is transforming our economy and society" (2001, 219).

A range of significant events gave momentum to these movements, including the rise of NGOs such as the World Wildlife Fund (WWF) in Switzerland in 1961 and Greenpeace in Canada in 1971. Urgent calls to action were also included in persuasive books. One of the most accessible and important books that influenced the gathering force of the environmental movement is Rachel Carson's *Silent Spring*, first published in 1962. It gained wide popularity for its lucid, considered and values-based argument which translated complex scientific and social debates into the everyday. Her book targeted the chemical industry and its irresponsible and cavalier use of insecticides to control agriculture and its detrimental effects on nature. This passage from her book does not use the words "public relations" but it alludes to the communicative processes involved in shaping public opinion and how invested power relations affect a citizen's ability to make a clear and rational judgement based on truthful and sound information.

> The citizen who wishes to make a fair judgement of the question of wildlife loss is today confronted with a dilemma. On the one hand conservationists and many wildlife biologists assert that the losses have been severe and in some cases even catastrophic. On the other hand the control agencies tend to deny flatly and categorically that such losses have occurred, or that they are of any importance if they have. Which view are we to accept? (Carson 1971, 87)

Stauber and Rampton say that, in an attempt to prevent her words being heard, the forces of public relations were turned on Carson. "*Silent Spring* also created a crisis—a PR crisis—for the powerful agricultural chemical industry which had emerged after World War II based in large part on the military's widespread use of DDT and its development of 2,4-D and 2,4,5-T herbicides. The agrichemical industry hit back at Carson with the PR equivalent of a prolonged carpet bombing campaign. Even before her book was published, Velsicol Chemical Corporation tried unsuccessfully to intimidate its publisher into changing it or cancelling publication" (1995, 123–124).

In 1970 Gordon Rattray Taylor's *The Doomsday Book* delivered the piercing call to curb the population explosion and reign in growth to prevent species extinction, pollution and ecological imbalance which could "change the climate" (1970, 12). In response to these concerns Rattray Taylor documented the rise of activist groups: "Two hundred students from forty campuses met recently at Stanford University and formed the Student Environmental Confederation, to co-ordinate existing student bodies, such as Students for a Better Environment, and to act as a clearing house for information" (1970, 261). The rise of activist groups, intersecting with these anxieties, strengthened the wave of social action. Another influential book was Saul Alinsky's *Rules for Radicals, A Pragmatic Primer for Realistic Radicals,* published in 1971. Alinsky crystallised connections between youth culture, social structures and the allocation of social, political and cultural resources with the urgent need for action. In drawing these elements together, he constructed an ideal of moral authority and social renewal progressed through a bright generation of protestors:

> Today's generation is desperately trying to make some sense out of their lives and out of the world. Most of them are products of the middle class. They have rejected their materialistic backgrounds, the goal of a well-paid job, suburban home, automobile, country club membership,

first class travel, status, security, and everything that meant success to their parents. They have had it. (Alinsky 1971, xiv)

The momentum was sustained in 1972 when *Limits to Growth* was published. Challenging the orthodoxy of capitalism and acknowledging the human relationship with nature, this book had impact in analysing the sustainability of population and natural resource growth.

> LTG pleaded for profound, proactive, societal innovation through technological, cultural, and institutional change in order to avoid an increase in the sociological footprint of humanity beyond the carrying capacity of planet Earth. (Meadows, Meadows and Rander 2005, x)

Ideological conviction to take environmental action brought in a new radical style of guerrilla activism. At the far end of the spectrum environmentalism embraced the idea of Deep Ecology, a holistic philosophy, and indeed an anathema to functionalism, in which nature is regarded as an "interconnected whole, embracing humans and non-humans as well as the inanimate world" (Heywood 2007, 259). Earth First! is one such group that proclaims "the spiritual and visceral recognition of the intrinsic, sacred value of every living thing." Castells details their activities as "an uncompromising movement that engaged in civil disobedience and even 'ecotage' against dam construction, logging, and other aggressions to nature, thus facing prosecution and jail" (2000, 117). While sharing some of these values, many other environmental groups diverged on a range of points.

Not surprisingly, the interplay between the activists and business and government sectors was often a source of bitter tension played out in the media. Around the 1970s and 1980s, public relations campaigns ramped up and spearheaded a range of high level, and unethical, persuasive tactics such as front groups and false public representations by business of environmental values and action, precisely because the movement's gathering force challenged accepted and unquestioned notions of legitimacy and authority in democratic society. This approach collided with the new directions in activism, often "Because conservationists had nothing material to offer in their political bargaining with government and industry, they offered threats instead, particularly the threat of media pressure" (Watson 1990, 118). In turn, deep and enduring tensions were embedded between activists and corporations.

A long-standing, seemingly "intractable" conflict between Australian timber workers and conservationists in Terania Creek area of New South Wales (NSW) is one example. Watson's account and his pessimistic findings indicated that this conflict was so deeply rooted in the structural limitations of class and capitalism that it was a fixed set of social relations (1990, 119). Writing a decade later, Doyle (2001, 156) argued that sometime in the 1980s anti-environmentalists, such as corporations and political institutions, changed communication tactics with activists and instead of conflict to secure their power, they promoted the idea of "sustainable development." However, rather than being a genuine attempt to resolve debates with rational discussion, Doyle claims that this new strategy was a self-serving form of public relations designed to undermine the growing authority of environmentalists, exploit the limitations of their marginal status and therefore weaken their legitimacy to lead or engage in the debate.

Transformations in social movements over this period can also be explained using the ideas of Habermasian ideas of reason as the system or technological progress and the lifeworld or moral progress (1989, 118). He defines old politics as revolving around questions of the system to do with economic, military and social security supported by "employers, workers and middle-class tradesmen" (392). New politics was responding to needs such as "quality of life, equal rights, individual self-realization, participation, and human rights," and support for this tended to be found amongst the younger, better educated, middle classes (392). He predicted changes to traditional forms of conflict within societies because, while these groups are disparate, the bond that unites them is the "critique of growth" evident in social movements, such as anti-nuclear and environmental movements (393). Indeed, he argues that green protests are a response to industrialisation and the pollution affecting the organic foundations of the lifeworld and denying people their "sensual-aesthetic background needs" (394). Habermas conceptualises the new activist conflicts as occurring along "the seams between system and lifeworld," where they are in fact reacting to the system's colonisation of the lifeworld (395).

ACTIVIST IDENTITY IN THE INFORMATION AGE

> Globalization and informationalization, enacted by networks of wealth, technology, and power, are transforming our world. They are enhancing our productive capacity, cultural creativity, and communication potential. At the same time, they are disenfranchising societies. (Castells 2001, 68)

Adding momentum to the development of new activism are developments such as the Internet and mobile digital technologies. These have empowered activists to create change and communicate within contemporary social structures by providing them with valuable tools previously denied. In the past, media power was centralised in television, radio and press newsrooms and guarded by media gatekeepers, like editors. These constraints restricted public access and ensured a level of exclusivity in political debates. Thus from a public relations point of view developments in technology that opened access were concerning:

Activists have taken to the Internet like ducks to water. They see the benefits of instantaneous global distribution of their messages at minimal financial or environment cost. Like-minded individuals communicate back and forth facilitating the snowballing of issues. (Deegan 2001, 13)

The effects of new communicative technologies facilitate more than just transmission of information. Castells (2001) discusses transformative effects on activism and communication, especially around mobilisation, meaning making and the creation of identity. He argues that the Internet, characterised by the unprecedented decentralisation of stakeholders, is an ideal tool to enable grassroots activists to develop virtual communities, and to use powerful websites for communication (68–133). Castells explains how the Internet assisted right-wing U.S. militia group "The Patriots" to coordinate action and stabilise their association (91). Castells argues that under these conditions social movements find agency to reproduce and distribute cultural codes within the logic of decentralised information networks. "These networks do more than organizing activity and sharing information. *They are the actual producers, and distributors, of cultural codes*" (2001, 362, italics in original). He argues that new activist identities are being forged in the "electronic networks or in grassrooted networks of communal resistance" (2000, 362).

GRASSROOTS ACTIVISM

Towards the end of the twentieth century, a form of activism emerged as a distinct category. It was not overtly politically aligned, and involved diverse local groups of empowered citizens focussed on a single-issue cause. Esteva and Prakash (1998, 1) examine grassroots activism as a subdivision of activism that has characteristics such as creativity and intellectual re-invention in resisting the "Global Project," which they define as the dominant ideology's imposition and promotion of programmes and policies to achieve global economic integration in modernity. Grassroots activism refers to a concept of diverse citizen collectives focused on local issues which work to achieve change outside and on the fringes of legitimate institutions, such as government or corporations. These grassroots activist groups draw on the concept of community, which Hamilton defines as a multilayered concept that people believe in as an ideal and which implies technical, symbolic and ideological meaning and values (Hamilton 1985, 8).

Signficantly, the grassroots activists critique the sometimes overlooked social, economic and environmental consequences of the modernisation of the industrial societies in which they live. They also benefit from these societies, for example by higher education, multiple entry points of political debate, improved health and access to the plethora of technological and informational resources available. However, compared to other contemporary business and state organisations, these groups have limited resources, such as time and money, to mount their campaigns. As a result, they tend to have bold and inventive approaches to communication and a willingness to adopt and experiment with new technologies to coordinate action and promote their cause. The participants' commitment is often long term and linked to beliefs about community and its relationship to the individual. This shapes a construction of citizenship and activist identity. Grassroots activist organisations are likely to have loose non-hierarchical and adaptive structures where participants unite, often from diverse socio-cultural, political and educational backgrounds. These participants operate in communities in ways characterised by extensive networking of ideas and action. Grassroots activism can lead to social change, by which I mean local or small-scale social and political policy shifts, rather than extended or large-scale social reformations (Abercrombie, Hill and Turner 1994, 382–383). However, while particular expressions of grassroots activism may be local and relatively small in scale, the issues they represent are embedded within larger or significant social or global trends.

Although concerned with a range of different issues, the case studies of grassroots activism in Chapter 4 are united in that they oppose the unintended effects of risk producing industries. The focus on the communicative activities of grassroots activist groups contributes to the furthering of understanding in public relations. In particular, they provide new perspectives about how public relations works and its role in communities. In Chapter 6 an analysis of grassroots activist activities will inform a discussion on ethical, effective and socially cohesive communicative campaigns that establish the legitimacy of activist groups and can be applied more widely.

LENSES OF TRUTH: VIEWS OF SOCIAL RELATIONS

At the Ethical Corporation's Third Annual Conference in May 2004, held in North London, placard-bearing protesters, wearing pig masks and suits, banged drums and shouted anti-big business slogans to "all the corporate scum under one roof" (Demetrious 2004, 20). Organised by Indymedia, a collective protest group, the activists' view was that corporate social responsibility (CSR) was no more than an exercise in elaborate "spin" for business to advance its environmental credentials or to "greenwash" the main game of increasing market share and maximising profits. However, on this occasion the business agenda was to take action around the environmental and social spillage caused by its activities—ostensibly the same agenda as the activists.

This section looks at activism and why it has historically adopted very different "models of society" from public relations, that set into play social relations anchoring each other in conflict. It reviews a small but representative selection of social theory to illustrate the historical interplay between public relations and activism and argues that relations of conflict and control had been firmly established over the nineteenth and twentieth centuries. The different models of society represented show how structures emerge and reproduce themselves to effect agency in different ways. The first model of society is based on a conception of conflict and draws on the influential theories of Marx and Engels (original text in McLellan 1984). These theories are used as the major social framework to account for collective activist behaviour in early modernity (Burgmann 1993; Pakulski 1991). The second model of society is based on a conception of a conglomeration of individuals and uses Durkheim's (1957) theories of the modern state and its relationship to the individual. These theories provide insight into business ethics and its relationship to society in ways that are important to understand the genesis of contemporary notions of corporate social responsibility (Freeman 1984; Greenwood 2001; McIntosh et al. 1998).

SOCIETY AS CONFLICT

The Marxist legacy remains one of the enduring influences that shaped political and social thought in the twentieth century, and germane to a deeper understanding of activism, public relations and social change. Marx's powerful intellect and creative energy brought together an unusual synthesis of history, politics, philosophy and economics to analyse the rapidly changing social and economic conditions and relationships brought about through the modernisation of Europe. This section concentrates on *The Communist Manifesto*, a key 1848 work in which he collaborated with Fredrick Engels. For Noble (2000, 71) this work "deserves attention in its own right" as it is "extensive, immensely rich in ideas and rhetoric." For McLellan the ideas presented were not new but "simply brilliant summaries of views put forward in *The German Ideology*" (1984, 220).

The Communist Manifesto begins with a short authoritative statement that discusses the totality of history as a battle between different groups: "The history of all hitherto existing society is the history of class struggles" (Marx and Engels quoted in McLellan 1984, 221–247). In modern industrial society, they claimed that there were two major and mutually antagonistic groups at the centre of political and social action, the bourgeoisie and the proletariat. This tension, according to Marx and Engels, arose in the seventeenth and eighteenth centuries when the feudal system of industry, which was monopolised by closed guilds, was replaced by a manufacturing system of industry, which was controlled by a middle class or the modern bourgeoisie. The bourgeoisie's industrial dominance was entrenched by technical developments such as steam and machinery. At the same time, international trade opportunities opened up global markets which resulted in an accumulation of vast wealth. For Marx and Engels, this radical redistribution of wealth enabled the bourgeoisie to monopolise the ownership of factories and industries, or "all the instruments of production," which in turn led to immense political and social power (McLellan 1984, 237). Technological developments, like navigation and communication, further empowered and entrenched the owners' domination over an economically dependent and growing workforce and the owners eventually became "leaders of whole industrial armies" (Marx and Engels quoted in McLellan 1984, 233).

In this setting, the contemporary State's power grew out of the bourgeoisie's need to have its interests safeguarded against the old aristocratic regimes that had previously controlled most of the wealth in society (Marx and Engels quoted in McLellan 1984). However, in contrast to a pluralist view of the state as impartial or an umpire to administer fairness and equity, Marx and Engels saw it as an instrument of business that did, somewhat obediently, as it was bid. Marx and Engels write, "The executive of the modern State is but a committee for managing the common affairs of the whole bourgeoisie" (McLellan 1984, 223). But for Marx and Engels, society's main problem is that the capitalist system has inherent flaws and cycles that disadvantage workers. For example, they argue that to be competitive and profitable, industry is bound to create incessant change and reinvention. However, this activity results in major disturbances in areas such as urbanisation, family, gender, the nature of work and spirituality. The owners of capital therefore cannot "exist without constantly revolutionizing the instruments of production, and thereby the relations of production, and then the whole relations of society" (Marx and Engels quoted in McLellan 1984, 224). Marx and Engels therefore argue that the social changes distinctive to early industrialisation lead to a condition of "rapid development" (McLellan 1984, 222). In fact, they claim, in only one hundred years the bourgeoisie's frenzy of production has subjugated nature at an incomparable pace to previous epochs. They claim that it is the dehumanised proletariat that will suffer the negative consequences of this action, not the owners of production (Marx and Engels quoted in McLellan 1984, 224). This theme of rapid change as an essential element of capitalism and its unintended effects should be noted, as later Ulrich Beck and Anthony Giddens theorise how this has played out in dangerous ways in late modernity. In particular, Marx and Engels' prescience is remarkable for forecasting a range of contemporary social debates such as globalisation, the decline of the nation-State, the expansion of communication and environmental degradation.

This insight shows that industrialisation is highly complex and bound up in economic and social anxiety that in turn disturbs collective social continuities in areas like family, religion and sentimentality. Under these conditions, workers' known and understood patterns of living constantly dissolves and leads to an era dominated by "uncertainty and agitation" (Marx and Engels quoted in McLellan 1984, 224). In fact, Marx and Engels argue that the bourgeoisie, in pursuit of their self-interest, deprive the proletariat of fundamental rights in unusual and cruel ways, unique to the period of industrialisation. The authors use strong discourse to depict the bourgeoisie as unholy and profane, for example, "The bourgeoisie has stripped of its halo every occupation hitherto honoured and looked up to with reverent awe" (Marx and Engels quoted in McLellan 1984, 223). With the proletariat on one side and the capitalist owners of production on the other, this overarching social dichotomy mapped out key actors and their settings, which for some have remained fixed, and underpinned relations and thinking in both activism and public relations. Interpreted through the lens of Marxism, activism's origins are rooted in resistance to these pressures, particularly trade unions, while public relations is positioned as the instrument of expansionist capitalism.

One of the most powerful ideas underpinning activist thinking is that political action has to be radical in order to reorganise modern society for the better. For this to succeed, Marx and Engels argue that revolution is necessary. They write: "The Communist revolution is the most radical rupture with traditional property relations; no wonder that its development involves the most radical rupture with traditional ideas" (Marx and Engels quoted in McLellan 1984, 237). To explain their socially controversial ideas more precisely, they engage in dialectic where the reader is made aware of several unidentified, but dissenting voices—sometimes the proletariat doubter, sometimes the bourgeois owners of production. Through this process, Marx and Engels argue that reform begins by elevating the workers' social status: "The first step in the revolution by the working class is to raise the proletariat to the position of the ruling class to win the battle for democracy" (McLellan 1984, 237). Following this, they propose that the State acquire all instruments of production, such as factories and industry. The authors make the point that while the acquisition of the instruments of production would initially cause social and economic upheaval, over time these matters would be resolved. The more significant outcome is that, as a result, class distinction and exploitation would disappear because the bourgeoisie would no longer be in charge of production. Furthermore, the State, which they claim developed as an instrument to protect the bourgeoisie's interests, would lose its political character and work to protect all. In particular, Marx and Engels are at pains to refute an implied argument that the abolition of private property means work would cease and a social malaise would take root. They argue, rather, that the exploitation of wage labour would disappear because the machine of production would be eradicated.

Despite having a clear contention to change modern society, Marx and Engels (original in McLellan 1984, 221–247) are somewhat ambiguous about the social conditions or political frameworks in which revolution can occur. For example, early in the work they state that radical changes that lead to better conditions for workers should take place gradually and within democratic social frameworks. Under these conditions the proletariat use "political supremacy to wrest, by degrees, all capital from the bourgeoisie" (Marx and Engels quoted in McLellan 1984, 237). But in the last section of the work they state that "forcible overthrow," not democracy, will be the mechanism for change. "They openly declare that their ends can be attained only by the forcible overthrow of all existing social conditions. Let the ruling classes tremble at a Communistic revolution" (Marx and Engels quoted in McLellan 1984, 246; in this quotation the term "they" refers to the Communists). This inconsistency is significant because it reveals that, while the authors attempt to produce a definitive guide for social action, their thinking about the repositioning of the proletariat in society by working within or outside the prevailing systems, is still forming or confused. It may also account for the various interpretations of Marxist ideas, and perhaps for their broad endurance.

In the last section of *The Communist Manifesto*, Marx and Engels critique three major strands of socialism and communism: "Reactionary Socialism," "Conservative or Bourgeois Socialism," and "Critical-Utopian Socialism and Communism" (McLellan 1984, 238–245). By describing and critiquing these categories, the authors define more precisely their own model of Communism. Of interest, Marx and Engels are particularly scathing about the social reformers and middle-class thinkers who argue against radical revolutionary methods to overthrow the bourgeoisie, in favour of negotiation. They claim this moderate form of socialism only serves to comfort those who benefit in some way from the capitalist society, and appease their conscience at the same time. Of course today, negotiation and compromise are central tenets of reformist corporate social responsibility (CSR) and corporate citizenship business models.

Significantly, for a discussion of public relations' relationship to activism and social change, the ideas of Marx and Engels shed light on historical activist attitudes and stances. In particular, the notion of the bourgeoisie's systematic exploitation of workers explains adversarial positioning between workers and the industrialist owners of production. Workers represented by trade unions, in their struggle to achieve better working conditions, were in conflict with capitalist owners of production who sought to maintain their business profitability. The legacy of these beliefs and attitudes contributes to a continuing antagonistic relationship between public relations and activism. For example, many contemporary activists who mount information and communication campaigns to achieve their goals view the world according to the Marxist dichotomy, where the two dominating social groups are the bourgeoisie and the proletariat. In the course of these campaigns, they position themselves in an adversarial tradition employing communication tactics and strategies that reflect deep division and entrenched hostility.

On another level Marx and Engels' theories are limited because they are unable to explain fully contemporary changes to activism. In the light of post-1945 social and political developments, Burgmann (1993) says that they do not explain activism that is not associated with workers' immediate interests. For example it is inadequate to explain more recent relationships between political action and social change, such as peace movements, Aboriginal land rights and gay rights (Burgmann 1993, 9). Beck (1992) characterises the Marxist couplet of 'base' and 'superstructure', as simplistic. This is the idea that the base, that is forces of production, such as workers, capital and infrastructure, determine the overall social conditions or superstructure. He says this idea "misapprehends the degree of autonomization of political action in the developed parliamentary democracies" and moreover "misunderstands" the variations evident modern political situations (1992, 189). Nonetheless an understanding of activism, particularly as it was played out in the twentieth century, is richly informed by an understanding of Marxist traditions. In particular, the key Marxist theme of the oppressive bourgeoisie and the oppressed proletariat helps to recognise that, when activists use the term public relations or "PR" they refer pejoratively to capitalists' or State organisations'" manipulation, propaganda and undemocratic communication practices. Marx's theories help to understand why activists overlook or dismiss the public relations industry and perhaps why their own communication activities are not described in an equivalent unity.

SOCIETY AS INDIVIDUALS

Émile Durkheim is a prominent social theorist from the nineteenth century who presented complex but more moderate view than Marx and Engels. His theories about individuals, public opinion and communication in large-scale modern industrial societies and their relationship to authority and moral discipline contributed substantially to sociology's establishment as an academic discipline. In particular he canvassed, not just the relationship between the individual and the state, but also what he refers to as "secondary groups" in society. These ideas are valuable in any discussion about public relations, activism and social change because they provide a greater understanding about the issues of power and communication in early modernity but also legitimacy ascribed in relation to social change.

The work discussed here is a series of lectures concerning the character of the State and civic morals delivered between 1890 and 1912 which remained unpublished, in part, until 1947. These writings show how collective behaviour and laws are established in modern industrial societies, their purpose and how individuals apply them (Durkheim 1957, 3). Durkheim's views on economic activity in modern societies are enlightened, far-sighted, and related to contemporary debates about corporate social responsibility. For example, he (1957, 9–10) discusses how business codes of ethics are ineffective because the principle of competition pits individuals and groups against each other and as a result the sector is loath to regulate its activities.

He claims that classical economists (without naming them) argued for a culture in which economics was an end in itself and without a place in the broader social order or structure. As a result, Durkheim predicts business and industry will dominate society and for this reason it is imperative to regulate and raise its moral standards to avoid a new set of social ills and crises that are of serious concern (1957, 16). These sentiments, like those of Marx and Engels, flagged far reaching problems currently confronting late modernity.

Like Marx and Engels, Durkheim (1957, 69–93) pays attention to the rise of the modern State but focuses on its relationship to the individual. Foremost, he believes that the State's core responsibility is to decide what is best for the collective good, after weighing up diverse representations from the masses. Indeed, more precisely, the State's role is to administer for the welfare and development of society as an aggregate of individuals, which is why the State continues to expand. But, he argues that the individual can continue to develop in modern societies without causing a decline in the State, precisely because the State liberates the individual. In this sense, Durkheim argues, it is not "you" or "me" as particular individuals that the State wants to develop but "individualism *in genere*," (Durkheim 1957, 69, italics in original). Durkheim says that a consequence of large-scale society is that collective culture is weakened, partly because it is "incompatible with the spirit of scrutiny and free criticism" (1957, 93). He claims also that the notion of collectivism, associated with the religious sphere, sits with the idea of the modern State. He argues that individuals, in a fusion of religious and civic morals, yield to the symbols and beliefs absorbed into mass society. But social antagonism occurs sometimes when the good of the group conflicts with the individual good or when some individuals appear not to see the social good at all. However, on balance Durkheim claims that, for society to function smoothly, the State and individuals must work together. These ideas about fusions of discourses might explain some of the modalities adopted by public relations in its persuasive strategies.

Durkheim argues that the larger a society becomes, the more rules are necessary for its enforcement partly because the individual becomes distanced from the collective good. But ironically most do not even notice the State's expanding and embedded control. Therefore, secondary or special interest groups that make effective representations to the State, institutions and the citizenry, which result in the formation of public opinion, are vital to stop the State from getting too powerful and repressing the individual (Durkheim 1957, 63). He says that their presence within democracies creates conditions that provide the individual with liberty. Durkheim (1957, 79–84) discusses also the idea that public opinion has an important role in shaping individuals' understandings of their civic duties that are of benefit to society. This is of particular interest because it shows how marginal groups and communication are necessary to achieve a representational democracy. Durkheim argues that in modern societies there are essentially two strands of thinking: bottom-up, from the social mass, and top-down, through the State. He says that public opinion from the masses is diffused, haphazard and "stays in the half-light of the sub-conscious," while State-generated thought is formed reflectively and "has structure and is centralized" (Durkheim 1957, 79). Activism is not named but implied in the concept of secondary groups. Clear in Durkheim's thinking is the idea of structural change and agency being affected through communicative processes. These ideas position the communicative activities of public relations and activism and their relationship as centrally important to the democratic ideal.

Shedding light on individuals' moral motivation and agency to act for social change, Durkheim (1957, 80–93) discusses the role of communicative deliberation in democracies and secondary groups. He says that, when individuals have a clear consciousness, then reflection and consideration of facts occurs without interference from ego and diffused thought. Durkheim says that the State acts in the same role in society, metaphorically depicting it as a brain that reflects the collective consciousness, and he argues that social groups should yield to its clear judgement to decide what is best for the common good (1957, 80). But Durkheim qualifies this statement by arguing that, for the State to promote the common good, it has to be open to public debates and to be transparent, so that citizens can participate and share in the decision making. He says that the extent to which this happens will vary and will depend on how many ways there are to encourage participation in public life. He argues that if the State makes no attempt to know what is going on, its influence will be limited. But, for Durkheim, open participation can go too far and can weaken the State. Therefore activism, not named but implied, acting outside the institutions, can undermine the clear consciousness of the State by working in opposition to progressive and innovative ideas being driven by the legitimate leadership. Durkheim notes that, while the State can be all-powerful against the individual, it is less powerful against social conditions, customs or beliefs and that this explains State political inertia on certain issues such as the Church and marriage. This may explain why secondary activist groups concentrate their attention in these areas. He also points out that, while some societies are stormy with tension, this does not necessarily lead to change. Indeed, he argues that excessive interaction in society leads to social fatigue, exhaustion, inertia and routine (Durkheim 1957, 82). Change, according to Durkheim, comes with rational debate between the State and individuals. For Durkheim, if the State exercises a balanced communication with the citizenry through secondary contact, it has the double insulating effect of making sure the State does not tyrannise individuals or individuals overwhelm the State. Similarly his ideas show how appearances can be misleading. Equally, activism purporting to progress new agendas, or working to protect or apply correctives may not lead to constructive change but rather deepen social division.

Durkheim's (1957, 101–108) ideas on civic duty also have relevance to contemporary debates about civil disobedience as a way to achieve social change. He argues that citizens must obey the laws that are derived from the direct will of the people, but must contribute in the formation of those laws and take part in public life. Of laws that society does not want, he says that "what my will has done, my will can undo" (Durkheim 1957, 107). However, he cautions that individuals will not respect the law if there are too many changes (Durkheim 1957, 108). To be respected, laws must express the interrelationship of the individual and democracy with its notions of deliberation for the common good. For Durkheim, people submit to laws not because they are laws, but because they are confident that they are good and appropriate. He argues that the whole notion of democracy lies in our understanding that we are individual parts of a whole. Therefore citizens have a duty to shape the society in which they live and it is "legitimate for every citizen to some extent to turn into a Statesman" (Durkheim 1957, 108). Durkheim's ideas are an interesting intersection of communication, (Habermas 1995; 1981; 1989), and community, (Bottomore 1996; Turner 1994a; Pixley 2000), and relevant to activism research because they show how citizens operate to communicate and contribute to notions of the common good with State institutions. His ideas legitimise activities such as civil disobedience as one of the important symbolic repertoires of communicative action in activism.

SOCIAL REPRESENTATION OF ACTIVISM

Informed by varying iterations of these ideas, the media represents activists within a broad spectrum. They can be portrayed as naive, spiritually connected dreamers; grim placard-carrying workers; young, clever, challenging and precocious; passionate and morally grounded communitarians, or extreme zealots living on the margins, or plain stupid or criminal. The shadowy dynamics of the Habermasian public sphere is a social space where the cultural resources of both public relations and activists are pitted against each other and "truths" are developed. Ryan conceptualises this process as a contest between competing interests fought out in an arena and writes: "Gaining attention alone is not what a social movement wants; the real battle is over whose interpretation, whose framing of reality, gets the floor" (1991, 53). For Ryan, framing is significant: "Frames are not consciously or deliberately constructed, but operate as underlying mind sets that prompt one to notice elements that are familiar and ignore those that are different" (1991, 54). Therefore to understand the processes of framing for activists in the public sphere, by public relations and other agents, it is important to excavate deeply into the communicative structures which shape meaning-making in media processes and institutions.

Central to this position is an understanding that the media is a social institution, not just invested with ideology in its own right, but also as a forum through which hidden relations of power promote and vie for ideological dominance. It is this layered complexity in media processes and institutions which make it such a powerful social site for the production and reproduction of meaning, and such a difficult social site to understand in terms of its capacity to influence thought and action. Therefore it is worth pausing briefly at this point to understand better the central concept of ideology. Ideologies are belief systems, which Oliver and Johnston argue "couple understandings of how the world works with ethical, moral, and normative principles that guide personal and collective action" (2005, 192). Fairclough contends that ideologies become most effective when they are naturalised into discursive practice and "achieve the status of 'common sense'" and social restructuring results (Fairclough 1999, 89). The extent to which ideology is naturalised means some people do not know that they are investing ideology in their texts. For Habermas public relations is part of the apparatus of media, particularly around the production of news that generates public opinion. The subject (individuals or groups, or in public relations parlance, "publics") is shaped by this process as the receiver of discourse that potentially can shape identity and act as a conduit for ideology. Therefore the media is a key institutional site for struggles of discourse. In other words, it is a social site of discursive action in which texts, designed to define meaning around contested notions of "truth" circulate with political consequences.

The media, broadly conceptualised, therefore is significant for its potential in social control. Fine-tuning these ideas, Fairclough's (1999) work also shows intertextuality hybridises and transforms textual meanings. He defines intertextuality as "the property texts have of being full of snatches of other texts, which may be explicitly demarcated or merged in, and which the text may assimilate, contradict, ironically echo, and so forth" (Fairclough 1999, 84). Therefore intertextuality is a subtle effect where, often unconsciously, the reader absorbs various discourses. He says this concept is particularly useful in understanding how texts "move along" or transform from one site to another, such as when a political speech is distributed into media such as television and then into homes through the six o'clock news and then into discussion around the dinner table (Fairclough 1999, 84). It comes in two forms: manifest intertextuality—where specific texts occur in a text such as a quotation and interdiscursivity—where orders of discourse are drawn on to constitute the text as well as conventions such as genre and narrative. Intertextuality, by influencing discourse, can influence social change. Thus for public relations, if activists are framed as "extremists," the somewhat prosaic practice of developing, distributing and monitoring "key messages" and "boilermaker statements" in the media is highly political since it influences political interpretations that have conseqeunces for social action.

Given that public relations has access to considerably more economic resources than activist groups, its practitioners are more centrally involved in developing strategies, tactics and representations, particularly around contested issues and ideas. From a Marxist perspective this social positioning provides public relations with other cultural resources as well, including the support of state. Because the public is unaware of its presence within the bourgeois public sphere, Habermas argued that in public relations it is vital that an advertisement is not recognisable as the presentation of self-interest, but rather that it creates the illusion of public interest mimicking the original intention of the public sphere (Habermas 1995, 194). In developing powerful textual frames, either through the written word or in pictures, hidden sectional interests like public relations may invisibly frame "truth" in relation to activist groups as extremist, unhinged and incoherent, time and time again in ways that garner public opinion and position them as outcasts.

"Truth" once naturalised gains traction and influences social change. According to Philogène "[N]aming plays a crucial role in the anchoring of new objects (2001, 114). She argues that "The stipulation that a thing be given a specific name thus carries with it certain commonly shared presumptions about concepts and categories. These in turn determine what the name does in the minds' of individuals and shapes how its meaning is communicated between them" (Philogène 2001, 114). Foucault also discusses the discursive anchoring of objects and their social construction. He argues that objects do not exist somewhere waiting to be found. Instead, they have a "normative" relationship with a society or one which can be defined as conforming to social expectations. Foucault cites the normative example of "motor disturbances, hallucinations and speech disorders" that were once understood to be manifestations of madness, but were subsequently redefined through psychopathology (1972, 40). Following on, an example is that what we know today as "vivisection" might tomorrow be designated "specieism" if arguments for animal equality by activists gains traction. As discussed, Foucault's analysis of these socially constructed "objects" is to find out "the first *surfaces* of their *emergence*" (italics in original) in order to understand what they do (Foucault 1972, 41). He argues that to understand the object and its definition other social phenomena of the day, such as the authority that limits its use, must be investigated. In the case of madness, Foucault names medicine as the authority that established, named and set limits around the object (1972, 42). Foucault says that a particular mix of social conditions is necessary for the appearance of an object, and that an underlying system of rules enables its transformation. For Foucault "these rules define not the dumb existence of a reality, nor the canonical use of a vocabulary, but the ordering of objects" (1972, 49). A discourse is therefore the normative communicative ordering of the object. The object once named, is socially anchored and framed through the media processes which refines and reinforces the preferred interpretation.

Therefore framing activists and developing social "truths" influences social directions, policy making, and the shape of society. An over-representation of sectional interest in the media that is determining public opinion through the instrument of public relations, overrides activist agendas developed around the common good. This, in turn, weakens collective cultures that are important for the aggregated welfare of individuals. For some activists these "truths" become entrenched and embedded hegemonically as common sense. For Philogène (2001, 114), "Once a thing has been determined as namable, the name chosen for it assigns that thing to a defining structure of functions and properties." Considering that Fairclough argued that ideologies are most effective when they appear "common sense," it is at this precise point that limitations to agency occur and social restructuring results (Fairclough 1999, 89). Understanding the significance of this is to understand communicative action, and how bitter interrelations have been established between public relations and activism.

In summary, these communicative frameworks reveal structural relationships between the activist groups, public relations and society, and how the meaning making processes affects representations. To illicit the less obvious or second order meanings embedded in the media, the public need the critical capacity to investigate the language of the culture and its relationships to power structures and institutions. The public must also be educated to analyse what has been included and what has been excluded to produce the language of the culture and work out how this determines what can be known about it and how this affects action. Without such knowledge, the processes of public opinion and the progression of ideas in society is weakened and compromised.

CONCLUSION

This chapter examined activist groups as the proponents of social change and mapped forms of activism which reflect changing norms and social mores. It has theorised this in relation to different conceptions of society, for example, characterised as conflict, as individuals and as groups. In this it aimed to develop a deeper and more nuanced understanding of the thinking and modes of activism as it changed over the twentieth century. Mapping activist terrain from Marxism to Durkheim's ideas of individualism shows that not only are activists legitimate, but that they are essential to nourish democracy. Without activists identifying and progressing issues of social, political and environmental significance, there would be inertia, repression and stagnation. But Durkheim's ideas clearly show that there are limits to this as well. Thus the process of public deliberation is important. This appreciation is relevant because it shows the complexity of social relations between public relations and activist that has led to similar mindsets of conflict. In doing so it demonstrates the importance of developing ethical substance in public relations and greater awareness of its dysfunctional side effects, particularly in view of the important role media plays in representing and distributing "truth". Thus it is increasingly evident that in public relations a discussion of ethics needs to reorient towards meaningful far reaching reform in all its social and political complexity. Significant changes in activism occurred in the 1970s and, around that time, the full extent of power play could be seen in the relations between public relations and activists groups.

The next chapter will use different case studies to show the extent to which repression and suppression of ideas took place over this period and the role of public relations within these circumstances. It will show that the effects of public relations in countering activist activity are socially far reaching and dire, and in particular, the extent to which public relations and its relations with activists and society are characterised by multilayered and complex contradictions. It will also show the conceptual and practical flaws in applying ideas of "symmetrical" communication to real-life circumstances and dynamic contentious social and political debates, and the constraints therein for public relations practitioners to think and act independently and ethically—no matter how meritorious they may be as individuals.

3 "No Protest Zone"
Public Relations and the Management of Activism

> Once a controversy is metamorphosed, or translated into a technical problem, the opinions and evidence of victims becomes worthless. Men and women who have worked in asbestos plants or who have consumed asbestos products are held to be incompetent as a source of reliable and objective information. They cannot be relied upon to give evidence about dust levels, or their own illness and its cause. In this context, access to information is the key to successful litigation, and this information is monopolized by industry. (McCulloch 1986, 257)

This chapter develops a critical description of public relations used towards activists in the twentieth century. It argues that at that time public relations worked in lesser-known but powerful communicative ways that reflected uneven social relations within the broader cultural and social landscape. Moreover, public relations was deeply hostile and adversarial in its relations to activism and at this time abused its power in unprecedented ways. This stifled important social change that was responding to significant environmental and social risks brought about through industrialisation. A consequence was that "PR" caused intolerable social havoc in a range of ways. As a corollary, the public orientation to public relations was not as an entity that promoted social cohesion and "harmony". Rather, it was as a self-centred and politically aggressive practice, ill-defined and ill understood, operating in ethically thin and opaque ways behind the public centres of action. This positioning represents more broadly some of the problems that have dogged public relations in modernity and stifled innovation and development within its ranks. Importantly, it signifies why public relations must be viewed through a new lens, to be understood, explained, regulated and practised.

Three activist campaigns are explored, in particular, the responses to activists by public relations practitioners acting on behalf of the organisations opposed, and the ensuing public debate. The first case study is of James Hardie Industries Limited, the principal Australian company that manufactured asbestos products used in both public and private buildings for the Australian and British markets. The core question at the centre of this debate is whether James Hardie was aware of the health risks associated with this commodity and product and if public relations were central

56 *Public Relations, Activisim, and Social Change*

to this. We examine another aspect of public relations' used throughout the controversy, to maintain the company's respectability in the community. The second case study is North American and focuses on the installation of a toxic waste incinerator. Waste Technology Industries (WTI) was planned and constructed in Ohio from 1979. Originally "[m]arketed to the community as a way to bring jobs to East Liverpool" (Ohio Citizen Action 8/ 7/2012), the potential hazards associated with its site, and the incinerator's proximity to homes and schools, caused a deep and bitter public controversy. This compelling case draws attention, not only to the ethical responsibilities of communicative practice, but its intersections with race and class. The third case study focuses on the public relations activities of a New Zealand state-owned company, Timberlands West Coast Ltd. Providing extraordinary insight into this event are media releases, planning documents and briefing notes that were reproduced in Hager and Burton's *Secrets and Lies: The Anatomy of an Anti-environmental PR Campaign*. The documents show the extent and ways activists were "managed" and a number of unethical and ambiguous practices designed to undermine public debate about the future of west coast New Zealand's temperate rainforest. The internal workings of public relations are closely guarded; therefore it is rare to see strategy and planning documents of any campaign, least of all one which has a covert political intent to silence and discredit activists. Together the case studies reveal the conceptual weaknesses in theories of public relations and of corporate social responsibility that present almost unresolvable issues for practitioners who seek an ethical approach to communication. Empirically they demonstrate that public relations is one of the most difficult industries to regulate and that very little is known about how it operates. Cases like these are an important reminder about the role ethics plays in an individual practitioner's decision making and how this affects, and is affected, by the social habitus of workplaces.

JAMES HARDIE INDUSTRIES: "NO RISK TO HEALTH"

> There is considerable confusion about asbestos as used in James Hardie products, and respirable asbestos dust. It is only airborne asbestos dust that is the potential health hazard. Because the small amount of asbestos fibre in our products is locked in by cement, it cannot escape into the atmosphere as dust, and therefore poses NO RISK TO HEALTH. (Pamphlet by James Hardie 1979)

In Australia, James Hardie Industries is closely associated with the manufacturing of asbestos products. In 1979 the company, then known as James Hardie and Coy Pty Ltd, (hereafter referred to as "Hardie") engaged with a public relations campaign to "set the record straight" addressing what it termed "considerable confusion" about the safety of asbestos dust, asbestos cement water pipes, the health hazards of dumping, the health risk to Hardie employees and finally the company's commitment to expansion and long-term prosperity. The pamphlet was push-back from Hardie to counter the "recent publicity" which had steadily accelerated since the early 1970s. Between 1969 and 1975 independent and public broadcasters such as Britain's BBC and ITV and Australia's ABC, televised documentaries about the pervasiveness of the deadly fibres. But even so, asbestos production remained profitable, and in 1973, "sales were holding up: American consumption ascended a peak of 800,000 tonnes" (Haigh 2006, 110). Public relations was now playing an active role in the management of communication around asbestos. Haigh writes: "In a speech in June, Matthew Swetonic of the industry's newly formed public relations group, the Asbestos International Association, insisted: 'The good news is, despite all the negative articles on asbestos-health that have appeared in the press over the past half-dozen years, very few people have been paying attention'" (2006, 110–112). The public relations had had the desired effect. He said that shortly after "When Jock Reid presided as chairman over his last Hardie annual meeting at Asbestos House the following month, the seventy shareholders attending asked exactly one innocuous question" (Haigh 2006, 111).

Asbestos is a naturally occurring mineral, now known to have dangerous carcinogenic properties, that was mined, commoditised, manufactured and sold commonly throughout the twentieth century as a building material and in other products. Its industrial production dates back to the nineteenth century and occurred in many countries including Australia, South Africa, Canada and the US. The major global players were U.K.-based Cape Asbestos, and Turner & Newall, and the U.S.-based Johns-Manville Corporation "which became the biggest asbestos miner and manufacturer in the world" (Hills 1989, 10). Hills said that the "Big Three" "dominated the industry that was to put "tens of millions of tons (an estimated 20 million tons in the US alone) of asbestos into ships and planes, office blocks and suburban homes, cars and kitchens, railway carriages and water pipes on every continent, even Antarctica" (1989, 10). The popularity of asbestos in Australia, Britain, the US and Canada was due to its versatility, competitive price and insulating properties that were fire and sound resistant. Asbestos appeared to be another modern "wonder product," similar to plastic, that epitomised the progressive, do-it-yourself and egalitarian spirit of the twentieth century. Indeed, riding on the back of post-war optimism asbestos was marketed to the middle classes as cheap, attractive and durable materials that would transform their daily lives with comfort and new possibilities for living. So popular was it in Australia that "[m]ost public buildings and about one third of private dwellings built in this era contained asbestos in the forms of concrete, asbestos cement sheeting (AC sheeting or fibro), vinyl floor coverings, lagging of pipes and boilers, and insulation (laid or sprayed)" (Australian Government National Health and Medical Research

Council 8/9/2012). However it is now publicly known that asbestos contains microscopic fibres that can be inhaled and incubate over twenty to forty years, eventually causing fatal diseases such as asbestosis, lung cancer and mesothelioma. People at greatest risk of these diseases are "exposed to the loose fibres" as were miners working in Wittenoom in Western Australia. Exposure to asbestos fibres can also occur through their removal in home renovations. Thus the widespread usage of asbestos in the construction of public and private buildings in Australia now means that it has one of the highest rates of asbestos-related death in the world. According to the Australian Government National Health and Medical Research Council the health risks associated with asbestos are long term and growing: "As these can take a number decades to develop, it is likely that the effects on the Australian community of exposure to asbestos will continue to increase into the 21st Century".

CONTEXTUALISING ASBESTOS PRODUCTION

Public relations was a key tool in the suppression of information about the lethal and long term effects of asbestos and in the management of the activist groups that mobilised to expose the hazardous nature of the material and to seek reparation. The known risks of the industrial production of asbestos can be traced to the nineteenth century, when people began to notice the ill effects on millworkers from asbestos factories in Manchester and Birmingham. Hills (1989) states that in 1906 the British Government established a Parliamentary Commission to investigate conditions in the factories which, by 1927, led to the classification of the disease "asbestosis." This was followed by more conclusive evidence in 1930 when:

> A Home Office doctor named Merewether and a ventilation engineer named Price examined workers and workplaces in the asbestos industry: 363 men and women were examined, and gave detailed histories of their occupational exposure to the dust; 35 per cent were found to have asbestosis, more than one in three. The two investigations found that the disease could develop after as little as six months' exposure, and after twenty years in the industry, four out of five workers could expect to develop the chronic symptoms of cyanosis (blue lips) dyspnea (shortage of breath), lungs that crackled like cornflakes, and a racking cough. (Hills 1989, 13)

Further epidemiologic studies of asbestos in Europe and the USA took place in the 1940s and 1950s but the alarming health and social effects were also prominently canvassed in 1964 in a conference hosted by the New York Academy of Sciences. According to Greeenberg, the conference "added little new to the knowledge of asbestos and its diseases, but it raised their profile, and reiterated to industry that, despite protestations to the contrary, urgent attention required to be paid to a major hazard" (2003, 550). In particular, attention was focused on Dr Irving Selikoff, whose empirical study of US insulation workers traced their medical histories and found a strong correlation between rates of exposure to asbestos and disease. His work gained media attention, not just for its integrity, but because he seemed to understand media processes and the role that he could play in agenda setting. Asbestos products and production were a social threat that required urgent action to control and avert. Despite this, Greenberg writes: "Selikoff was demonized as shameless and irresponsibly exploiting the media for self promotion, but could be seen as ahead of his time in recognizing the value of the media in altering policy makers and those who influence them, to an awareness of a major international public health hazard" (2003, 547). Monitoring this activity was the American Textiles Institute. The committee was concerned about the growing publicity and discussion in its minutes reflected the level of concern amongst its members:

> ... the picture has changed somewhat [since their June meeting] as recent publications again point out the intention of this conference headed by Dr. Selikoff. Since they are linking asbestos with cancer, the committee feels this conference will have an effect on the entire industry and are concerned as how best the results of the conference can be investigated and rebutted. After considerable discussion it was agreed a public relations man with our help would be quickest way to get accurate publicity to the public. (Minutes of the June 6, 1963 American Textiles Institute Meeting, quoted in Greenberg 2003, 547)

However, as Tweedale and McCulloch argue, production of asbestos continued to increase between 1960 and approximately 1980 despite the growing concerns about the health risks it presented (2011, 1). They explain that "[t]he asbestos multinationals—Johns-Manville, Turner & Newall, Cape Asbestos, Eternit, and James Hardie—were powerful enough to influence the media and scientific debate. Most leading asbestos scientists had links to the industry. The asbestos industry's critics were dismissed as subversives or accused of having links with trade unions and personal-injury lawyers" (1).

A PUBLIC RELATIONS MAN

> When I told Russell years later that Hardie's first asbestos compensation claim had occurred in 1939, he was quiet for a moment. Did it surprise him I asked to find that Hardie had been sued so long ago? He gave a dry chuckle. "Well, it's par for the course, really," he replied. "The question you ask is, 'How did they get away with it for so long?'

It just got covered up. It was all kept secret. James Hardie was fairly influential." (Peacock 2009, 54)

Public relations was a key instrument used by the asbestos industry to ensure that their reputations were put ahead of the risk incurred by the dissemination of knowledge about asbestos products and production. Australian investigative journalist Matt Peacock has specialised in investigating the public relations activity of James Hardie Industries Ltd. He said that in 1977 Neilson, McCarthy & Partners were employed by Hardie to monitor media about the organisation. In fact their query relating to the granting of permission to reproduce part of the program for "internal and external community relations" triggered his interest in the asbestos issue. He surmised that the part of the program that they were interested in was the simple declaration that: "The asbestos industry in Australia is no longer a problem," uttered by Gersh Major, a physicist in Sydney University's School of Public Health and Tropical Medicine. The School was articulated to the federal Department of Health which was "specialising in occupational health," and which according to Peacock had also been "receiving a research grant from James Hardie Asbestos." (Peacock, 2009, 25).

It was cascading failures and inaction of government and business that provided the catalyst for numerous grassroots activist groups to form in response to the asbestos crisis. Men and women associated with the production of asbestos, mobilised to provide social justice for victims and changes in policy and to alert the public of the dangers of asbestos. In Australia, one of the strongest and most effective of these was the Asbestos Diseases Society of Western Australia formed in 1979. Typical of many activist groups it drew on the social infrastructure of another community collective: "The new organisation drew the bulk of its members from those who had worked and lived at Wittenoom and was supported by the Ex-Wittenoom residents Association" (Australian Asbestos Network 8/ 9/ 2012). The driving force in the group was Robert Vojakovic: "the Croatian miner who had taken over as president of the society, and whose voice was soon heard loudly on Perth radio demanding that the government go back and have another look (Hills 1989, 52). According to Tweedale and McCulloch (2011, 3) individuals and groups affected by asbestos began writing literature warning of the lethal health risks, one was Nancy Tait who wrote *Asbestos Kills* in 1976, another was Alan Dalton who wrote *Asbestos Killer Dust* in 1979. "Inevitably, these campaigns groups were attacked. The asbestos industry published a critical *Commentary* on *Asbestos Kills* that took Tait to task for her 'extreme view'. Alan Dalton was sued for libel and bankrupted by Dr Robert Murray, the medical adviser to the Trades Union Congress (who later worked for the asbestos industry)" (Tweedale and McCulloch, 3). Yet despite the accumulating evidence about the risks associated with asbestos, there was marked intransigence in business and government to address the crisis.

> The negligence of those who knew the dangers so clearly associated with the material continued till as late as 1979 in this country, although by then some belated attempts were being made to control and eliminate the substance in some industries. These belated and often secretive attempts to get rid of the material without the workforce knowing why it was being removed, could not continue for a very long before workers and their unions discovered what was happening, and took action to find out what had previously been hidden from them. (Wragg 1995, 4)

The framing of asbestos victims and activists as simple minded not-in-my-backyarders or "NIMBYs", "malingers", "interlopers" and "extremists" shows how public relations practices sought to control identity within bounded limits that are infused with negative connotations. Hardie was able to assimilate these meanings successfully into the political discourses and thus maintain its reputation as a good-hearted business, successful, proper and socially useful. Published in 1987, *"A Very Good Business": One Hundred Years of James Hardie Industries Limited 1888–1988* by Brian Carroll, was an opportunity to cement the proud narrative of the organisation into the history books. Other methods were also deployed to ensure Hardie was perceived as respectable. One included a barrage of statements invoking legal discourse to maintain a form of third party endorsement through the support of science. In respect of this, Hardie continually and vexatiously disputed links between asbestos to cancer. According to McCulloch:

> The politicization of science is used by industry to immobilize debate, by excluding the victims and the public from participation in the conflict. That exclusion is a political strategy which is rarely, if ever, justified by the nature of the explanations involved, or by the methodology physicians use in researching diseases and their cause. What needs to be done is to transfer the asbestos controversy into the public arena, so that the issue is no longer seen or defined as a technical problem for experts in the legal, medical, technocratic and bureaucratic spheres to debate unhindered by an informed public. (McCulloch 1986, 257)

These baseline public relations practices helped to buttress the institutional authority of Hardie as a source of credible information.

More oppressive tactics to suppress information included threats in relation to jobs or legal action for its opponents. Peacock writes that "[f]ootage of Hardie's two factories in Brisbane had also featured in a follow-up story to the radio series on ABC TV. David McPherson, a delegate for the manufacturing workers' union in one of the Brisbane factories, called me after the broadcast to say his manager had suggested that following this unwanted publicity they 'play it cool . . . because all of our jobs depend on it'" (2009, 36–37).

In the Hardie case it was evident that the active concealment of sometimes privileged information affected stakeholders to which it had a moral responsibility. Peacock details the views of Neil Gilbert, an insider who worked at Hardie and played a "key role in developing the company's response to the health hazard" (2009, 60). He writes "Gilbert was aware of the accumulating evidence that asbestos caused cancer, a fact he told me was 'well known' within the company by 1961" (2009, 63).

WASTE TECHNOLOGIES INDUSTRIES, INC.

> Public opposition to waste disposal facilities is a recent phenomenon. Prior to the rise of the environmental movement in the 1970s, waste facilities aroused little public concern, and rarely were facilities closed due to local opposition. (Cerrell Associates Inc. 1984, 4)

It remains unclear why in 1979 "[o]ne of the world's largest capacity hazardous waste incinerators" was proposed in the poor industrial area of East Liverpool, Ohio ("Background on WTI"). Its planning and eventual construction in the early 1990s caused a bitter and ongoing controversy in the USA that reached high political levels. From the outset key concerns were that the location of the facility—in a valley prone to air inversions, over an aquifer and in the flood plain of the Ohio River was "about the worst place you could imagine siting a giant hazardous waste facility." These factors compounded the health risks associated with emissions and contamination in the incineration process for nearby residents and the school community, particularly if permit conditions were breached or accidents occurred. According to the activist group Ohio Citizen Action, in the early 1980s, and when approvals processes were in carriage "Ohio had virtually no siting criteria for hazardous waste facilities and a rubber-stamp facility siting board" ("Background on WTI").

Thomas Shevory's authoritative 2007 book *Toxic Burn: The Grassroots Struggle against the WTI Incinerator* is used to inform much of this section. Apart from the geological conditions, he argues that another key factor in the siting of this facility was the deindustrialisation of East Liverpool. The WTI incinerator was located in the East End of the city, a manufacturing precinct which previously had been home to flourishing pottery and steel industries. However, economic decline in the potteries had been marked since the post war period when lower tariffs contributed to Japanese imports. Other industries were also under pressure. Shevory writes that "[b]y the mid-1980s, the steel industry had also fallen on difficult times. The Jones and Laughlin Steel Company, which had closed down, reopened after concessions from the United Steelworkers Union. While operations continued, it had become "a shell of its former self" (2007, 37). By the 1970s this trend of deindustrialisation "was unfolding not only in

East Liverpool but throughout industrial America" (39). Moreover, socially disadvantaged and politically disempowered, the East End of the city was predominately where "the city's black residents live" (6).

The social-economic implications of the site's location for public resistance are an important consideration, given the unsuitable geophysical features of the site. Of particular interest, Shevory discusses "the now infamous Cerrell Report" commissioned by the California Waste Management Board to gauge and address, more generally, public resistance to hazardous waste repositories referred to in the report as "Waste-to-Energy" facilities (Cerrell Associates Inc. 1984 1). The report entitled "Political Difficulties Facing Waste-to-Energy Conversion Plant Siting," prepared by Los Angeles public affairs company Cerrell Associates is a public relations plan that responds to these questions:

> What are the issues raised against Waste to-Energy projects? Who in the community objects most vociferously? And who objects least? And, finally, what decisions can be made in selecting a site that encourage community acceptance of the project? (1984, 1)

The Cerrell Report is very significant for a range of reasons. For one, it assesses in detail the demographic and psychographic factors influencing individuals and groups that oppose sites for "waste-to-energy" facilities. These factors focus on the inhabitants' greater or lesser capacity to defend social and democratic rights according to "educational level, age, and political ideology" (Cerrell Associates Inc. 1984, 18). Secondly, while the exact reasons for the siting of the incinerator in the East End of East Liverpool are unclear, the profile of the area and its inhabitants matches the lower-socio economic demographic profile identified in the report as "least resistant" (50). Lastly, the report shows that countering activism was a key consideration for public relations. The term "activist' is used freely throughout the document, in conjunction a list of communicative activities "to contribute to a balanced understanding of the proposed Waste-to-Energy project" (37). This revealing paragraph in the report discussed "public relations" as the key tool in breaking down strong opposition.

> The first decision facility proponents need to make regarding the encouragement of community acceptance is whether a public relations campaign may even be necessary. In terms of small, private on-site facilities, past experiences suggest that a community acceptance program would not be necessary. However, in virtually all major facilities that directly affect the surrounding community, public opposition should be expected. (28)

Of interest communities that had mobilised through activism were seen to be highly resistant to what were euphemistically termed "encouragement" strategies.

> In addition, a community that has a recent history of public activism against major facilities and support for environmental regulation will probably be aroused and suspicious of any new major facilities. Regardless of whether the earlier struggles of the environmental protection group were successful, the organizational apparatus and the spirit of the group will persist. Furthermore, a community history of environmental activism should be viewed as indicative of adverse community attitudes. (17)

A key activist group involved in countering the incinerator's construction was the "Tri-State Environmental Council." According to Rembert, "The threat of the incinerator led [Terri] Swearingen to co-found the Tri-State Environmental Council—a grassroots coalition of citizens from West Virginia, Ohio and Pennsylvania whose mission is to stop environmental racism" (1997, 1). Another early activist group was "Save Our Country" which began to network with similar groups, fighting similar issues in other locations. Shevory writes: "Save Our Country began to make connections with other antitoxics activists across the state and eventually the country (2007, 76). In response to the activist backlash, WTI deployed what was to become a familiar disparaging narrative: "Antitoxics activists were branded with the 'NIMBY' label. The implication was that they were often simply obstructionists, or worse, representatives of an ignorant mass whose members were unable or unwilling to grasp the scientific 'facts' involved with waste disposal, particularly in terms of the concept of 'risk'" (111–112).

The ownership of the WTI was always a vexed question. Ohio Citizen Action states that "[t]here were originally four investors in the facility. In 1990, the current owner—Von Roll America, Inc., a subsidiary of Swiss-based Von Roll AG—bought out the other partners, without properly informing the regulatory authorities or seeking the required permit modification" (2011, 2). According to Shevory, "Terri and a diverse group of researchers had uncovered more than forty-four possible owners through the mid-1990s" (2007, 10). In addition, minor descriptive changes about the known elements of the corporation contributed to identity obfuscation. In respect of the WTI: "At one point, one of the partners had evolved from Waste Technologies Inc. to Waste Technologies, Inc. The comma indicated a different legal owner" (10).

To gain a measure of acceptance in the face of community resistance it was important for WTI to spread some of its economic benefits. In respect of this, the WTI paid a gratuity to the Council. Seemingly innocuous, this behaviour can set the groundwork for control. Fostering economic co-dependency had the dual advantage of enabling favourable treatment. Shevory writes: "The plant's owners considered the fee to be a 'gift' to the city, and one that they could conceivably withdraw at their discretion. The city's budget was now, however, highly dependent on these funds" (2007, 11).

Public ignorance about the WTI was understandable as early proposals for development pointed to an entirely different development, which frustrated opposition. This irony is demonstrated when, according to Shevory "The first step to siting the incinerator was the creation of Columbiana Country Port Authority" (2007, 59). In 1979 the Ohio state legislature provided the Department of Transportation with considerable funds ostensibly to purchase property to improve river usage, which implied "some kind of port facility" that was state owned (Shevory 2007, 60) However, the process, which involved grants, agreements, and public notification, obscured the intent. "During the initial public hearing, the Port Authority's chair, Russell Albright, mentioned some of its goals, which included establishing an industrial park and leasing unused space to WTI and to a grain elevator company. Albright described the proposed WTI operation as an 'industrial waste facility,' which would receive waste from barges on the Ohio River. No mention was made of hazardous wastes or of incineration" (60–61). Ohio Citizen Action (2011) states bluntly: "There were numerous irregularities and probable illegalities in the permit process for WTI". In this case, inaccessibly and general ignorance surrounding the proposal, affected the ability of the public to prepare formal objections to the site.

Long term strategies to gain hegemonic acceptance were deployed in this case. One was to disperse and integrate political statements relating to other powerful lifeworld discourses. In relation to the WTI facility this strategy included "picnics in the parking lot for the local residents. School children would be encouraged to visit, take a free balloon, a hotdog, and maybe an ice cream cone. These regular events are even spotlighted on the Webpage of Von Roll, the corporation that owns the plant" (Shevory 2007, 7). It comes as little surprise that this strategy and its objective to "bolster the image of trustworthiness" was outlined in the Cerrell Report:

> Escorted tours of the proposed site area and/or of existing waste energy facilities should be an on-going invitation. Public concerns can sometimes be alleviated by familiarity with the facility and site. If the site is compatible with adjacent land uses, or an existing facility well maintained, many fears of the public could be eliminated. A facility open to the public would also help to bolster the image of trustworthiness. (Cerrell Associates Inc. 1984, 38)

An example of greenwashing was when the WTI was promoted by its owners as a environmentally friendly plant that adopted the language of Cerrell Report. Shevory writes: "In fact, a brochure entitled 'Waste-to-Energy' was published by WTI in September 1981, the company's first stab at public relations" (2007, 65).

Creating obfuscation and barricades to understanding can take a number of forms. Activists found that people put forward as officials seemed unaware of the complexities and oblivious to their concerns. Shevory reports on the experience of Save Our Country's Alonzo Spencer who struggled to get any depth of understanding about the WTI from a spokesperson: "The council member who attempted to respond to Alonzo's questions seemed rather clueless. He exhibited a notable lack of curiosity about the ownership issue and had apparently taken at face value what the plant managers had told him" (Shevory 2007, 10).

Activists were also intimidated by legal action. In 1997 Ohio activists speaking out about the environmental and associated social and health issues encountered a strategic lawsuit against public participation (SLAPP) when "the company had decided to initiate a lawsuit against some of the incinerator's main opponents. Von Roll was seeking $34 million in damages against thirty-three individuals" (Shevory 2007, 138). According to Terri Swearingen,

> I'm also being sued for libel. WTI put a SLAPP [Strategic Lawsuit Against Public Participation] suit against me. I think that WTI is the epitome of everything that's wrong with the regulatory system and our government. The WTI SLAPP suit is a camouflage to divert attention away from the issue—the incinerator. They attack your position and your First Amendment rights-and your children's security. They can come into a community and say, "We're going to build this because the EPA gave us permission to, and if you try and stop us, we'll sue you." (Rembert 1997)

The activist campaign gained national exposure. However, despite high profile politicians such as Vice President Al Gore in 1992, promising that the "new Clinton-Gore administration will not give WTI a test burn permit until all questions have been satisfactorily answered" (Environmental Research Foundation 1992); the WTI proposal proceeded and today operates as Heritage-WTI, Inc. in East Liverpool, Ohio. It is claimed that a legacy of health and environmental problems in the area remains. In a 1992 interview Terri Swearingen said that in East Liverpool "the breast cancer rate per 100,000 between 1992 and 1995 was 41.5. The Ohio rate for the same period of time was 28.2. The U.S. average was 26.2." (Rembert 1997). According to Shevory, between 2003 and 2004, to meet permit compliance WTI failed three "test burns" which are intended to "give an accurate reading of what is generally flowing from the stack, leaking from the seams, and in general being deposited in the local community" (2007, 208). Even so, he says that the validity of test burns to gauge the quality of emissions is disputed. "The first test burn was undertaken in September 2003. WTI failed. Another was taken in December 2003. Again WTI failed. . . . In February 2004 the Title V permit was authorized by the Ohio EPA. In March, WTI failed another test burn. In April, a fourth test burn was undertaken, and WTI finally passed. Thus the already-accepted permit was legitimized by a fourth test". Shevory also reported that in 2004 "the EPA imposed a $643,908 fine on WTI" for permit violations.

TIMBERLANDS WEST COAST LTD

New Zealand's native forests are characterised not just by their beauty, diverse climates and ecosystems, but also by activism that they engender. Originally politically benign, conservation organisations such as the Native Bird Protection Society existed as early as 1923 (Dann 2003, 396). However over the 1970s and 1980s the New Zealand timber industry's harvesting of indigenous forests and the plantation of exotics spearheaded a different reaction in civil society. Dann writes: "It was not until the 1960s that nature conversation, as it was popularly conceived, ran up against a new type of industrial development in New Zealand" (Dann 2003, 370). The Native Forest Action Committee (NFAC) was one group that developed from an existing group, and also presented a more politicised and co-ordinated activist response.

> The Beech Forest Action Committee (BFAC) became the Native Forest Action Committee (NFAC) in 1975. In its heyday in the late 1970s, NFAC was the second largest conservation organisation in New Zealand and collected 341,160 signatures on its "Maruia Declaration" petition, which called for an end to the logging and the burning of native forests. (Dann 2003, 371–372)

Roche argues that "NFAC challenged the New Zealand Forest Service (NZFS) plans for indigenous harvesting and expansion of exotic plantations throughout the remainder of the 1970s and into the 1980s. The exchanges were acrimonious on both sides with the NZFS over time losing some critical public support" (Roche 2008, Australian Forest History Society Inc., 3). Thus, rather than abating, the clashes over conservation and commercialism continued in to the 1990s. In particular, "when most New Zealanders would have presumed that logging native forests was settled and a thing of the past, proposals appeared to dramatically expand the scale of West Coast logging" (Hager and Burton 1999, 11–12).

Hager and Burton have paid particular attention to the problems associated with a state-owned enterprise (SOE). The logging company Timberlands West Coast Ltd which is owned by the New Zealand government, focused on the logging of ancient beech forests of the West Coast. They identified that the internationally networked PR company Shandwick New Zealand was employed by Timberlands to manage the opposition to its operations. The $1 million public relations campaign informed much of Hager and Burton's book. They reference one strategy document that outlined that "[t]he main thrust of the Communications Strategy . . . is to limit public support for environmentally based campaigns against Timberlands, thereby limiting public pressure on the political process" (1999, 31).

From the outset the tenor of the public relations campaign was aggressive and intimidating and working on a number of levels. According to Hager and Burton, Timberlands was conscious that activists, and their cause, had garnered respect and standing in the community. "Aware of this, and of its own lack of broad support, Timberlands' next strategy was in the language of the PR trade, to 'position' its opponents as being 'extreme.' They argue that in 1997, the CEO of Timberlands, Dave Hillard wrote "The company is accused of environmental vandalism. . . . by a group of extreme activists who are self-appointed, misinformed, and politically motivated" (1999, 37).

Repetition of key messages reinforces media framing and this was also used in the Timberlands campaign. A good example is: "The thing I like about Timberlands" in the advertisement (below) which Hager and Burton claim was "played at saturation levels during the period when Timberlands was attempting to ensure a flood of local submissions in favour of its beech logging plans":

Presenter: What did you like about Timberlands?
Child: The thing that I like about Timberlands is because they take care of our forest and show what they can do.
Child: The thing I like about Timberlands is you learn quite a lot.
Child: The best thing I liked about Timberlands was pruning the trees.
Child: The thing I like about Timberlands was going to the skid.
Presenter: What a great impression Timberlands have left in these kids' minds. Next time you're out about in the forest, have a think about what Timberlands are doing for the West Coast. (Hager and Burton 1999, 175–176, italics in original)

According to Hager and Burton, "In a 1997 communication strategy Shandwick explained the line: "Current environmental opposition is based on a small but determined group of relatively extreme environmentalists who do not support the sustainable management philosophy, enshrined in legislation and supported by the more responsible environmental groups" (1999, 38). In a similar way to the WTI case, low level support was also compounded through the thickening of relationships between Timberlands and the local council. "The local newspaper pictured Mayor Kevin Brown holding his new name-tag, which had the council's and Timberlands' logos side by side at the top followed by the words 'I support sustainable resource management.' The badges were made of native timber" (Hager and Burton 1999, 174).

They claim that the company used misinformation to confuse the public. "Constantly defending itself against claims its opponents had not made helped Timberlands to define its opposition as engaged in 'misinformation.' Without having to cite evidence, Timberlands turned defence into attack, forcing its opponents to disprove a negative" (Hager and Burton 1999, 39).

Public relations companies are sometimes likened to quasi-intelligence units or private detectives. In particular, practices such as information gathering can involve invasion of privacy and stealth. In the Timberlands case study: "the Body Shop's support for NFA was listed on the PR telephone conference agenda. 'Franchise owners of Body Shop are pro-active in green movement. Need to develop a campaign targeting them,' the minutes said . . . Shandwick then sent requests to consultants in overseas Shandwick offices looking for dirt on the Body Shop" (Hager and Burton 1999, 51).

Forming the basis of much public relations work, the media monitoring of a corporation is the review and analysis of discursive activity in the public sphere. In general it refers to the measurement of media reporting as data in news and other broadcasts, in the main to see if the "message is getting through" or if reputation and/or issue management is required. Media transcripts are provided by a range of in-house, or consultative services, whereby analysis can take place. In this sense this activity is a pre-response or general indicator that determines whether public relations action should occur at all.

However, targeted intelligence gathering is different and involves the intent to develop detailed profiles of activists. "In several known instances [in New Zealand], 'moles' attended conservation group meeting to collect information. . . . Shandwick arranged monitoring of VEG (Victoria University Environment Group) by finding a student on the Victoria University campus prepared to attend its meetings for payment and report back to the PR company on what was said. . . . He was paid $50 per hour for these services" (Hager and Burton, 1999, 32).

Like the WTI activists, the New Zealand activists experienced the intimidation of proposed legal action through SLAPPs. Hager and Burton write: "Timberlands had become obsessed with finding any opportunity to make legal threats against its opponents. Minutes of another teleconference recorded 'To discuss with Pitt & Moore the NFA pamphlet from Rotorua (a forest industries conference). Could be libellous?' Shandwick's Rob McGregor was charged with following through" (Hager and Burton 1999, 47).

Strategic reframing emphasising environmental rather than commercial objectives, or "greenwashing" was evident in the Timberlands case when "a 1997 'communications strategy" (Hager and Burton 1999, 98) prepared by Shandwick considered in detail how to portray the company as being environmentally responsible. To enhance its image, Timberlands was advised to upgrade, not its actual environmental research, but publicity about this. Shandwick also proposed that it publish an 'Environmental Report,' upgrade the company's self-promoting *Green Monitor*, host environmental media facility visits (to coincide with the launching of the beech plans) and establish the 'open forests' policy" (Hager and Burton 1999, 98).

Deceptive and manufactured grassroots activist groups by the public relations industry is sometimes called "astroturfing." Hager and Burton discuss the creation of one such group in 1997: "The main tool used by Shandwick was the creation of a new group called the Global Climate Information Project (GCIP), backed by trade associations representing the companies with most to lose from trying to control global warming: leading oil, coal and automobile producers, including some of the most notorious polluters in the United States" (1999, 23). In another example, the PR firm Shandwick "was assigned the job of replying to the latest pro-forest conservation letters to the editor" (Hager and Burton, 1999, 19).

With serious concerns about the ethics of Shandwick's New Zealand campaign, in late 1999 Nicky Hager and Bob Burton lodged a formal complaint to the Public Relations Institute of New Zealand (PRINZ). After internal ructions, PRINZ referred the complaint to an independent QC, Hugh Rennie. According to Harrison, Rennie investigated five of Hager and Burton's 18 claims against Shandwick and upheld two of those five claims. He agreed that a student was paid to spy on the activists and secondly that a "mindset of conflict" was adopted in relation to the activists (2004, 4–5). Harrison said that on the same day the Rennie Report was released, "Shandwick executives did further damage to the principles of industry self-regulation and peer review of professional practice by publicly resigning from PRINZ" (2004, 6).

PANOPTICON PR: A TERRIBLE ERA

> On a given day, public relations practitioners may prepare press releases, help a reporter develop a story, edit a employee publication, prepare an exhibit, interview a government official, conduct a scientific survey of public opinion, counsel management on the public relations impact of a major policy decision, write a speech, raise funds, or prepare an annual report. Practitioners do so many varied jobs that some scholars who study public relations question whether it can be conceptualized as a single activity. (Grunig and Hunt 1984, 13)

Twentieth-century public relations practices directed at activists were underpinned by a strong expectation that obedient publics, blind to the discursive mechanisms at play, would behave submissively as directed. Indeed the social world Bernays described in his 1928 book *Propaganda* was a utopian one for public relations. Publics he described were "herds" that followed leaders who formed their thinking (2005, 73–74). However, the social and political awakenings of the 1960s and 1970s fundamentally changed the reception of public relations. Some publics now challenged the authority of the "invisible government" and the naturalised view that it somehow "knew better." Moreover, the push-back from empowered publics over these years brought to the fore critical perspectives that highlighted theoretical weaknesses, tensions and contradictions that underpinning Bernays' conception of public relations. In particular, these critiques challenged his argument that the unworkable fiction of democracy justified a public relations intervention.

Robust public conversations about important and complex issues are essential to democracy. In the 1970s, activist groups worked in focused ways to expose contradictions in business and state policy and practices that shattered the passive acceptance of these policies and practices as "truth." At this juncture, and in response to this resistance, a public relations response was launched to manage the disturbed discourses. Privileged by the conditions of early modernity and responding to the pressures of capitalism, public relations had transmogrified social arrangements based on the oppressed and oppressor into a conception of the "weak" guided by the wisdom of the "strong." Having been given this "gift," the public relations industry assumed a sense of entitlement. Its objective was to maintain and increase influence in power relations. In terms of its conduct, the means justified ends. This teleological slant discouraged workplace cultures that analysed the complex consequences of communicative action. Cosy relationships with editors predicated on mutual self-interest were influential in persuading publics on matters of public policy. In turn, economic success was used as validation. Moreover, large sections of the media advantaged public relations practitioners and contributed to their discursive dominance either by failing to take a position or enquire into the disputes, or by being a conduit to circulate their "truths." At the same time, while quite inaccessible, the media reduced activists' subtle and thoughtful arguments to simplified "bites" of information. Panopticon-like, public relations was designed to see all but remain unseen. Its surveillance, undetected, would invisibly manage activists and restore "harmony." As the case studies reveal, the effect of this was devastating for real democracy and was an abuse of power.

The case studies also suggest that a culture of impunity existed around the communicative activities of business. Largely unscrutinised by the state authorities, their programmes were conducted in self-regulating ways. The "Public Relations Action Plan for James Hardie Asbestos" (September 1978) justified the company's programme of activity on the basis that it countered "unfounded and misinformed criticism"; however, this was a fallacious foundation. The situation analysis used in this document did not accurately include all the relevant facts: for example, it omitted to consider that the health risks were real and known since the UK Merewether and Price study in 1928 (Peacock 2009, 53). The Plan also used this unjustifiably as a basis for framing opposition as "elements of the trade union movement and fringe environmental groups attempting to kindle widespread public interest in the issue." (September 1978).

Democratic process, regarded as "unworkable" by Bernays, was but a slight consideration for big PR. However, the cost of this was considerable, not just for the individuals and communities affected, but also for the environment and social responsibility more broadly. It cost people's lives, health, well-being and their right to democratic process. The production of statements and the erasure of others through public relations practices propped up failing discourses, masked contradictions and buttressed the authority of business to continue in their erroneous ways.

The exposure of public relations' abuses is little consolation to those activists pitted against them. The activists examined in this chapter had strong arguments in the public interest and their communicative activities were respectful of democratic systems. Arguably, in the 1970s a level of collusion between public relations organisations existed, that enabled the sharing of information and in particular learnt techniques in dealing with activists. In doing so, unethical behaviour was embedded and normalised. Was there collusion between large public relations firms across the globe? Did they share information; indeed did they teach each other unethical practices? Collusion between public relations organisations is evident in the James Hardie case as there is clear sharing of information between the asbestos manufacturers and the companies that represented the asbestos producer. For example, in response to managing the media exposure of health issues linked to asbestos, Leslie Anderson from the Australian public relations firm Eric White Associates (EWA) wrote to the Managing Director of Hardie:

> Hill & Knowlton, our parent company, has been very much involved in this whole matter. In the U.K., our office was instrumental in the establishment of the Asbestos Information Committee in 1969 and worked for that Committee for some four or five years. In the U.S. Hill & Knowlton began work for Johns Manville in 1967 and in 1971, at the instigation of that client, began work for the Asbestos Information Association. Work on that assignment lasted for about five years. (Anderson 1978)

Significantly, this section from the Cerrell Report also reveals that "unpopular" risk producing industries, from toxic dumps to the nuclear industry, networked and shared information in relation to public relations strategies to manage public opposition:

> Many of the complaints people have against toxic chemical dumps, landfills, offshore oil rigs, nuclear power plants, and other unpopular facilities reflect similar fears held against Waste-to-Energy facilities. Understandably, opposition movements in each case would draw from similar circumstances and similar backgrounds (Cerrell Associates 1984, 11)

Therefore the case studies reveal, not just calculated and manipulative repertories of communicative practice in relation to the issues at hand, but broad patterns in unethical public relations practices, suggesting a systematic approach that was not accidental or unplanned.

Up to the 1960s, few "publics" outside the labour movement had mobilised and counter-campaigned against businesses. After this time, activists who mobilised and intervened in the wealth and expansion opportunities of industry were attacked with fiercely aggressive and unacceptable tactics. How is this explained? A consideration is whether the public relations practitioners and the organisations launching these communicative actions action understood fully the social ramifications. Were they extraordinarily naïve in social territory was that was unexplored, unknown and unregulated? Were they not privy to all industry information, did they in fact believe their own arguments? These are speculations only, which may or may not, form part of an explanation.

Not surprisingly, a slew of scathing critiques emerged over the 1980s and 1990s contesting the role of public relations in society, and in particular these critiques sought to shed light on the more prominent unethical practices. Nelson's 1989 work provides a bleak view of the public relations industry and its relation to society:

> The power of the PR industry is demonstrated not only by its hegemonic manoeuvrings within and for every area of government and business, but also by its remarkable ability to function as a virtually invisible "grey eminence" behind the scenes, gliding in and out of troubled situations with the ease of a Cardinal Richelieu and the conscience of a mercenary. (Nelson 1989, 19)

Nelson examines many examples of manipulation of the mass media by corporations to provide the public with misinformation and the responses by activist groups. One is an account of the antagonism between Action for Corporate Accountability, a group opposing multinational food giant Nestlé's "marketing of infant formula worldwide" and Ogilvy & Mather Public Relations, the firm that represented them (1989, 13). She said that the confidential PR report: "advised a strategy of 'neutralizing or defusing the issue by working quietly with key interest groups' and "building relationships with individuals and groups that share Nestlé's interest, in order to cultivate institutional allies." Nelson also focused a chapter on "greenwashing" in the 1970s, and gave the example of Hooker Chemical activities in Niagara Falls arguing: "Having dumped 43.6 million pounds of waste solvents and pesticide residues into the Love Canal from 1942 to 1953, Hooker nevertheless maintains to this day that the resulting toxic mess and health disaster were not its fault" (Nelson 1989, 131–132).

In 1995, Stauber and Rampton's *Toxic Sludge is Good for You*, published by Common Courage Press, fused satire with informed political, media and cultural perspectives to expose the inner workings and relations of power in the public relations industry. Bringing the shadowy industry into the light, they listed the Top 15 Public Relations Firms in 1994 with a total net fee income of $1.04 billion as Burson-Marsteller; Shandwick; Hill & Knowlton; Communications International-Porter/Novelli; Edelman PR Worldwide; Fleishman-Hillard; Ketchum PR; Ogilvy, Adams & Rinehart; Robinson Lake/Sawyer Miller; The Rowland Company; Manning, Selvage & Lee; GCI Group; Ruder Finn; Financial Relations Board; and Cohn & Wolf (1995, 208). The book delved into the minutiae of the PR world and sharpened understandings in powerful ways. For example, it described a political lobbying practice that a Hill & Knowlton executive referred to as "grasstops communication." This involved elaborate nepotistic hiring practices to employ "old friends, businessmen from the state or congressional district and ordinary constituents" when dealing with a political target (1995, 80). This practice was so successful it was applied more broadly to private industry. Beder, (1997, 133) also detailed disturbing public relations practices, in particular, "cross-pollination," or the subtle but systemic binding of opposing groups. She says "This can be done by donating public relations work to charities in order to be able to pressure them into supporting other clients later on." Beder outlines an example which took place between public relations company Porter/Novelli that represented pesticide manufacturers and produce growers and the American Cancer Society. Having provided the Society with "free services for decades", she says the public relations company managed to get it to issue a memo disputing the validity of documentary that was "about to be screened claiming that pesticides caused cancer in children" (1997, 133). The memo "was then used by the pesticide industry to lobby against the broadcasting of the documentary" (1997, 133). Public relations' reliance on the logic of early modernity was characterised by numerous problems within the late twentieth century. The critiques of public relations activity over this time set out to show that, rather than democracy, public relations was the great "fiction" which could not be sustained.

PUBLIC RELATIONS AND SOCIAL HAVOC

By the end of the twentieth century the relationship of public relations to activism was devoid of trust. This was highlighted in 1999 when the intergovernmental World Trade Organisation (WTO) held its November meeting in Seattle. The WTO was established four years earlier to open international trade through negotiating agreements and policies in order to achieve "a more prosperous, peaceful and accountable economic world" (WTO 2012). However, at that time activists, such as the collective Independent Media Centre, had a different view (Roper 2002, 121). They saw in carriage a neoliberal agenda using trade as a key dynamic—much like the imperial powers in previous centuries—to secure power and influence for the wealthy member nations, notably the USA, which was seen to play a leading role. Thousands of protestors with well organised rallies and anti-corporatist messages attended the second meeting of the WTO in Seattle with an agenda to "stop the destructive march of economic globalization." The media framing of the event focused on direct action and the theatre of activism: parody, blockades, pickets, human chains and graffiti amongst others. It also focused on the violent clashes occurring on the boundaries of the "no protest zone" set by local authorities and enforced by armed, helmeted black-clad paramilitary. Amid acrid clouds of tear gas, the fire of rubber bullets and concussion grenades directed towards the largely unprotected protestors presented a distorted and frightening visualisation of society and democracy. The compelling images on television, the Internet and in newspapers gained international notoriety as the "Five Days that Shook the World" and the "Battle for Seattle."

Indeed for the corporate world, and for those in public relations, the threat of activist movements at the 1999 WTO meeting flagged the potential of the Internet as an organising tool for disseminating independent messages and bypassing the media gatekeepers, which over the course of the twentieth century had maintained a tight rein on who could get media exposure (Ryan 1991; Roper 2002). To counsel influential corporate clients on these uncharted trends a "Guide to the Seattle Meltdown" was prepared by Gardner G. Peckham, Managing Director of a subsidiary of global PR colossus Burson Marsteller. The guide contained profiles of key activist groups participating in the Seattle protests, together with a cover letter that warned publics now had capacity to take action. The leaked document spread through global email systems reaching many activist groups, seeming to confirm that something extraordinary had happened at Seattle

> The spectacle created in Seattle during the WTO Ministerial meeting by a diverse collection of activists may have significant short-term ramifications for the business community. . . . These high profile battles will allow activists to further institutionalise and consolidate their gains, increase coordination, garner greater media attention and expand their targeting of business interests. . . . More recently, some environmental groups have resorted to targeting corporations for contributions in return for suspending their public ire. (Leaked Memo 2000):

Recanting in an interview in 2001, however, Gardner took a "business as usual" stance and distanced himself from these comments. He said, "My sense at the time of Seattle was that these groups had the potential to achieve an awful lot with all of those targets of opportunity in the following six to 12 months. I am interested to note now that they really I think achieved very little and they seemed to be allergic to having much in the way of leadership" (ABC Radio National 2001). Peckham said "I believe that at some point the corporate community is going to have to come to grips with the activists. Their traditional response to activism is to either ignore it or try to isolate it and deal with it in a vacuum, and they can get away with that as long the activists are separate, not united, as long as they are basically operating on the fringes and not in the mainstream" (ABC Radio National 2001). The assumptions embedded in this interview are that despite presenting a threat and despite the co-ordinating features of the Internet, corporations regard activists as predicable in their thinking and action. Peckham's comments also suggest that the public displays of conflict and angst by activists actually benefits public relations by bolstering its standing as rational player in the debate. Agitating, sometimes violent behaviour works to undermine the activists' claim to be working for the common good, muddies the water, and provides the public with evidence of extremism and possibly threat to society. Activism, in this social space, has worked to public relations' advantage over the twentieth century.

CONCLUSION

This chapter has focussed on the public relations practice of risk producing industries in the 1970s, 80s and 90s and in particular its role in stifling activism, creating consent and resisting social change. In doing so, it has catalogued a range of intrinsic and extrinsic public relations practices, a frightening repertoire. Moreover once revealed, these practices show that the institutionalised systemised use and abuse of discursive power had profound social effects, in nature and society beyond the immediate objectives.

This chapter has also tried to understand the activists' relationship to public relations, and why their concerns were overridden. The activists had strong arguments that engaged with science, technology, economics and the social, which within democratic society should have been considered. What made it acceptable for public relations companies to conceal key information, to lie, to spy and keep dossiers on activists, to threaten and harass and to produce counter-science and inflated support for their industries? Moreover to act with misplaced conviction, amoral detachment and a sense of impunity? Was it fear driving these brutal public relations campaigns that encroached on social and democratic rights? Was it fear, not just of being denied the project at hand, but of the environmental social movement, its scale and its gathering force and what this meant for industry more generally? According to Beck, once social risks become politicised, as an effect of industrialisation and shown in the case studies, a particular social and discursive space opens up that releases a range of new possibilities and solutions in ways that profoundly threaten the producers: "The insecurity within industry intensifies: no one knows who will be struck next by the anathema of ecological morality. Good arguments or at least arguments capable of convincing the public become a condition of business success.

Publicity people the "argumentation craftsmen" get their opportunity in the organization" (Beck 1992, 32). The case studies of James Hardie, Waste Technologies Industries and Timberlands evidenced the opening up of such a social and discursive space that Beck refers to; an intense, energetic, communal and creative space in which ideas and alternatives flourished. And it is precisely this social and discursive space that public relations was used to control in unseen and unseemly ways. However, there is more at stake here than a quarrel with activists. The principle of competition embedded in a market-based economy does not give antagonistic public relations a mandate to shut down these spaces which are the lifeblood of democracy. Nor should governments and other institutions waive concern for such events. More needs to be done.

In redressing these circumstances, this book argues that urgent reform in public relations is required to understand these developments and to deal with the social realities, because according to Kevin Moloney "We cannot wish PR away" (2006, 176). Therefore one possibility is that change within the ranks of public relations occurs, given its embedded status, position and prestige in late modern society. However, it should be noted that the cooptation (Dutta 2011, 260) of large activist organisations to become part of the "public relations story" not only misunderstands the problem but serves also to mask it yet again. Another possibility for reform is through the disarticulating communicative practices from public relations, and deinstitutionalising the field. Focussing on social, economic, environmental and political *variations and contexts in communicative practice* therefore may offer more scope for reflexivity and in confronting the harmful side effects of public relations.

4 Worlds Collide
Public Relations, Activism and Late Modernity

> For years Burson-Marsteller has been involved in major environmental issues all over the world, not hesitating to give polluters a helping hand when confronted by activist groups and/or government regulations. Many transnational corporations have turned to B-M for help in the creation of a pedantic, elitist and corporate-oriented brand of environmentalism. It is the hope of entrepreneurial sectors and neoliberal demagogues that this type of safe and harmless environmental activism will displace the more militant and agressive [sic] grassroots groups. (Ruiz 24/10/2012)

When activism changes direction, so too does public relations. This chapter argues that in the twenty-first century politics and conditions have transformed and affect both activism and public relations in ways that have implications for current and future developments. In particular the chapter explores how activism has moved into a more central social space, without being mainstreamed, as was sometimes the case in the mid 1980s and 1990s. Activism is on the rise, and together with the Internet and digital technologies, comes in many forms. Notably in this movement, socially and politically disparate people and groups mobilise and challenge from a community base, and on a myriad of issues: from environment to social justice, equality and media independence. Questioning science, power relations and the status quo, these activists have set agendas successfully advocating for change. Opening new ground, the changed social conditions allow for different viewpoints and diverse approaches to communicative practice which are important for reform in public relations. This chapter theorises these changed social conditions and observes how they are being expressed in other sites, such as corporate social responsibility and corporate citizenship and analyses what this means for public relations.

In 2000, public relations theorist James Grunig (2000) argued that, while most activist groups have some form of power, small community groups are the exception. However I argue that grassroots activism, once delegitimised and regarded as socially ineffective, has instead become highly effective. As a corollary, the ethically dubious public relations idea of "publics" as a commodity to be managed and manipulated is anachronistic in late modernity because "self-interest" is redefined around ecological debates. To understand the social contexts and conditions that explain these changes, this chapter sets out three pillars of theory: risk and reflexivity theory, communicative theory and citizenship theory, which together provide new perspectives on public relations and activism in the twentieth and twenty-first centuries. Socio-political, communicative and cultural theories may appear an unusual combination to view these public relations and activist activities, but it precisely this convergence of ideas that provides powerful insight into these relations. Communicative and citizenship theories shed light on some of the invisible effects of discourse on society, particularly unethical practices. The first pillar is Ulrich Beck's theory of risk society and reflexive modernisation[1] (1992; 2000; 2004). Refreshing modernity debates with a boldness of vision, Beck's work explains the logic of grassroots activism within the changing social context of late modernity.[2] When used to explain activism in relation to high emitting industries and developments in contemporary society, Beck's theories provide the means to speculate about future social and political developments that will have profound impact on the relationship between public relations and activism. The second pillar is communicative theory (Habermas 1984; 1989; 1995) which links ideas about modernity with the media's ambivalent relationship to self-interest and rational critical debate in democratic society (discussed also in Chapter 1). Lastly, citizenship theory is a pillar that sheds light on the conditions and influences that affect participation and belonging in late modern society (Marshall 1996; Turner 1994; Hudson and Kane 2000; Carter 2001). Together, these theories explain the growth of activist networks, what they seek to promote and their capacity to create change in state and business sectors.

REFLEXIVELY ORGANISING CHAOS

The idea of "publics" as largely cooperative and malleable has been a central premise in public relations since Edward Bernays penned *Propaganda* in 1928. It has been used to predict behaviour and develop strategies in communicative activities to neutralise opposition or build support for industry over the course of the twentieth century (Seitel 2011). Thus the extent to which people are apathetic, compliant or resistant in relation to a "problem" has been widely discussed and theorised. An example is James Gruing's "Situational Theory to Identify Publics" in which analysis is predicated on three variable factors: "problem recognition," "constraint recognition" and "level of involvement" (1984, 149). McElreath endorses this approach and says that by "using each factor as a variable, a number of provocative theoretical statements can be developed about communication behaviours of publics. For example, the more a public recognises a problem, perceives the problem as being relevant to its life, and feels that it can do something about it, the more likely that members of the public will appreciate and participate in communication about the problem" (McElreath 1997, 174). This view is underpinned by a structural functionalist belief that publics can be switched on and switched off. As such, McElreath argues that "an example of deactivating an active public would be an industry, faced with an organised consumers' boycott and potentially restrictive legislation, having its trade association establish a quasi-independent commission to investigate the public's concerns and to serve as an industry watchdog. From the industry's point of view, this would diffuse the active publics by providing a more management predicable forum for public discussion" (McElreath 1997, 172). Thus public relations practitioners, in the implementation of their programs of action, have generally expected that people and groups affected by their organisations can be finely managed and unconsciously controlled, even in difficult circumstances. But contemporary industrialised society's social, political and ecological conditions have changed radically, undermining this premise. The next section draws on the three variables in Grunig's framework: "problem recognition," "constraint recognition" and "level of involvement" (Grunig and Hunt 1984, 149) to explore social and political shifts in late modernity.

"PROBLEM RECOGNITION" IN LATE MODERNITY

New publics see new problems that cannot be switched on or off. Central to this is an underlying a change in the logic driving society, and its social, political and economic flows. Beck expresses this in the notion of "risk society"; a social phenomenon in advanced capitalist society in which "the social production of wealth is systematically accompanied by the social production of *risks*" (Beck 1992, 19; italics in original). In other words, the material goods which alleviate need and lack are inevitably co-produced with risk and hazards. Beck discusses conditions propelling these changes in present and future tense. Firstly, he says today, there are enough goods to satisfy and meet genuine demand, as well as "legal and welfare state protections and regulations" (Beck 192, 19). Secondly, there is knowledge that if the momentum of co-production of goods and risks is not slowed, there is a heavy price to pay tomorrow.

As discussed in Chapter 1, Beck's (1992, 21–22) definition of contemporary risk differs from an understanding that involves corporations managing the frightened publics' perceptions in relation to the extent of the problem, its sense of control and trust in the organisation. For example, Deegan argues "Communication about risk, termed 'risk communications' seeks to reduce concerns proactively by being open about and seeking to build an understanding of risk" (Deegan 2008, 94). Different again, according to Beck are personal risks that directly affect an individual because that person has been unlucky or has engaged with certain, avoidable behaviours.

Generally these risks were obvious "assaulting the nose or the eyes" (Beck, 1992, 21). Another difference is that the causes of contemporary risk are an inversion of a traditional definition of risk:

> In the past, the hazards could be traced back to an *under*supply of hygienic technology. Today they have their basis in industrial *over*production. The risks and hazards of today thus differ in an essential way from the superficially similar ones in the Middle Ages through the global nature of their threat (people, animals and plants) and through their *modern* causes. They are risks *of modernization*. They are *wholesale product* of industrialization, and are systematically intensified as it becomes global. (Beck 1992, 21; italics in original)

The canvas on which Beck maps out these changes is large, both temporally and spatially. The long-term incubating and globally threatening nature of these threats cannot be expunged or eradicated by a specific treatment. Beyond human control, their cumulative effects will affect the "unborn" in different times and places. For Beck, this changed logic manifests in social, political and economic realms. It has replaced simple beliefs, such as teleological or goal-oriented advancement of industrial society, which drove economics, and public relations, to this point. It has replaced the domination of institutionalised left and right politics, which to either a greater or lesser extent supported these beliefs. It has replaced the passive unpolitical "publics" that put their trust in these political and economic institutions. At this point in modernity he argues that "[W]e are therefore concerned no longer exclusively with making nature useful, or with releasing mankind from traditional constraints, but also and essentially with problems resulting from techno-economic development itself" (Beck 1992, 19). Echoing sentiments expressed by Rachel Carson in *Silent Spring*, he argues that exposure to risk is linked to products and practices that have in the past been considered safe, even banal, like asbestos which once had gained trust and earned a place in cultural biographies of Australians, British, Canadians and Americans: "In other words, the insignificances can add up quite significantly" (Beck 1992, 26). Therefore in late modern society, the "risk" concept encapsulates a paradox: the sophisticated medical and techno/economic advances that society applauds as "progress", and the act of risk minimisation itself, are the likely causes of further risk (Beck 1992, 14). For Beck these risks are writ large. He cites the example of radioactivity resulting from an atomic accident that will have intergenerational effects as well as widespread immediate threat. Another example is the long-term, culminate effects of carbon pollution. "The affected even include those not yet alive at the time or in the place where the accident occurred but born years later and long distances away" (Beck 1992, 22). Because these threats cannot be entirely controlled and managed, life is different in risk society because the powerful elites in charge of production will also be victims of risk.

Therefore in risk society it is the failures of modernity, rather than the successes, that dominate the social world and the constitution of what is a "problem" and for whom.

"CONSTRAINT RECOGNITION" IN LATE MODERNITY

There is a public groundswell "to do" something about these newly defined problems in the conditions of risk society. This social reorientation is not an isolated phenomenon linked to an oil spill or chemical accident, and its problems are not discrete or a single issue. Risk society is temporally related to the social, political and communicative conditions of late modernity which have defining characteristics. Thus Beck's second major thesis is the related idea of "reflexive modernisation." This describes the possibility of industrial society's demise, not through revolution as predicted by Marx and Engels (1984) but through "the victory of Western modernization" (Beck 2000, 2). In other words, at this stage of modernity, society is concerned not with underproduction as was the case for previous generations, but over-production. Our society has too much product and it is the pollution, the waste and its unwanted side-effects which undermine capitalism's claim to progress in society. This change is highly significant for public relations, because in the past it had predicated much of its communicative strategies on persuading people that they needed "more." "Problems" were defined when there was resistance to expansion plans or impediments to progress. Now the reverse is true, legitimatised "problems" for the public are when expansion plans and progress are unchecked.

In these conditions constraints are broken down and as Beck predicts, a massive public critique will take place and a rethinking of the means, goals and objectives of the scientific and techno-economic production process that led to the problems (Beck 2000). He says "an alert and critical public" will appear in the form of social movements, asking contentious questions about risks and tabling them for public discussion by drawing on the expanding knowledge bases available (Beck 1992, 20). Hence a foremost characteristic of this era is a public, persistent and articulate, that contests science's claim to represent logic and reason. This contrasts with previous eras, when progress and science could operate without much public controversy: "Until the sixties, science could count on an uncontroversial public that believed in science, but today its efforts and progress are followed with mistrust. People suspect the unsaid, add in the side effects and expect the worst" (Beck 1992, 169). The converse; people who do not "suspect the unsaid" and do not "add in the side effects" and do not "expect the worst" are precisely the type of "publics" desired and sometimes expected by public relations. As a result of this powerful public scepticism in the changed conditions of risk society, *"the sciences' monopoly on rationality is broken,"* and groups who have a stake in risk society will jostle, claim and counter claim and, in doing so, invalidate the notion that expertise is the pathway to rationality (Beck 1992, 29; italics in original). Consequently, the locus of politics will shift and sub-political social movements will be more influential in decision-making and will occupy a far more powerful and critical position in a risk society redefined by the new global dangers and threats. Beck's two related theses of risk society and reflexive modernisation reposition social movements in late modernity. His ideas recast the political role of activists and explain their media prominence and effective use of communication. But this also flags changed conditions and the possibility of obsolescence for public relations. New "publics" in these conditions recognise new "problems" and this represents a radical change in thinking and action.

Beck contrasts these contemporary social conditions with earlier ones that were based on class systems of social control organised around the question of how wealth could be produced and distributed in a "socially unequal and also 'legitimate' way" (Beck 1992, 19). In the early stages of industrialisation, the public tended to overlook serious consequences of the production processes, precisely because they believed that progress would make their lives easier and better. In that way they were blinded to the smoking industrial chimneys, the filthy rivers and desolate landscape. Instead they battled over labour, wages and working conditions. But this is no longer the case in late modernity. In this setting the public is less likely to tolerate the by-products of the industrial production processes and is far more likely to challenge the institutions that produce risk. Therefore collectives of citizens, such as activists, will question and dispute authorities, especially on issues of concealed and embedded risk. If, as Beck forecasts, this widespread public critique of modernity becomes culturally embedded, then public relations becomes obsolete, along with much of early modernity. As a result, business orthodoxy, its hierarchies, legitimacy and ideas, are more likely to be questioned. In these circumstances, debates do not die, nor can backlash be controlled. The gates have opened.

Media, in its many forms will be used by activists to define, challenge and amplify debate about rationality and expertise, because "everyday life is culturally blinded; the senses announce normalcy where—possibly—threats lurk" (Beck 2000, 30). Therefore, the interpretation and communication of risk to other groups in society is a distinguishing characteristic of this era. Beck argues that in risk society science can be understood broadly in two different ways that have specific social consequences, public benefits and limitations. The first is as "laboratory science," a traditional scientific form concerned with looking for answers through exact measurement (Beck 2000, 30). For Beck, the problem with this form is that "it is blind to the consequences which accompany and threaten its successes"; an example is chemistry that leads to pesticide production (30). Beck describes the second scientific form as the "public discursivity of experience"; one that asks questions rather than seeks definitive answers (30–31). For Beck, this second scientific form develops in public forums such as media and "is related to everyday life, drenched with experience and plays with cultural symbols" (31). The access of social movements to the media, when combined with questions about the logic of producing and distributing wealth which is embedded with hazardous risks, will construct and define knowledge in late modernity. A distinguishing characteristic of activist examples I have selected for study in this book is the activists' strong critique of scientific knowledge and technology surrounding risk-producing industries using the media and new information technologies. Beck's (2000) theories about different forms of science, and their relationship to culture and symbolism, therefore shed light on these complex relationships and developments. Constraints collapse because not only are individuals empowered by communicative tools and access to knowledge defining and interrogating new problems, but the overarching social conditions impel them to make use of these tools and knowledge.

"LEVEL OF INVOLVEMENT" IN LATE MODERNITY

The level of people's political involvement in society is greater in risk society because there are more access points. A consequence of these changes is an increase in expertise outside mainstream institutions or the "demonopolization of expertise" and a rise in sub-political activism or bottom-up politics (Beck 2000, 29). Terms such as "sub-political" and "bottom-up politics" refer to extra-parliamentary political activity occurring outside traditional party domains: left and right politics (Beck 2000, 19). Beck claims that in risk society there is ample evidence that citizen initiative groups now provide leadership and set public agendas in ways usually associated with the state and with the business sectors. In this sense "sub-politics has won a quite improbably thematic victory" (Beck 19). By this he means that collectives of citizens working for social change are resource-poor in technology and money, and operate in less powerful political positions in society—yet nonetheless can influence social change in power structures that favour the dominant ruling groups. He cites the example of East Europe where citizen groups contributed to the collapse of the communist nation-states. For Beck this is evidence that "[S]ystems theory, which conceives of society as independent of the subject, has also been thoroughly refuted" (Beck 2000, 19). He argues that it is possible, therefore, for groups of individuals to determine outcomes that may seem implausible given the social constraints imposed upon them by power structures. His theories show that in these conditions activists have the potential to restructure power relations that results in significant social change.

Thus the potential for public involvement is opened through a dynamic intersection of Beck's (1992, 22–24) five theses:

1. Risks such as radioactivity produced in late modernity "induce systematic and often *irreversible* harm, generally remain *invisible*, are based on *casual interpretations* and thus initially only exist in terms of the (scientific or anti-scientific) *knowledge* about them" (Beck 1992, 22–23; italics in original). Therefore, the knowledge produced by the "mass media, scientific and legal professions" can control the extent to which they are perceived as risk and in that sense risk is "*open to social definition and construction*" (23; italics in original).
2. Social risk positions, or points of risk intensity that arise in risk society, occur because risk is subject to the "boomerang effect" and has been redistributed from old industrial society (23). This means that the producers of risk are now caught up in its unforeseen global consequences, such as the greenhouse effect. Beck (43–44) argues that these positions will be determined by the extent to which a community is exposed to risk geographically, socially or even chronologically. He illustrates with an example of the difference between the first world and third world impact of risk in 1984 when poisonous toxic vapours escaped from the Union Carbide chemical plant in Bhopal, India, killing up to 30,000 people (Lapierre and Moro 2002).
3. The changes in the logic of wealth distribution to risk distribution do not necessarily break the logic of capitalism—but rather take it to a new stage. For example, risks, such as carbon pollution, will be subject to exploration by the capitalist system in order to resolve the problems, but if the risk is not resolved then industrial society remains static (23).
4. In risk society "[K]nowledge gains a new political significance" and disputes take place about "the social definition of risk" (24). Therefore, a sociological theory that considers the construction of knowledge and its origin is necessary to investigate and understand this stage of modernity.
5. In risk society the unpolitical becomes political, and its social economic and political consequences lead to a "*reorganization of power and authority*" (24; italics in original).

Anthony Giddens, like Beck (1992, 2000) explores the complex and contradictory consequences of industrialisation for social reorganisation. His (1995) work seeks to understand the features of late modernity and define the characteristics of its social institutions. He argues that contemporary modernity is characterised by industrialisation's detrimental ecological consequences and that the inevitability of globalisation is intrinsically linked to its unprecedented power and influence. Giddens also argues that the "future-oriented thought and the 'emptying out' of progress by continuous change" has created a radical shift in the way people think about modernity (51).

Deborah Lupton (1999) examines Beck (1992, 2000) and Giddens (1991, 1995) and her work highlights the various nuances and differences between their respective theories of risk and reflexivity. She argues that there are a number of convergences, but also some divergences. An example is the notion of reflexivity. For Lupton (1999, 81), Beck suggests that reflexivity is an outcome of more risk production, while Giddens presents risk and self-reflexivity as a matter of greater perception in contemporary societies. Another area of difference, according to Lupton (1999, 77–80), is their notions of experts and public trust. For Beck, people distrust the instruments and institutions that produce risk, whereas for Giddens it is the other way around: trust is necessary to give rise to critical thinking.

While risk and reflexivity theories provide new frameworks to view and interpret developments and activity in public relations and activism in the twenty-first century, Lupton's (1999) work is valuable for identifying key inconsistency in views of "risk" as, on the one hand, deepening inequity and on the other "democratising, creating a global citizenship" (1999, 68). Lupton argues that this schism in Beck's argument remains unresolved and that "Risk Society is thus characterized by the contradiction that the privileged have greater access to knowledge, but not enough, so that they become anxious without being able to reconcile or act upon their anxiety" (69). Given that Beck's theories explore the effects of overproduction in industrial society in the latter part of the twentieth century in respect of environmental degradation and catastrophes like "atomic accidents" (Beck 1992, 23), it is easy to speculate that Marx's and Engels' views may have influenced Beck's sociological theories. The significant difference for Beck, however, is that in contemporary society the owners of production are not able to shield themselves from the consequences of their actions, as has been the case in the past, because "hazards and potential threats have been unleashed to an extent previously unknown" (Beck 1992, 19). Another critique that Lupton voices is that Beck and Giddens do not adequately acknowledge the complexity of early modernity, and its diversity of views and the competing frameworks at work on critical issues like science, social justice and knowledge. Rather that "the reflective critique of science and other expert knowledge systems, as well as social movements, are features solely of late modernity, and were not found in earlier modernity" (1999, 82).

Notable is that Beck's argument, that society has the capacity to repair problems caused by early modernity, has intense spiritual connotations. It contains powerful words like: "constellation," "salvation," "sinfulness," "absolved," and "self-reformation," and "providential."(Beck 2000, 51–52). He also alludes to a form of global redemption occurring in "the public exhibition and self-castigation of the great industrial sinners" (Beck 2000, 52). Beck's unusual use of language reveals an element of zeal that confronts the conventional objective approaches which separate logic and religion. On the other hand, this orientation may also suggest that Beck is prepared to see the world differently from early Enlightenment concepts of rationality and to rethink the role of spirituality and morality.

On balance, however, the risk society thesis has much to offer. Beck's notion of scarcity society positions activism in early modernity as a marginal activity practised by isolated collectives that exist on the fringes of the legitimate institutions which society has invested with the authority to create and implement change. It is precisely this interpretation of activism that is reflected in the adversarial public relations writings of Deegan:

> Environmentalists, workers' rights activists, animal rights groups, human rights campaigners, protestors against genetically modified foods or nuclear power, community groups opposing the siting of incinerators, dumps, factories etc. Any group that pressures for change can be given the title "activist group". While their concerns may vary, they are universally united in their commitment to forcing change. Their campaigns can have widespread implications for those they target and beyond. (Deegan 2001, 1)

And yet, there is acknowledgment within public relations that risk society in reflexive modernity repositions activists as legitimate and politically relevant. This is reflected in this quotation from Burson-Marseller, one of the largest global public relations companies.

> Today, social responsibility is no longer a matter of corporate discretion, due in large part to the NGO community's growing influence," said Bennett Freeman, Managing Director, Corporate Responsibility at Burson-Marsteller. "NGOs and other stakeholders are more likely to acknowledge progress and success if companies are candid about problems and even mistakes. Corporations need to focus on the implementation of substantive policy commitments even if that process is uneven or incomplete." (Burson-Marsteller 24/10/2012.)

This statement demonstrates clearly that within public relations institutions there is recognition that cultural and social changes have taken place. But are the same ideologies represented in Deegan's writings underpinning this apparent awareness? From the theoretical discussion presented in Chapter 1, it is argued that at Burson-Marsteller's comments are, at best, a recognition that the conventional understandings of public relations around crisis and issue management are out of step with current developments. But there is little to suggest more broadly that any significant cultural change has transpired, precisely because the rigid ideological and paradigmatic constraints that have led to public relations' success in the marketplace and its consigning of limits on thinking and practice.

The three-variables situational model of public relations—problem recognition, problem constraint, and level of involvement—for McElreath "can be influenced by an effective public relations manager (1997, 175). But risk theory shows that it is naïve to presume that public relations managers can either switch on or switch off "publics" awareness and activity in relation to delegitimised problems. Assumptions in public relations about finetuning the manipulation of publics are not just fused with a level of misplaced arrogance, but in risk society they can also be fused with foolhardiness.

LOSS, FRAGMENTATION AND SPIRIT

Disruption in a risk society leads to loss of meaning and requires new knowledge that rebuilds stability and community. For Habermas, the rebuilding of meaning, certainty and coherence is important in the wake of "legitimation and orientation crises" and necessarily involves the "cultural reproduction of the lifeworld" with "existing conditions in the world in the semantic dimension" (1989, 140). As discussed in Chapter 1, the lifeworld is a concept of communicative action characterised by interpretive understandings, negotiation and agreement which is essential for a fair and just society.

> The lifeworld is, so to speak, the transcendental site where speaker and hearer meet, where they can reciprocally raise claims that their utterances fit the world (objective, social, or subjective), and where they can criticize and confirm those validity claims, settle their disagreements and arrive at agreements. (1989, 126)

Habermas points out that the bringing about of consensus can be equated with the achievement of success in teleological systems (1989, 126–127). He says that action is normally around "situation management" which have been conceptualised within the two streams of reason (the system) and the lifeworld (moral progress): in his words "the teleological aspect of realizing one's aims (or carrying out a plan of action) and the communicative aspect of interpreting a situation and arriving at some agreement" (126). Transposing these ideas into risk society "situations" concerned with the embedded threats and hazards will be "managed" in the period of reflexive modernisation according to these two streams. Hence knowledge will be dismantled and rebuilt in the wake of risk society within the semantic realm of the public sphere. Yet, this is the same social space which public relations seeks to influence, manipulate and tilt to form public views and opinions in ways that bolster and revive flawed contradictions. Developing complex psychographic and infographic profiles for "target publics" public relations has colonised the media with both intent and a systematic approach to manage situations according to its own instrumental goals, rather than attempt to find shared understandings. Thus, public relations in this form is central to the problem of rebuilding knowledge in risk society. Reproducing self-reinforcing meaning within its limited range has a narrowing effect, perhaps explaining why public relations' ethics are widely criticised.

> The life conduct of specialists is dominated by cognitive-instrumental attitudes towards themselves and others. Ethical obligations to one's calling give way to instrumental attitudes towards an occupational role that offers the opportunity for income and advancement, but no longer for ascertaining one's personal salvation or for fulfilling oneself in a secular sense. (Habermas 1989, 323)

Habermasian theories of communicative action are rich and can unlock new understanding of what communicative practice and strands of rationality mean for individuals, groups and society. In particular, his theories expose the thin reference system of rationality within which public relations sits and how social dominance of this form, contributes to intolerance and insularity within the ranks of public relations and more broadly through their communications and influence via the media. Hence the public relations idea of "deactivating publics" which axiomatically involves media processes (McElreath 1997); is significant not just for the issue at hand but in thwarting the rebuilding of coherence and knowledge against the legitimation and orientation crisis of risk society. deeper understanding in this area is important for enduring and meaningful reform in public relations.

CITIZENSHIP, COMMUNITIES AND COMMUNICATION

> [T]he emergence of citizen journalism and the mobilisation of community action groups and NGOs means that the public are increasingly being drawn into the professional communication processes. (Breit 2007, 342)

In the conditions of late modernity, grassroots activists embedded in communities are advocating for change, but what differentiates these from public relations' approaches? The new public in risk society, unbound from conventionality, often conceive and produce novel communications that reposition boundaries, and as such have increased potential for social impact. To discover the relationship between forms of community and the communicative sub-political expressions, this section focuses on the changing political theories of citizenship in late western modernity in order to analyse the "social interconnectedness and political responsibility" (Carter 2001, 5). Citizenship theory provides a standard to show whether this repositioning affects political participation in the public sphere and the production of public opinion (Habermas 1995, 236–50); and furthermore, if it is of wider "holistic" community value (Breit 2007, 346).

The repositioning of holistic community value and contribution to citizenship as a measure to understand the impact of action is relevant to a discussion of public relations and activism. In relation to this, Clifford Christians argues that many codes of ethics governing professional practice suffer from relativistic fields of vision, especially within the context of rapid techno-economic social change. Instead, he claims that society should embrace an ontological and sustainable grounding for ethics where "moral principles have objective applications independent of the societies within which they are constituted" (1997, 5). He argues that this is achieved by adopting shared understandings of behaviour that transcend specific situations. By adopting a universal ethical framework, Christians argues that society can avoid the limiting constrictions of relativism. He looks to the notion of the protonorm to find the basis for a universal ethical framework. A protonorm is a conceptual universal norm in which is reflected "our common condition as a species" (Christians 1997, 12). One protonorm is that "life is sacred" and unites humans as a unique species (Christians 1997, 12–15). Christians argues that this could be used as an overarching framework to guide ethical communication and ultimately contribute to a fair and just society that upholds the sacredness of life and our reason for being. Christians isolates three principles from the protonorm that life is sacred: human dignity, truth telling and a commitment to living together peacefully. Human dignity requires people to value and respect each member of society as equally worthy and sacrosanct, without regard to religion, class, gender or ethnicity. Truth telling refers to respecting the fact that language is powerful and the means to social formation. The notion of non-violence extends beyond physical abuse and embraces a commitment to live together peacefully. Christians cites examples like Mahatma Gandhi and Martin Luther King who used this philosophy politically (1997, 12–15).

Citizenship theory also provides the tools to analyse new forms of community emerging around the grassroots activist debates and whether this is a positive development within prevailing social frameworks, or if it contributes to the further fracturing of understandings in modernity in ways discussed by Christians (1997, 5). In particular, it provides the lens to view the characteristics of the long-term commitments made by the activists to work together for a common goal, and whether this is a factor in a process of politicisation that has led to the repositioning of the civil sector in late modernity (Beck 1992; 2000; Beck and Willms 2004; Giddens 1991; 1995; Habermas 1984; 1989; 1995). Lastly, the inclusion of citizenship theory serves another important purpose; and that is to provide depth and understanding to the embedded assumptions about the role of the individual in modernity implicit in the work of Beck (1992; 2000; Beck and Willms 2004) and Giddens (1991; 1995). Citizenship theory, in its changing and multifarious forms, is also assisted by the ideas of Habermas (1984; 1989; 1995) by expounding the formation of public opinion within the public sphere in the politicisation process for individuals and groups in democratic society.

T. H. Marshall's (Marshall and Bottomore 1996) foundational writings are considered a useful basis for any discussion on the concept of citizenship (Carter 2001, 6). Published first in 1950, Marshall's influential work seeks a universal definition of the term citizenship (Turner 1994; Hudson and Kane 2000). Indeed, he defines the notion of "citizenship" as a collection of rights and responsibilities that form a social status which constitutes full membership of society. However, Marshall qualifies this by saying that the status bestowed on individuals is a socially constructed one and that therefore these rights and responsibilities will vary, depending on the values and ideals that society holds as appropriate in the particular times, place and context (Marshall and Bottomore 1996). Marshall's critics, however, argue that he promotes a particular relationship between culture and politics that needs to be explained further. For some, the very idea of a formal totalising definition of citizenship promotes a uniformity that stifles diversity in societies (Bloomfield and Bianchini 2001; Hudson and Kane 2000). Indeed, Hudson and Kane (2000, 5–6) claim that Marshall's interpretation of citizenship is linked strongly to obsolete notions of class and society. Similarly, Bloomfield and Bianchini (2001) criticise Marshall for his hegemonic assumptions about the social obligation of workers to participate in the agenda for advancement of Western modernisation. Turner (1994, 6–9) also critiques Marshall's views as teleological, simplistic and ambiguous with regard to whether he supports or opposes capitalism. In totalising the definition of citizenship, Marks (2001, 167–168) says that Marshall fails to acknowledge the variety of situations which different social groups inhabit, such as the disabled. Hindess (2000, 33–50) claims that Marshall assumes that citizenship has been realised in Western democratic countries like Britain. He argues that citizenship is more accurately described as "one of the central organising features of Western political discourse" (Turner 1994, 19). However, Vandenberg says that Marshall's contribution to citizenship theory is enduring and "remain[s] conventional wisdom" (Vandenberg 2000, 8).

The legitimisation crisis of risk society is rebuilding knowledge and reviving the concept of citizenship as a political theory in late modernity. Like Beck (1992) and Giddens (1995), April Carter (2001, 3) argues that social and economic change is forced because of the "global nature of the threat posed to the survival of the human race and of the planet by nuclear and chemical weapons and environmental degradation and . . . the trend towards a global economy" (Carter 2001, 3). For Turner the idea of citizenship is being revived in Western society because there is greater awareness of the idea of statelessness through issues such as the refugee crisis. He claims that issues like these have "raised once more the complicated relationship between nationalism, political identity and citizen participation" (Turner 1994, 1). Turner explains that citizenship is essentially a Western idea linked to democracy and modernity, with particular structural and cultural preconditions including "a city culture, secularization, the decline of particularistic values, the emergence of the idea of the public realm, the erosion of the particularistic commitments and the administrative framework of the nation-state" (Turner 1994, vii). So while traditional citizenship theory focuses on universal entitlement to resources and on issues of exclusion and inclusion, to recast concepts of citizenship, the distribution of particularistic cultural resources needs to be considered. For Turner, a cultural dimension to citizenship ameliorates the universal totalising effect of conventional citizenship and "cultural citizenship can be described as cultural empowerment, namely the capacity to participate effectively, creatively and successfully within a national culture" (Turner 2001, 12). Examples of cultural citizenship are access to education and the capacity to acquire the language and heritage that form a cultural identity that can be exchanged intergenerationally. Turner, by redefining resources in cultural terms, attempted to expand Marshall's notion of citizenship to be a collection of state and legal rights and responsibilities. These ideas of citizenship inform a deeper understanding of public relations activities which attempt to intervene in a citizen's access or utilisation of cultural resources as a prelude to management and control.

ACTIVE AND PASSIVE CITIZENSHIP

Ethical scrutiny in public relations, even with its critics, tends to focus on the activities of an offending organisation or an individual practitioner. But what is the collective impact of normatively accepted public relations activities in social terms? In particular, its practice of influencing or manipulating citizens as "publics" within the categories of "latent", "aware" and "active" (Grunig 1984, 145). The ideas of inclusion and political participation are interwoven and relate broadly to the ideas of passive and active citizenship (Kane 2000, 223–224). As discussed in Chapter 1, the dichotomy of active and passive citizenship is of particular value to shed light on citizens and the extent of their political inclusion and participation. Kane (224–225) links passive citizenship to the notion of "thin community" and associates it with "liberal individualism" where, in a fragmented modern society, personal freedom of choice and the pursuit of personal economic goals override the individual's responsibility to the collective common good. On the other hand, Kane links active citizenship to the notion of "thick community" which together produce "civil communitarianism", a form of citizenship where involvement in a community is a virtue of value in its own right (224–225). Lyons defines communitarianism as "an approach to constructing relations between people and their governments that involves responsibilities as well as rights, and emphasises the importance of rebuilding a moral economy of mutual rights and responsibilities at the neighbourhood level" (Lyons 2001, 208). Kane (2000, 219), however, argues that communitarianism is not the antithesis of liberal individualism but a corrective view that emphasises the common role of creating a strong social fabric that nurtures the social, political and cultural conditions that allow the individual to flourish. "These communitarians, rather than destroying liberal values, mostly sought to apply a corrective by pointing out that the social fabric sustains, nourishes, and enables individuality rather than diminishes it" (Kane 2000, 219). Carter (2001, 6) also argues that there are competing models of citizenship that relate to political positions. She states that "[T]here is a long-standing distinction between republican and liberal ideas of citizenship, the former implying a much stronger commitment to the political community and the latter allowing more scope for individual pursuit of private goals and with a more limited sense of necessary citizen obligations." She suggests that a socialist movement or grassroots activist would "incorporate in principle republican rather than liberal ideals of democracy and citizenship, though with important differences of emphasis" (2001, 6). The notions of active and passive citizenship and "thick" republican and "thin" liberal community are therefore useful to provide frameworks to illustrate the consequences for influencing participation and commitment and how this relates more broadly to politicisation and values. The dichotomy of active and passive citizenship has its critics, however, because it simplifies a far more nuanced and complex social landscape situated within dominant sites and contexts. For example, Bloomfield and Bianchini (2001, 108–109) caution that passive citizenship promotes a neo-conservative view that advocates a minimalist role for the state confined to such things as the maintenance of property and contracts and national security. Marks (2001, 170–172) makes a strong critique of active citizenship and its underlying assumptions. She argues that the notion is linked to ideals of physical and mental ability, Social Darwinism and utilitarianism because it largely excludes those who do not conform to this ideal, such as people with disabilities.

DIFFERENTIAL CITIZENSHIP

Differential citizenship opens up the concept more broadly for interpretation and diverse application. In particular, Hudson (2000, 15–25) says differential citizenship is significant for "disarticulating" the broader notion of citizenship from the nostalgic idea of the nation-state and, as a corollary, its totalising effects and cultural uniformity (15). Furthermore, he says that differential citizenship is a response to the social differentiation of society defined by notions of reflexivity where the politics of self-identity have arisen from the multiple options of choices and pathways. Therefore a differential perspective "recognises multiple and irreducible types of citizenship negotiated by the exercises of civic capacities" (Hudson 2000, 17). So while there are influential site specific, heterogeneous citizenships working in society, for example—"political, social, economic, cultural, sexual or military and environmental", expanding the concept, can bring these together to develop coherence and a wider understanding and application (24). For Hudson (16) differential citizenship is an unusual synthesis that consists of traditional membership based on inclusion and exclusion, different capacities exercised within different domains and contexts, the evaluation of what is good behaviour, and the application of that good behaviour as an ethic. Hudson's views on differential citizenship offer ways to analyse organisations that adopt an ethic of citizenship for their causes to further extend their activities and ideological positions. Paying attention to the capacity of individuals to participate in public debates and the social impact of these activities is an important standard of fairness and equity to which groups publicly communicating should attend.

Citizenship theory and its revisions (Marshall 1996; Turner 1994; Hudson and Kane 2000; Carter 2001) raises new questions and answers about how communities are formed and participation is defined. Firstly, it provides a workable framework of thought in which the broader politicisation process can be viewed through the holistic communicative activities of grassroots activists and others involved in public debates. Secondly, it gives a sharper understanding of the history of the civil sector in Western modern society and the ethics the concept embodies. Thirdly, it helps to define benchmarks more precisely to gauge capacities for participation, as well as expectations and responsibilities, such as the ideals being sought and the ways in which this relates to their communication. Lastly, contemporary citizenship theory introduces a number of key debates that explain and reflect changing values and beliefs in late modernity. Knowledge of these debates deepens our understanding of new forms of communication in activism and whether sites like public relations contribute or not, to these values and beliefs. In particular, it suggests that "publics' are more analogous to "subjects" than "citizens".

NEW BUSINESS CULTURE: PR OR CSR?

Within business there appears to be a schism between older style functionalist approaches and those infused with a more holistic and values-based approach. Corporate social responsibility (CSR) is a theoretical expression of the latter which reorientates around the changing relationships between economies, society and state. As such it could open new ground for public relations but a central concern to CSR theorists is that much of this approach is seen as the new "PR", with its associations of manipulation and discursive control.

Usually, CSR literature (Andriof et al. 2002; Lyons 2001; Greenwood 2001; McIntosh et al. 1998) claims that it is possible to achieve an acceptable intersection between profit-making on the one hand, and social, economic and environmental responsibility on the other, to create sustainability that has a "positive social and environmental impact" (Birch 2001, 62). Andriof and Waddock define CSR as an approach based on an understanding that "business exists at the pleasure of society and, second, business acts as a moral agent within society" (2002, 21).

Lyons (2001) links the growth of sustainable business development concepts with communitarianism and its doctrines of strengthening common social networks on a local level so that the individual can flourish (Lyons 2001, 208). Indeed, Leeper, a public relations academic, discusses communitarianism as alternative public relations "meta-theoretical" approach to liberalism that reflects the principles of corporate social responsibility (2001, 93–104). He states that public relations "as the quest for harmony, fits comfortably within communitarian meta-theory" (104). In particular, he refers to core values of social cohesion, citizen empowerment and acceptance of responsibility enmeshed in a CSR communitarian approach that "will go beyond even the most enlightened public relations theory based on symmetrical communication and reciprocity" (102). While it appears that Leeper flags a paradigmatic shift for the profession, by defining public relations "as the quest for harmony" (104), he flags yet again, the field's deep links to teleological, liberal pluralism frameworks and that, to affect a real change, deeper rethinking is necessary (Smith 1993, 25).

Writing more than twenty years ago, Freeman (1984) is a precursor to corporate social responsibility who paid particular attention to the domain of public relations. Freeman's concept of stakeholders is an example of the CSR nexus between profit-making and social responsibility. He argues that, "Organizations have stakeholders. That is, there are groups and individuals who can affect, or are affected by the achievement of an organization's mission" (Freeman 1984, 52). According to Greenwood, (2001, 2) this concept involves principles of protecting the rights of individuals, and organisations being responsible for the effects of their actions. Freeman's stakeholder theory orientates business to include the civil sector and flags an environment in which activism, the state and business may interact in less adversarial ways.

In fact Freeman forecasts a range of grim outlooks for public relations while at the same time opening up potential for its development. He describes one negative scenario where offending organisations maintain a public relations or "PR" department merely to act as a sacrificial lamb, offered up only in times of crisis. Furthermore, Freeman regards marketing-based concepts, used in public relations, like "target publics" and "target audiences" as limited because they are organisationally selfish and outward:

> Most PR people are trained as communications experts in schools of journalism. Typical stakeholder interactions revolve around 'communications' programs, where the PR people tell the stakeholders or 'publics' or worse still 'audiences,' about the company's plans and how the plans affect the stakeholder. (Freeman 1984, 166)

Freeman's ideas about stakeholders present a reasonably sound theory that can redefine activist and business relationships, but Grunigs and Hunt's

(1984, 41) two-way symmetrical model shows how this theory can be adopted and adapted in such a way as to render it difficult for this to happen. For example, Grunig and Hunt use statements that imply a fair and unbiased relationship, but which, in fact, privilege business and marginalise activism. Like Grunig and Hunt, Freeman's notion of stakeholders (1984) is also expressed from a business outlook, but, Freeman's ideas are open, innovative and insightful because he defines with clarity and certainty alternative business approaches that are structured to be less antagonistic and selfish. This work is also important as a cultural marker where business theorised communication practices and sought to disarticulate itself from public relations for ethical reasons.

Writing over a decade later, McIntosh et al. (1998, 50–51) describe corporate citizenship as a relationship between companies and society based on rights and responsibilities. Like CSR, corporate citizenship also seeks to change the relationship between economy, society and state. They present a framework to explain four different positions business can adopt towards society that determine its social and economic obligations and responsibilities. At one extreme, McIntosh et al. present a business model based on profit-making where the organisation "has no responsibility other than its economic and legal obligations." At the other, they present a business model based on profit-making that aims to contribute to a better society, beyond just legal obligations. McIntosh et al. use terms like 'stakeholder' and show that Freeman's (1984) ideas about the complexity of the relationship between business and society have become integrated into 1990s business discourse.

Greenwood (2001, 2–16) explores Freeman's (1984) concept of stakeholders further to show how other elements, such as community attitudes and understandings, can shape relations with business and state organisations. She argues that two organisational strategies dominate in stakeholder theory: "these are variously called social responsiveness and social responsibility" (Greenwood 2001, 4). She suggests that these models are predicated on the idea that the organisation's attitude is a determinant in relationships. For example, when a business or state organisation regards community groups as separate, and only in terms of how they affect their economic aspirations and legal requirements, they ignore the groups unless they become a problem. Greenwood called this a "strategic" view of relationships (2001, 8). She terms another strategy 'moral'. This is when business or state organisations view themselves as interconnected with community groups. Greenwood (2001, 8) argues that organisations with moral orientations will produce communication in new forms such as social and environmental reporting (SER). SER is a new communication practice associated with the notion of sustainable capitalism which Birch defines as organisational behaviour, policies and practices that should work, not only in economic terms, but as a holistic system connected to society (2001, 54). Sustainable capitalism is of interest because it again demonstrates a shift in organisational attitudes and social practices and hence a distinct change in how organisational communications are produced and consumed. Greenwood, however, identifies in her analysis (2001, 7–8) the various strategic approaches to SER in the community-organisation stakeholder relationship, appearing to flag that there are likely to be unethical communication practices within cultures of corporate social responsibility.

Raising concerns about CSR as a new form of unethical public relations, Leipziger (2003) argues that communication is critical to the implementation of corporate responsibility. She writes "much of what is written about CR (corporate responsibility) tools is public relations and marketing—an attempt to gain more members and attain critical mass" (2003, 15). In the main, however, this work is focused around measures to evaluate CSR in practice such as the AccountAbility 1000 Framework, the AA1000 Assurance Standard, and the Global Compact.

By adopting the principles of CSR, business and activists organisations can communicate in more productive and sustainable ways. Bliss (2002, 252) argues that there are various styles in which activists can mount campaigns. One style is adversarial and another is working together through a stakeholder collaborative campaign (2002, 252). Bliss' (2002) and Greenwood's (2001) views concur that an organisational attitude towards stakeholders determines the tenor of relations between them. Bliss (2002) and Greenwood (2001) help to clarify the types of relationships and responses to grassroots activists groups by CSR oriented organisations.

Phillips (2003), like Greenwood (2001), argues that an organisation will ultimately determine how stakeholder relations develop, but adds that, if an activist group is hostile and confrontational, then the organisation is not duty bound to treat them as "normative stakeholders" (Phillips 2003, 148), or with the expectations that provide guidelines for general interaction and behaviour (Abercrombie, Hill and Turner 1994, 287–8). I believe that Phillips' work signals that some organisations will consider some stakeholders more important than others in ways that determine their value and relationship. If this occurs, words like "cooperatively engaged" and "normative stakeholder" are open to subjective and multiple interpretations (Phillips 2003, 148). This suggests that the interpretation of Freeman's (1994) stakeholder concept may become indistinguishable from previous "target public" approaches.

Jones, however, proffers an alternative view of this new business approach (Alert and Alarmed 20/5/2006). In his blog,[3] he argues that CSR is ineffective and manipulative and merely "plays to youthful idealism." Furthermore, he argues that business is unaffected by it because no government agency "will take responsibility for its enforcement." He argues that, rather, "CSR is an academic growth industry" and that the concept is like one known as the "soulful corporation," invented by "American corporate PR departments and their academic counterparts" fifty years ago and used to stifle "inter-war antipathy to corporate business."

In summary, an examination of McIntosh et al. (1998), Freeman (1984), Greenwood (2001), Leipziger (2003), Bliss (2002) and Phillips (2003) shows that organisations which adopt the principles of social, economic and environmental sustainability recognise the use of communication by grassroots activists as significant. However, Jones' (Alert and Alarmed 20/5/2006) blog shows how this ideal needs to be structurally embedded in social institutions to be effective. On the one hand, the CSR literature shows how organisational communication espousing a relationship between making profit and social, economic and environmental sustainability, wittingly or unwittingly, may be used to advance a new era of the manipulation of information—or spin. On the other hand, it shows how business may be open to new and alternative ideas in ethical social relations between different groups in society (Leeper 2001, 93–104).

INDUSTRY PRACTITIONERS, CSR AND ACTIVISM

These theories, which are strongly infused with citizenship and an acknowledgement of the legitimate activities of activists seeking change, have permeated through to practitioners. However, a distancing from public relations and its associations is also evident. For example, at the cusp of the millennium Thomas and Eyers argued (1998, 11) that an organisation's approach to communication is a critical element in the development of a credible organisational CSR culture. Thomas and Eyers stated that, till then, "public relations" had been often superficial and used by industry to trumpet their achievements over their failures (1998, 12). Peters (1998) echoed those sentiments, saying that significant relationships between organisations and communities cannot be achieved by simple public relations communications: "building a great reputation is not about words and fancy value statements communicated via glossy brochures which languish on coffee tables in receptions lounges and in the department of corporate affairs" (1998, 38). Like Peters (1998), Newbold, Chair of the United Kingdom's (UK) Ethical Trading Initiative (c.2001) described limitations to traditional public relations practices. She stated that contemporary businesses cannot just spend money on public relations to buy a corporate reputation, because activist groups are increasingly effective in exposing companies who seek to cover up misdeeds. Therefore, Thomas and Eyers (1998, 11), Newbold (c. 2001, 12), and Peters (1998) not only acknowledged the impact of activism but demonstrate a recognition that public relations "gloss" and "spin" could work against a company. These industry views corroborate Freeman's (1984) earlier claims that organisational-centric public relations practices are limited and that public relations' avoidance of the complexities of its relationship with activism is no longer tenable.

Two themes are emerging. One is that that the locus of politics has moved and sub-political social movements such as grassroots activists are more influential in decision-making. The other is that communication as social action can take forms, such as public relations, that impact on the agency of citizens to take part in the formation of laws and participate fully in public life. These themes relate to the central theoretical frameworks of risk society and reflexive modernisation that argue that changes in contemporary industrialised society, driven by life-threatening hazards and threats such as global warming, are a result of the unquestioned logic of early modernity. In these conditions a tenacious and coherent public will appear in the form of social movements, or grassroots activists, asking contentious questions about risks and tabling them for public discussion. The relationship between public relations and activists is historically adversarial. Furthermore, the practice of public relations is seen by some as an instrument to silence activists in a way that is unethical and that offends democratic principles and ideals. In summary, activism, in its variety of forms, is necessary for rational debate in large-scale democratic societies and can nourish the principles of open participation and decision-making to bring about positive change. The ability of citizens to take part in the sub-political formation of laws and public life may be compromised by media practices, unethical public relations, as well as by social and economic conditions such as Internet access. However, an emerging theme is that new business cultures challenge liberal pluralist coherences that in the past have served to simplify complex relations of power that over-privilege business and government and have served to marginalise activism. Therefore public relations academics and practitioners may find how grassroots activist groups are communicating, and the ways this differs from other state and business organisational approaches, significant for reform and a deeper understanding of ethics.

CONCLUSION

Risk theories, changes to science, knowledge and the media in late modernity explain the willingness of diverse people coming together as activists to take action and communicate on matters once considered too technical for lay people; such as the impact that toxic dumps and incinerators, logging practices and toxic emissions on communities and environments have on different groups in society. Risk society means profound changes in the relationship between activists and public relations. It means that the public relations notion of passive and obedient "publics" should be no longer assumed. It also means there will be more protest groups with strong political agendas coupled with a widespread ability to develop, understand, predict and disseminate information through the Internet. Digital technologies will emerge as citizens mobilise around global threats like climate change. As the logic of scarcity society changes to that of risk society, corporations paying lip service to social responsibility do so at their peril. In tandem, public relations will have to acknowledge that NGOs and community action groups have important contributions to make in an era of change and uncertainty. "Reputation" will continue to be a key concern for business in a risk society—a company's track record cannot be hidden or concealed in risk society; just as gaining and maintaining "legitimacy" is a key concern for activist groups.

Beck's theories of risk society and reflexive modernisation describe important new social conditions transforming the contemporary world. In particular, they are relevant to explain the growth of sub-political networks, what grassroots activists seek to promote and their capacity to create change in state and business sectors. Other important concepts are communicative theory (Habermas 1995; 1984; 1989), communication ethics (Christians 1997) and citizenship theory (Marshall 1996; Turner 1994; Carter 2001; and Hudson and Kane 2000). Together, these theories provide an unusual lens to analyse social relations between different groups, particularly business, its instrument public relations and activist citizen collectives. The theories integrate to form a powerful new way of thinking about public relations and activism.

By using theories of risk society (Beck 1992; 2000; Giddens 1995), the normative elements positioning activism and public relations in the twenty-first century are shown. But importantly these theories, particularly Beck's theories of risk society, discuss what gave rise to this change. Thus the activities of public relations and activism can be viewed with new insight. Such insight opens up new subject positions not only for activists, but also for public relations practitioners. It shows how a differentiated approach to communicative practices is possible, and how the idea of variations in communicative practices occurring outside the gaze of institutional sites is valuable for reform in public relations. What remains after the grassroots activist debates, are the values and images of the campaign and redefined ideas of corporations. Grassroots activist groups have not only redefined what is in their "self-interest," but their actions are characterised by the promotion of the common good, an ethic of participative conduct and ideals of deliberative democracy. Thus the object in the grassroots campaigns is not just something to oppose in situ, but a longer term commitment to a more complex idea which frequently contradicts the profit interest which until now has been used to justify and advance ideas of "progress." Significantly, however, unlike previous eras, these contemporary grassroots activist groups rework, rather than break, the logic of capitalism. The theoretical frameworks set out in this chapter position the domain of public relations to think and act and interpret in new ways. In particular these theories show that it is time for scholars, practitioners and institutions to act with intent to stop the intervention in the development of debate in communities, and to rethink ideas about dissent. If public relations remains blind to the changes of a risk society and repeats the social relations of early modernity it will lead to the same stale concepts and thematic choices which compromise individual and collective agency and in the end are counter-productive for all. Not just is there an urgent case for further consideration and reform in public relations, but the time to do it is now.

5 New Social Realities
Grassroots Activism and Public Relations

> Behind the facades of the good old industrial society that are still being propped up, could it be that, alongside the many risks and dangers, forms of this new division of labor and power between politics and sub-politics are already beginning to stand out and be practiced today. (Beck 1992, 235)

What is it like to live in a risk society in a period of reflexive modernisation where politics is unbound and "centreless", and how do we recognise if these changes are being practiced today (Beck 1992, 231)? At the cusp of the new millennium I noticed that newspaper reports of local grassroots activist campaigns in the south-west region of Victoria, Australia appeared time and time again. Not only were campaigns becoming more visible, but I saw new communication practices and approaches emerging undescribed in public relations. Over this time, a period of low rainfall occurred in Victoria. Beginning in the mid 1990s, the drought would take another 14 years before average rainfall would resume. It would have critical impacts on water storages and power supplies. This chapter shows public relations and its relationship to activism through three sustained case studies of grassroots activism each responding to the threat of globalised risk society.

The first case study occurred between 1995 and 1999 in Werribee, in the state of Victoria, during a period of politically conservative, right-wing Liberal and National Party Coalition state government. Werribee is on the outskirts of Victoria's capital city, Melbourne, and it belongs to its western suburbs, strongly associated with heavy industry. Today however, growing populations of young residents seek value, lifestyle and a friendly community in a semi rural setting. The Werribee Residents Against Toxic Dump (WRATD) campaign is important for its grassroots activist response and role in influencing decision making on the location of a hazardous or "prescribed waste" storage facility. The second case study of Batesford and Geelong Action Group (BAGAG) took place between 2001 and 2002, and was situated further out of Melbourne in the industrial regional city of Geelong, 75 kilometres southwest. With port facilities and transport links, over the years Geelong has historically supported large and diverse manufacturing industries. However, since the 1970s this has been in decline, with some, such as the textile industry, completely disappearing. The BAGAG case study differs from the WRATD case study in two ways: it occurred during a period of socialist-democratic left-wing Australian Labor Party (ALP) state government and the Internet was accessible to the mainstream population and therefore used more in the campaign. The third case study is of environmental activism between 1995 and 2003 in the Otway Ranges, which are approximately 200 kilometres south-west of Melbourne. Over the length of the campaign, both Coalition and ALP state governments were in power. In this case study, the activities of the grassroots activist group Otway Ranges Environment Network (OREN) intervened in the long-standing relationship between government and the timber industry to achieve a landmark turnaround of state government forest policy. Examined from the lens of the activists, the case studies will be unpacked in terms of their focus on public relations.

WERRIBEE RESIDENTS AGAINST TOXIC DUMP

> Perhaps the thing that gets most residents angry is the fact that industry and government bodies seem to see Werribee as a general dump for anything they can't get rid of elsewhere. Residents are sick of having the area treated like a waste dump for industry. (WRATD 1996, 1)

In 1995, CSR,[1] an Australian sugar and building material company, announced its proposal to build a hazardous waste disposal facility in the outer-western suburb of Werribee. This was described by its Technical and Development Manager, David Maltby, as a "prescribed waste landfill (to replace the Cleanaway landfill at Tullamarine) and organic processing (composting) facility in part of a quarry hole owned by CSR in Wests Road, Werribee" (Strangio 2001, 48; brackets in original). Maltby suggested to the Minister for Planning and Local Government, Robert Maclelland that the proposal should go ahead without an Environmental Effects Statement (EES)[2] because of the "highly favourable site conditions" (Strangio 2001, 48–49). While Minster Maclelland encouraged the proposal, he disagreed about overriding the state approval process. He said that to progress its proposal, CSR had to prepare an EES to determine the facility's impact on the surrounding areas, as it "raised 'significant environmental issues, including the potential hazards and risks to the environment'" (Maclelland in Strangio 2001, 49). The Minister considered that an EES Consultative Committee would ensure that all parties had an opportunity to be represented and that this process "would assist in fostering community confidence in the planned facility" (Strangio 2001, 49). But for some the government approvals process was tokenistic. According to van Moorst (1998, 30) the EES Consultative Committee included "four elected residents, along with two representatives from environmental groups, various government and industry representatives, and a continual swag of CSR employees and consultants." van Moorst argued that the "only planning principle applied in this case was to facilitate market interests and proponent-driven developments, regardless of community interests, environmental risks or effective alternatives." He said that the process was no more than a charade in the form of a "well organised presentation by the proponent aimed at putting the proposal in the best possible light" (van Moorst 1998, 29–31).

Locals gained a sense of how CSR would present the case in its public relations brochure:

> [T]he proposed Wests Road landfill would not be a conventional tip of the type that generates odours and attracts vermin but rather a highly sophisticated facility, strictly regulated, using the latest in technology and employing every possible safeguard to protect the environment. (CSR c. 1996)

Designed to soothe public anxieties, CSR's brochure informed that "waste bound for the West Road facility would first have to undergo a testing procedure to determine that the waste was of a type accepted by the landfill." The company stated that the "area that would accept the waste would consist of a series of fifteen cells constructed progressively during the operational life of the landfill." Furthermore, CSR claimed that the hazardous waste, as staged landfill, would be eventually revegetated and possibly become parkland "for passive recreation, with cycling and walking trails." In particular, the company emphasised that another public benefit of the complex would be "an organic composting facility" to encourage waste minimisation practices in line with federal and state government policy. CSR described "prescribed hazardous waste" as having mainly a "nuisance value," arguing that "until it was classified as prescribed waste about 10 years ago, such waste went to ordinary municipal tips all over Victoria." To establish the proposal's credibility with the local community, CSR announced in the brochure that "project manager" David Maltby would provide information and answer questions at a Werribee office (CSR c. 1996).

However, despite CSR's attempt to gain community support and head off opposition, local residents and businesses received unofficial news that Werribee was the proposed location for a hazardous waste disposal facility (HWDF) in early 1996. Not surprisingly, the prospect of "acid sludges, electroplating residues, tars, asbestos and other prescribed chemicals too hazardous for normal tips" (Hosking 1996, 4) stored in a disused quarry three kilometres from the nearest housing estate, caused trepidation in the local community.

In response, eight residents met "around a kitchen table," to form 'Werribee Residents Against Toxic Dump," a community action group to raise concerns about the proposal (WRATD c. 1999, 1–5). Harry van Moorst was a resident and key activist in the WRATD campaign. He said that "there was no campaign at this stage, we got it to the point where there were ten, fifteen, twenty of us meeting and having done a lot of research and having got some information together through the local newspapers, we organised a public meeting" (Interview with the author November 18, Geelong, 2004). Following, at the public meeting, WRATD planned more community-mobilising action, such as a large public assembly and the launch of a petition against what it now termed the "toxic dump." The group also planned to investigate the risks that the HWDF posed and to write reports. According to WRATD, nineteen thousand people signed a petition opposing the facility over a five-month period (WRATD c. 1999, 2).

WRATD's response to the CSR proposal was decisive and organised, in part because it believed that the right wing Liberal-National Party Coalition state government had given the HWDF tacit approval. Since winning office in 1992, the Coalition state government, led by the self-assured and increasingly confrontational Premier Jeff Kennett, had used its strong electoral mandate to justify controversial changes to public policy, including the privatisation of public utilities such as gas and electricity, and competitive tendering of public services (Alford and O'Neill 1994, 101). The Coalition government had a radical change agenda for Victoria and had gained a reputation as inflexible and tough, which meant that no activist group at this time would have underestimated the tenacity with which it would fight to hold ground. For example, from 1993 to 1995, community action group Save Albert Park (SAP) had been unable to stop the infrastructure for the staging of an international car racing (Grand Prix) development in their suburb, despite a high-profile and a well-organised campaign. During that dispute, Premier Kennett referred to the SAP protestors as "stooges" for the ALP and for International Socialists (Lane 1995, 16) and "whingeing solely for NIMBY (Not In My Back-Yard) reasons" (Neales 1994, 20).

The tense social and political conditions pressured WRATD to define quickly the complex biological, environmental and social arguments against the proposal. Foremost, WRATD argued that the facility would not be able to operate safely and disputed CSR's definition of what was "acceptable." It used reports, pamphlets and media releases, amongst other techniques, to communicate this to the broader community. WRATD's slogan: "the wrong technology, the wrong location, the wrong company" helped the local community to organise the dense social, technological and political arguments into three key ideas simplifying the argument and making it easier for people to engage.

To manage campaign communications, van Moorst said CSR spent "hundreds and hundreds of thousands, possibly up to a million dollars on public relations" and that they hired three different PR consultancies. He said that an example of CSR's public relations was an extensive advertising campaign in Melbourne's largest daily newspapers and a broad-scale letterbox drop to convince householders in Melbourne and Geelong that the proposal had merit and the support of the Kennett government:

> They took out big advertisements, little advertisements and at one stage they ran an eight-week campaign of advertising in the *Herald Sun* and *The Age*—half page ads. In all of this, they tried to convince the rest of Melbourne, because they realised they weren't ever going to convince Werribee, that this was okay and that therefore the Kennett Government could impose it on Werribee and that it wouldn't be any problem. But they did this, they went and letterboxed all of Melbourne virtually with a leaflet, showing how good this was and they started to put more and more advertisements in. Now in one sense, that's a typical PR response. (van Moorst 2004)

In the early part of the campaign, both CSR and WRATD vied for the media to validate them as the authoritative source. In establishing their credentials, CSR's approach to communication was to convince locals to put their trust in them because "they knew best":

> CSR's tactics and strategy was to simply try and convince the locals that really they knew best and leave it to them. When they realised the farmers could see through the myths about clay liners—because after all farmers have got clay dams and things and they know they leak—and when they began to realise that people weren't being sidetracked by the potential composting facilities and other things, they began then to use the media and I think they did a lot of work also lobbying behind the scenes . . . lobbying the government. (van Moorst 2004)

However, a series of inept public relations moves over time lost CSR credibility, particularly as WRATD used these errors strategically to argue that it was the "wrong company" to manage such a facility (Strangio 2001, 141–143). In one example, in 1998, Bob Reid, CSR's General Manager Recycling and Waste Management, announced that the landfill would now operate as a "repository" as opposed to "landfill," meaning that the waste could be retrieved and recycled. He said that "global positioning satellite technology" could locate materials earmarked for recycling at a later date and that half the material could be turned into "environmentally friendly potting mix and other garden products" (Dent 1998). But according to Strangio (2001, 141–143) the proposal's 3D mapping capacity was outlined in the original plan and therefore not news to informed locals. Locals were also cynical that CSR's communications in relation to the composting aspect of the proposal were an opportunity for greenwashing. They believed it merely served as a CSR a talking point, in discussing its environmental credentials in ways that distracted attention from the "toxic dump."

Despite its considerable focus on public relations, CSR struggled to gain support from locals and the broader Melbourne community who were now beginning to become engaged in the debate. In what appears to be an acknowledgement of the effectiveness of WRATD's campaign, CSR's Bob Reid used WRATD's slogan reflexively in his comment, "it is the right technology and it is in the right place" (Dent 1998). Harry van Moorst explains that:

> They put out this absolutely ridiculous one page advertisement on Environment Day, where they used our logo of "No Toxic Dump" and they put another one next to it, saying "prescribed waste safe, prescribed waste landfill" with a big green tick. So they were trying to say that we don't want a toxic dump either. And again, that would have totally backfired. They obviously were protesting their innocence too much. And so they were using that typical PR style. It was their response. (van Moorst 2004)

Somewhat boldly, WRATD skilfully unpacked the CSR "public relations" for readers, presenting its campaign a complex instrument to filter truth:

> CSR makes a lot of false claims in its advertising and PR campaign, including their claims about EPA policy and about prescribed waste . . . CSR has spent a lot of money on advertising; they have lobbied politicians, held an "invitation only" press conference, and distributed more than 300,000 leaflets trying to convince the public that nothing could ever go wrong with their clay-lined toxic dumps. (WRATD c. 1998, 2)

WRATD's communication approach contrasted with CSR's in a number of ways. One was in the production and distribution of materials that used volunteer and "in-kind" assistance, such as support in producing full-colour brochures, the donation of office space, computers and signs (Strong 1998). Harry van Moorst recalls:

> We did exactly the opposite. We got free printing of about 50,000 leaflets but instead of letterboxing them, we handed them out to people and talked to them . . . at shopping centres in and outside of Werribee, in South Melbourne, in Pakenham, anywhere and everywhere we could go. So we're communicating with people directly and you could ask them; "Would you really want this in your backyard?" and if not and so on. Whereas they went to the typical PR style of advertising, as though that was going to convince people. (van Moorst, 2004)

But van Moorst believes that CSR was not concerned about negative public opinion because they thought that they had state government support that would ultimately override community dissent. He said "I think they were willing to leave it at that because they felt that they had the Kennett Government totally on side and they would simply impose it."

However, regardless of being given official approval to proceed with its installation, by November 1998, CSR and the Wyndham Council were engaged in talks "conducted in strict confidence, with all other parties, including the Kennett government, left in the dark" (Strangio 2001, 169). In effect, CSR had moved and was ready to abandon the proposal for the hazardous waste disposal facility and sell the quarry site to Wyndham City Council. Van Moorst said that CSR's "turning point in their own thinking was when we did meet with them in Sydney at their shareholders meeting." Furthermore, he said that CSR's withdrawal was influenced by economic considerations:

> The biggest problems CSR had at that stage were financial ones, which had nothing to do whatsoever with the toxic dump per se. But this didn't add to their image in any positive way. It didn't help. But I think the real thing was that that Kirby[3] was smart enough to realise that what we were saying was true and that it wasn't part of their core business, they didn't really know that they were doing. They weren't going to make lots of money out of it given the overall nature of the company and they were going to lose. They were never going to build it because we were determined enough. And, I think once he realised we were determined enough to stop it, everything else in a sense didn't matter. It wasn't going to happen. And so, he was willing to start winding it down. It unfortunately left Kennett on a limb. (van Moorst, 2004)

In response to CSR's extraordinary turn-around The *Herald Sun* reported that:

> CSR last night announced it had accepted an offer from Wyndham City Council for the council to purchase CSR's quarry site, shelving plans to dump 120,000 tonnes of toxic substances into the quarry ... Mr Reid (CSR Recycling and Waste Management General Manager) said the offer was an opportunity to end a protracted and expensive legal dispute that started 12 months ago and could continue for 12–18 months. (Dent 1998, 7)

CSR's policy change caused deep embarrassment for the Coalition state government. The Herald Sun reported Kennett as saying that "CSR would have to have been the most inept private sector organisation I have come across in trying to establish a facility ... the management of this issue has been appalling and in the end they simply didn't have the stomach for seeing it through" (Dent 1998, 9). *The Age* discussed the implications of WRATD's challenge to the state government: "It was, after all, an unaccustomed experience for the Premier to witness a project he has anointed being defeated by the actions of a group of ordinary citizens. For six years, his Government has successfully fended off the protests of organised lobby groups and the State opposition over everything from the privatisation of public utilities to the curtailment of powers of the auditor-general" ("Power To The People," *The Age* November 22, 1998, 24). Shortly after, WRATD issued a media release saying that the activists would celebrate their win over both the economically driven Kennett state government and CSR by planning the "biggest community party that Werribee has ever seen" and that this was a "victory for community rights and for the environment. It is victory for all Victorians, not just for Werribee" (WRATD).

Van Moorst said that CSR's back-down was an "important victory because it was the first really heavy defeat that the Kennett government had had, and in a sense it was the beginning of that decline in support for the Kennett government to the point where his own seat was lost eventually." Reflecting on the outcome, he said that he knew early in the campaign that WRATD would succeed:

> It was pretty clear that we were going to win this, the amounts of community support and the community initiatives that were being shown. It wasn't as though you had to drag it out of people to get their support. Rather, they were trying to drag you to come and speak to them, to give them petitions, to give them the posters to put up, whatever it was. . . . So my view was that so long as we run this sensibly and don't shoot ourselves in the foot, we can't lose this, partly because we had the arguments on our side. I mean, it was a stupid suggestion. It is a stupid technology and CSR didn't know anything about it. So, I mean all those arguments were correct anyway. So they should have won automatically, it should never have got to the stage it did. (van Moorst 2004)

BATESFORD AND GEELONG ACTION GROUP

On 18 September 1999, Victorians were taken aback when, at the next state election the seemingly impervious Kennett Coalition was narrowly ousted and replaced by a minority left-wing Bracks Labor state government. Jeff Kennett had lost the confidence of the people and shortly after resigned from politics altogether. Strangio writes:

> That the unthinkable happened at the September 1999 election was principally the result of a revolt by traditional Coalition supporters in regional and rural Victoria . . . There is little doubt that the Coalition was also brought undone by an electorate grown weary of the

characteristics of the government—especially the premier's leadership style—which had been so conspicuous during the struggle over the Werribee waste dump. (Strangio 2001, 178)

While in office, the Coalition state government led by Premier Kennett instigated some significant long-term policy changes for Victoria, including the privatisation of the state's power utilities. However, rather than resolve the issues about supply, the privatisation reduced the state's capacity to meet and/or manage energy demand. As the heat and drought intensified, the newly elected state ALP government was confronted with predictions of power shortages in the state's electricity grid, particularly given the use of air conditioners, and the potential for blackouts in the Geelong region (Gardiner 2002).

In 2001, in the small settlement of Stonehaven, about ten kilometres from Geelong, a multi-national US energy company, AES Corporation, had applied for a generation licence to build a peaking power station. The rationale was that the peaking power station would ease the pressure on the electricity network and provide timely back-up for the state's power reserves. The power station was to be known as AES Golden Plains and operated by a subsidiary of AES Corporation, AES Power One (AESPO). A local paper reported that "AES Power One chose to build their station in Victoria because . . . Stonehaven was an ideal location, being close to gas a pipeline [sic] and transmission lines" (Baird 2001, 13). AESPO stated that the Golden Plains facility "will consist of four combustion turbines of 125 megawatts of capacity, each burning natural gas for the supply of electricity during peak use hours on the hotter days of summer and the colder days of the winter . . . This type of generator is clean, quiet, safe and reliable" (AESPO 2001, 2). The Office of the Regulator-General, Victoria, called for public submissions to assist it to "grant or refuse an application for an electricity licence for any reason that it considers appropriate"; but stated that this did not imply that the AESPO proposal had permission to go ahead (c. 2001, 1).

On 28 June 2001, the local Golden Plains Shire issued AESPO a conditional planning permit, after receiving nine objections to the proposal that raised concerns about the environment, a lack of public consultation and the reputation of the applicant, amongst others (Golden Plains Shire 2001, 19–20). The officers' report to councillors made it clear that the Golden Plains Shire expected that the proposed 500 MW peak loading fossil fuel station would run at full load for only five per cent of the year and that this would be during summer's hottest days (11). It stated that the proposal's "use of fossil fuels is a Federal policy issue" and was therefore irrelevant to the Shire's sustainable development policy and planning assessment process (17). However, one condition was that "this permit shall have no force or effect until such time as a Works Approval for the proposal is issued by the Environment Protection Authority (EPA)" (23).

The AES Corporation had developed a high profile in the international energy industry. In its licence application to the State Government, AESPO refers to its parent as a "global power company committed to serving the world's needs for electricity by providing safe, clean, reliable power in a socially responsible way" (AESPO 2001, 1). The AES Corporation was founded in 1981 and "owns or has an interest in 166 power generation facilities totalling over 58,000 MW in 25 countries as well as distributing electricity in 9 countries through 19 businesses and has branches all over the world" (1).

In contrast to the bullish right wing Jeff Kennett, the state government was now led by the affable socialist-left Premier, Steve Bracks. Together with proponent AESPO, the new government wanted the power station operational as soon as possible to address the power shortage. AESPO's licence application stated that "Golden Plains is being fast-tracked in an attempt to address the current shortfall in reserve capacity" (AESPO 2001, 3). A spokesperson for Planning Minister John Thwaites said the government "believed key environmental issues would be addressed in the planning permit and the EPA approval processes" (Hodgson 2001, 39). However, residents in the semi-rural Dog Rocks estate, only a few kilometres from the proposed site, were upset that the project was proceeding so fast. Residents were uncomfortable, not only with the idea of a power station so close to their homes, but also with the way the supposedly family friendly ALP state government appeared to be circumventing the EES process to suit the proponent in ways disturbingly similar to the previous government.

In mid 2001, Batesford and Geelong Action Group (BAGAG) formed "to stop AES Corporation building a gas fired, peaking power station at Stonehaven" (Baird 2001, 13). In a letter to the Office of the Regulator-General, Victoria, the group's steering committee stated that widespread community concerns about the proposed power station had led to the group's formation. "Recent meetings have been attended by up to 150 people. Their opinions are representative of thousands more" (Batesford Action Group Steering Committee, 2001, 1).

Stuart McCallum was a core member of BAGAG who had had expertise in environmental conservation, in particular grasslands. He said that "within the people objecting to it, there were people who lived nearby who felt that the pollution aspects were not good and also people who were looking at the longer term issue of greenhouse gases and global warming."

BAGAG mounted arguments against the proposed power station's production of hazardous risks based on contradictions in local, state and federal policy, its location, its technology and the proponent's reputation for corporate irresponsibility and violations. It also argued that the proposed power station posed risks due to its fuel and its outmoded operating technology. They said that the power station's water use and thermal efficiency were also central issues of concern. The proposed power station would consist of four combustion turbines with a 125 MW capacity and was designed to run at periods of high electricity usage such as mid-summer or winter, i.e. an estimated five per cent of the year. It was to be fuelled largely by natural gas and would generate up to 500 MW of electricity. However, BAGAG argued that polluting fuels, such as kerosene and diesel, could also be run through the turbine system. The activists claimed that the proposed technology was first released in 1984 and was linked to the production of high emissions that would endanger public health. Since then, they said that substantial improvements in turbine technology and efficiency had occurred making them cleaner and safer. The BAGAG website (now defunct) argued that "this technology was currently being installed in Bangladesh and Peru". The group also drew public attention to the large quantity of water the turbines would use. They linked this argument to issues surrounding the region's dwindling water reserves caused by the intensifying drought.

On a state level, BAGAG questioned the government's commitment to reducing greenhouse gases and consumption, particularly of air conditioners which were known to create significant power demands and in high use due to the sweltering conditions. In reference to AESPO, BAGAG activist Iain Lygo said that: "Their PR work was at best ordinary and they failed to get across their message that they were here for the benefit of the people of Geelong" (interview with the author July 10, 2003). He describes how BAGAG made a strategic decision to highlight publicly its parent company's environmental track record:

> An early tactic was to actually make an enemy of AES and highlight their appalling environmental record and their dreadful record on corporate relations and that's certainly had an impact on people in Geelong and really set the scene where the local residents couldn't trust this company. (Iain Lygo, interview with the author, Geelong, July 10, 2003)

Not only did AESPO demonstrate that they had a poor understanding of the issues they were trying to promote but they provided the public with misleading information. According to Lygo:

> Their PR effort was dreadful. It had some significant errors. Their work process, the works approval paper that they had was appalling. It had glaring omissions that we picked up and broadcast to the people of Geelong. They put on a few tours out to their other power station in the La Trobe Valley and one of their major mistakes was, on the way back, they showed us the AES power station at Newport which was smoking profusely and one of the groups on the buses said "Oh well, what's that? That's polluting pretty badly isn't it?" And they said "Oh, don't worry about that. That's a coal fired power station" when clearly it's not, it's a gas fired one and that caused great embarrassment for them. Their spin was unbelievable on a lot of occasions and didn't

match the reality of what was happening on the ground, so they really hurt themselves there. (Lygo, 2003)

Stuart McCallum observed, "We had pretty good technical people who had a better understanding of the machinery than everyone except the AES people who were not very good with the PR as they did not know how to deal with well-informed opposition" (interview with the author, Geelong, July 10, 2003). He said that AESPO "was always on the back foot in terms of their communication, with the Shire and the community. In contrast, BAGAG had a good relationship with the local media: Stuart reflects:

> We were always very media friendly and if someone would ring up we'd be quite happy to go into as much detail as they had the time to discuss the issues, and they'd say "Oh look thanks very much for that. It's just so hard to get information out of the other side." So they were always on our side. They knew that if they rang up, we'd give them some time. We'd tell them what we knew and they could ring AES and they'd get a few terse lines and, you know, it always came out that way, in whatever was published, so that was on our side. (McCallum 2003)

In early October, AES produced a generic letter,[4] signed by AESPO's Golden Plains Manager Graham Dowers, stating that, having obtained EPA approval for the power station, construction was planned for early November. The letter conveyed that the proponent was very confident that the project would proceed:

> I am happy to report that, following an exhaustive investigation of the proposed plant, the Victorian Environment Protection Authority has provided AES with a Works Approval for the project. This approval will allow construction to commence in early November 2001, pending a successful outcome from the Planning Appeals scheduled to commence on October 15, 2001, at the Victorian Civil & Administrative Tribunal (VCAT).[5] (Dowers 2001)

Despite seeming like a fait accompli, the activists appealed against the Golden Plains Shire's decision to allow the construction of the plant to proceed. According to Stuart McCallum, "Golden Plains were always in a bit of a bind over granting a permit . . . Golden Plains figured the best strategy for them was to issue a building permit but to tie the power station down as tightly as they could in terms of conditions." He said that BAGAG had two justifications for arguing against the proposal: "the conservation grounds and the air pollution grounds."

For the activists, Dr Graeme Lorimer, a recognised authority on air pollution, who wrote the computer model that EPA used, provided expert evidence at VCAT on emissions for BAGAG. BAGAG's report challenged the modelling on which the EPA had based its assessments, saying they had used inferior methods, "not thorough or adequate to determine the worst case concentrations. Mr Hearn's modelling was not wrong but nor was it thorough nor adequate to determine the worst-case concentrations" (Lorimer 2001, 2). Dr Robert Burton, an expert on noise pollution, also presented evidence on behalf of the group. According to McCallum the "EPA had to then argue that this little bit of pollution wouldn't really matter terribly much."

BAGAG's representation at VCAT cost about AUD$50,000. To raise the funds the community held raffles, movie nights and auctions. Iain Lygo said: "AES made it difficult for us by stretching out the VCAT hearing to ten or so days, basically because they knew they had deeper pockets than us."

The recent sting of electoral defeat drew out a political opportunity for state Liberal MP Terry Mulder. He pointed out in a speech to Parliament that it was not the Labor Party but the mayor of the City of Greater Geelong and aspiring state parliament Liberal candidate Cr Stretch Kontelj who assisted the community activists in their VCAT campaign. "[N]amely, the issue of pure decency in relation to this whole process in Geelong. That was an act by the mayor of Geelong, Cr Stretch Kontelj, in making a donation of $1000 towards the action group to help it fight the cause at the Victorian Civil and Administrative Tribunal" (Victorian Parliamentary Debates, Legislative Assembly, 28 November, 2001, 2053). Mulder argued that the Labor state government "do not care about people. They do not care about people with respiratory diseases. They do not care about children. They do not care about the environment around Geelong. It is the Liberal Party representatives who are fighting to protect people's rights, as we always have done in the past and as we always will do in the future" (Victorian Parliamentary Debates, Legislative Assembly, 28 November, 2001, 2054).

However despite the appeal, on 14 December 2001, VCAT announced approval for the AESPO to build the $260 million, 500 MW peak power station (Mayne 2003, 5). Over the six-week period, the Tribunal considered the submissions and subsequently voted to protect grasslands and vermin-proof the fence but dismissed BAGAG's other pollution concerns (McCann 2001b, 5). According to Stuart McCallum "the outcome of VCAT was that the station was approved; that most of the conditions set by Golden Plains Shire were upheld. Our argument in relation to the grassland was upheld. We actually won that part—that is to use a power station to control serrated tussock." A Shire project manager, Ed Harvey had argued that building the plant would provide funding to control serrated tussock on the site. BAGAG argued that perhaps there were more cost-effective means of controlling weeds. BAGAG won the point.

Nevertheless Stuart McCallum said that AESPO argued successfully that the Golden Plains Shire planning permit condition which said that the power station could only run five per cent of the time was an uneconomical and unreasonable condition:

One of the conditions the Shire wanted to argue for was that the power station could only be run four or five per cent of the time. It couldn't be run more than that and VCAT was persuaded by lawyers for AES that that was unreasonable. It wouldn't be economic for them to run just at that time and maybe they could have a little bit more. And it was always a disappointment that the council didn't argue that fully, and actually win that point. (McCallum 2003)

AESPO Director Jerry O'Brien was reported to have said that "VCAT has made an independent assessment . . . and determined it won't be harmful to the community or the environment in Geelong. We would hope that people would be comforted by that assessment" (McCann 2001b, 5). The objectors were disappointed that VCAT upheld Golden Plains Shire's planning permit, but took consolation in the fact they had successfully stalled the project's construction so that it would not be operational over the 2002 summer period (McCann 2001a, 7). This allowed them further time to raise awareness and lobby for a full EES statement.

Community Picket Line (CPL) was formed in response to VCAT's decision to uphold the Golden Plains Shire's planning permit. According to a local paper, protest organiser Sue Kelly-Turner said "about 20 dedicated protesters would picket the site until building began, probably in February. We have an on-call list of about 20 people who are all very committed and in for the long haul. We are dedicated to occupying this site 24 hours around the clock for as long as it takes. We won't back down" (*Geelong Independent*, Objectors vow 24-hour picket of site, December 21, 2001, 3). CPL was separate to BAGAG, and designed to physically block access to the site. To facilitate public participation in the vigil, a caravan and signage was set up, as well as a website. The following statement from CPL's[6] website explains the picket line's purpose:

> The Community Picket Line is made up of individuals and groups all working together for a single aim. That being, to achieve the Right for the Community to have an Environmental Effects Statement (EES) [*sic*] done on the AES Stonehaven Power Plant. (Community Picket Line 2002).

In late 2002, the state government election was to be held, and the power shortages that had led to the proposal that took on renewed political relevance. In this 3AW radio talkback transcript, Acting Premier John Thwaites said that the "national electricity advisory group" [*sic*] "NEMMCO,"[7] had advised the state government that if "there was very hot weather and there was any further generators went down, then we wouldn't have sufficient capacity." Thwaites then criticised the effect of the Kennett government's privatisation policies on the State's current capacity to generate electricity:

> The Kennett government in their seven years of office did nothing to build new generation capacity for electricity. I think all they were interested in was privatising. They just simply were selling off the electricity and that means that we didn't have the building of generators that we needed and of course that takes some time. We're doing that as a government now but the shortfall as a result of seven years of inaction is effecting [sic] us. (Thwaites in Rehame transcript, January 1, 2002, 1–2)

In response, shadow treasurer Robert Clarke said that Mr Thwaites, Acting Premier, had "the nerve to blame the Kennett government for the failures of his own government to get generation capacity online" (Gardiner 2002, 13).

State Liberal Party candidate for the seat of Geelong and Mayor of the Greater Geelong City Council, Stretch Kontelj, debated the lack of an EES with 3AK radio presenter Brett De Hoedt. Kontelj said that the power station debate could determine the state election outcome:

> There's a state election coming up later this year. The seat of Geelong is held by only sixteen votes, the most marginal seat. And I understand that this group may put up a candidate on this specific issue. So I think it's a . . . it could well determine the outcome of the government." (Kontelj in Rehame transcript, January 7, 2002, 7)

The act of forming a picket line was a singularly effective communication tool, conveying the long-term commitment of the protesters. It provided a visual reference point for the protest and a means by which signage and the human face of the protest could be effectively communicated (Johnstone 2002a, 5; Box 2002, 14; McCann 2002, 1). The activists set up living arrangements that included a solar-powered caravan for accommodation, food, entertainment and secure parking. The protesters also established a vegetable garden to provide food over winter (McCann 2002, 1–3). CPL eventually celebrated 200 consecutive days of vigil at the site (Mayne 2003, 5).

However, at the same time as the Stonehaven activists were preparing for long-term community opposition to the proposal, the proponent was reconsidering its viability. AESPO had announced its USA parent company, energy giant ENRON, had lost money and investments and for this reason it was considering withdrawing its interest (Poehland 2002, 7). But an AES Project manager Matthew Barley explained that the current re-assessment did not necessarily mean that the power station would not be built. Rather, "AES would maintain its planning permits and could reconsider construction some time after this year" (Murphy 2002, 3).

In the confusion surrounding the withdrawal of AES Corporation, the state government took the opportunity to re-assess its decision regarding the power plant's construction. Because the completion of other electricity upgrades had catered for the shortfall, it now questioned whether the power station was needed at all, even though it had previously said the 500-megawatt power station was essential to service Victoria's power shortages (Johnstone 2002b, 5). Spokesperson for Energy Minister Candy Broad, Nick Peece said "the AES power station will not be needed in the immediate future" (Johnstone 2002b, 5).

In February 2003, AES Corporation announced that it would "off-load" the Stonehaven site "with other Australian assets" (Mayne 2003, 3). 5). Therefore, the construction of the AESPO station, previously promoted as providing 'peaking power capacity' for the next summer's electricity needs, had not even commenced. Meantime, the state government declared construction on the project was frozen, but that planning permits for the station were valid and could be transferred, although AES maintained the right to reconsider construction in the future (Mayne 2002, 7).

OTWAY RANGES ENVIRONMENT NETWORK

Further southwest of Werribee and Geelong are the magnificent Otway Ranges, a cool temperate rainforest containing remnant vegetation from the super continent Gondwanaland. It was here, in 1995, that a collective of environmentally concerned citizens sought to protect the Otway region's diminishing reserves of old growth and other native forest areas. The Otway Ranges Environment Network (OREN) was formed from "Save the Otways," a smaller community coalition that operated between 1981 and 1993 and, amongst other things, maintained a seven-year logging moratorium in the Otways at West Barham River. When OREN formed, its members were a mix of practised and novice activists. Some came to the group as experienced protesters from Save the Otways and from forest campaigns like those in East Gippsland, whereas others joined in response to current forest issues and debates. Through this campaign the drought continued on relentlessly, water storages diminished and the landscape transformed. Over time it provided a disconcerting but compelling environmental frame through which to view the group's arguments and their calls for urgent action.

An incorporated body, OREN's common objective was to stop clearfell logging in the Otways. Simon Birrell played a key role in the group as a spokesperson and in media liaison. He said that OREN used a system of deliberative democracy that was non-hierarchical and allowed members to act on initiatives linked to the group's strategic goals:

> I suppose the group is just nothing more than a gathering of people with common interests to stop native forests clearfell logging and that's probably pretty much the beginning and the end of the policy.

> It's pretty simple. How you go about actually achieving that objective ... the general philosophy of OREN was that people just go off and do whatever they want to do because there's a thousand different things you can do at different levels. Some people may feel that they need to go and protest in the forest, some people may feel too intimidated by that and do nothing more than write a letter to the editor or put together a documentary or do research on the impact of logging on different forest values, such as biodiversity or domestic water supply catchments. (Simon Birrell, interview with the author, Geelong, July 8 2003)

In particular Birrell said that OREN's aim is to unite a broad range of community members opposed to logging and that this diversity allows members the flexibility to adopt different roles. He claims that the group members' ages and cultural backgrounds differ significantly and that this shows potential supporters that the protesters are not fanatics or social outcasts.

The timber industry's deep association with the Otways can be traced to the nineteenth century, around 1850, when a sawmill was founded at the harbour town of Apollo Bay. Writings by George Facey (1979, 1), an early Otway sawmiller, suggest that the burgeoning colony's demands for building materials like weatherboards, shingles, floor joists and studs for walls, roofs and floors influenced the Otway region's social and economic development over the next century. Facey wrote that timber workers, using axes and early versions of cut cross saws, supplied settlers with materials to build their town by forging bullock tracks, rough roads and later railway lines into the bountiful but inaccessible Otway Ranges forest. He wrote that in the ensuing years sawmills proliferated in the region until "there was a mill on nearly every ridge" (2). Further, he claimed that timber mill workers contributed to the Otway's growing population and that, as a result, towns such as Forrest, Barramunga and Apollo Bay grew into supporting, resourceful communities. However, he wrote that by the 1950s, the timber industry had begun to change. Some of the locally operated mills closed, replaced by larger-scale commercial operations using plantation practices. This quote from his self-published memoirs demonstrates his ambivalence about these changing timber production practices and the consequences for the native forest:

> Barramunga was a very close knit lot of people, always out to help one another if things took an adverse turn. A big blow to Barramunga was the closure of the sawmills in the district. These mills had given regular employment to quite a few men of the district. The Forestry[8] claiming they were fire hazards. Big companies with outside interests planted various farms with pine trees [where they] should have been let revert back to the native trees. (Facey 1979, 18)

This view about the imposition of large-scale industry in the Otways is corroborated by Pescott (1998) who said that in the twentieth century softwood plantations were established on a commercial basis. Pescott said that in the 1970s radiata pine was the preferred plantation species and was established on public and private land holdings and that "in most cases, the new plantings were on land specifically cleared of its indigenous vegetation for the purpose" (1998, 37). Another significant timber industry forestry practice around this time was the granting of licences to extract hardwood for pulp and papermaking. From around the 1980s, local environmental activist groups, such as Save the Otways and the Geelong Environment Council, mobilised to actively politicise the deforestation of indigenous vegetation in the Otways. To stop large-scale commercial logging practices in the Otway's, OREN focused its arguments on the forest's multiplicity of values. The group's activities can be organised into three key areas: the definition of value, timber practices and policy. OREN contested definitions of value that the timber industry and the state government assigned to different forest resources, such as timber, water and wildlife. They defined the value of biodiversity and of tourism holistically, not predominantly by economic indicators such as woodchipping yields set by forestry practices. To support this, they researched scientific, economic and social effects of commercial timber practices. Examples are in relation to the use of large-scale logging machinery and its relationship to diseases like myrtle wilt and erosion; and hydrology research studies to determine the impact of logging in the Otways on the water catchments quality and supply capacity. Concerns also focused on the timber industry practice of clearfell logging. Clearfell logging removes the entire understorey, such as tree ferns and grasses and they argued that this affects water quality and yields and therefore reduces the forest's economic value as well as removing the habitat of endangered species, such as the spot-tailed quoll. In terms of government process, OREN also argued that the Otways supplied 300,000 people with water and that the state's logging policies, in particular, woodchipping in native forests, were putting this at risk.

The campaign and sub campaigns was multi-layered and extensive but one particularly effective part was the boycott in December 1996, with key support from the National Union of Students (NUS), of paper and pulp manufacturer Kimberly-Clark:

> My understanding was the NUS—the National Union of Students—helped put out a flyer for us that Kimberly-Clark were in the Otways and that woodchips were being used to make their products. The NUS were able to distribute materials, flyers and stickers through the student union movement and we gradually saw these stickers physically making their way out across Australia. They ended up in the Northern Territory; they ended up in Western Australia. (Rue Lees, interview with the author, Geelong, 8 July 2003)

Lees said that the product boycott "was one of the most effective campaigns . . . that had a very broad appeal right throughout Australia."

At this time, Kimberly-Clark Australia (KCA), a subsidiary company of a US-based corporation, had a licence to source up to 44,000 tonnes of timber from the Otway state forest for "the hardwood woodchips to manufacture tissue paper" according to OREN's website. OREN argued that its clearfell logging "was having a devastating effect on the Otway forests and potential economic growth in the region" and that if KCA wanted to it could "find its woodchips from other sources" ("Campaigns: Kleenex Boycott" 2006).

OREN's campaign supported the boycott call by promoting alternative products made from post-consumer (recycled) waste paper. For example, it asked consumers to avoid Kleenex tissues and toilet paper and instead buy Safe and Softex brands among others. Lees said the OREN campaign called on boycotters to contact KCA to voice their protests and to take direct action. Indeed, OREN's website urged people to "Hand out information, talk to your local supermarket, tell friends and family. It all helps because people are not aware and do not think about where tissue paper comes from" ("Campaigns: Kleenex Boycott" 2006).

As a result of a workshop OREN conducted, it argued that " . . . Latrobe University, Royal Melbourne Institute of Technology, Deakin University and Woolongong University have ceased purchasing or are well on the way to not buying Kleenex products" ("Campaigns: Kleenex Boycott" 2006).

Kimberly-Clark was clearly concerned by the momentum of protest action as drought conditions deepened. Lees said that it contacted OREN with an invitation to meet and negotiate:

> Kimberly-Clark wanted to directly negotiate with members of OREN. The group decided there was actually no advantage for us to negotiate with Kimberly-Clark because we knew where we stood on the issue. We didn't have a moving point in that we were very sure that we wanted Kimberly-Clark out of the Otways. There was no negotiating with that and the only thing that meeting with Kimberly-Clark would do would be give them more information about our group. (Lees 2003)

In particular, she said the slogan "don't wipe your bum on the Otways" contributed to the success of the campaign:

> Then there were these stickers, these very luminous, fluoro green stickers that were made. By having a slightly humourous slogan, "don't wipe your bum on the Otways" like it was very effective in that it was saying these forests have higher value than just wiping your bum on, basically. (Lees 2003)

Indeed, the extent to which the Kimberly-Clark boycott campaign was effective is indicated in this *Melbourne Times* newspaper article sourced from OREN's website:

Toilet tissue giant Kimberly-Clark wants to get to the bottom of why the Moreland Council is no longer buying its products. The council made the decision recently in a bid to prop up support for the ailing recycling industry, conservation co-ordinator Paul Murfitt said. He said the council would not use Kimberly-Clark products because they were made from logged forests rather than recycled paper. The company produces Kleenex goods. Instead, the council will use paper produced by Queensland Cosco company. ("Oren News—What the Papers Say")

According to Boycott Woodchipping Campaign Victoria, a conglomerate of thirty of Australia's major national, state and regional conservation groups, the Otways' sticker and slogan "appeared in almost every toilet throughout Victoria" and the campaign had a "dramatic impact on sales"

Similarly, OREN had evidence directly from KCA that the boycott was successful:

> I'm not sure how it happened, but we managed to get hold of a document that was put out by Kimberly-Clark. I think they turned up to a public relations seminar or something like that and were using the Otways group as a case study on how to deal with pressure groups. And so we actually got feedback directly from Kimberly-Clark that we were successful, because I think within that document Kimberly-Clark had decided that, from a public relations perspective, this was a "no win" situation for them and the best idea was for them to get out, which is eventually what they did. (Lees 2003)

In December 1998, two years after the OREN boycott was actioned, Kimberly-Clark announced they would no longer source woodchips from the Otways. For OREN, the boycott campaign had unforeseen benefits. The group's exposure to the process helped them to understand the structure of the timber industry. Rue Lees said that:

> In the first couple of years we had the Kimberly-Clark campaign and that was something I felt consolidated OREN as a group in that we did have a target to focus on and we were all, those of us who were new to it, were starting to get our heads around the industry and how it was structured and the importance of the woodchip industry to the timber industry down there. (Lees 2003)

Simon Birrell agreed and said that after the boycott, OREN was seen as an organisation that was prepared to conduct a pro-active rather than reactive social action:

> If you're promoting a consumer awareness campaign, such as don't buy the Kleenex brand name, or talking about water, you're running

a proactive campaign. You're on the offensive and the industry is then trying to catch up and deal with your issues, and you're running and driving the agenda. And that's the challenge, I suppose, for conservation groups to run proactive campaigns. It's very hard because conservation groups don't normally have a lot of resources. People feel very passionate about their patches of forest, wherever they are across the state or across the country, and when they see things getting logged and destroyed, it is very hard to know what to do and it's sort of instinctive to just want to go and protest at the time at the site. (Birrell 2003)

However, these views about the OREN campaign were not shared by Daryl McLure. This *Geelong Advertiser* opinion piece, demonstrates that he views the protesters as "ferals" and fanatics, despite the fact that he is concerned about the sustainability of logging in water catchments:

The Greens, feral and otherwise, were given a lesson in how a non-violent demonstration should be run by the Victorian loggers who set up shop outside the Victorian ALP's election campaign launch in Melbourne last week . . . I don't know who to believe in the arguments which rage about whether Otways logging is sustainable or not. I tend not to believe the Greens because I don't trust them and don't think their leadership is honest at international or national levels. At the grassroots level, the fanaticism of their foot-soldiers, their confrontational demonstrations against ordinary workers, annoys and angers me. If they want to protest, they should do it outside State Parliament where the people who make the decision congregate. Why disrupt the livelihood of loggers who are making an honest quid within the law? Maybe logging of old growth forests, especially in a water catchment area, does have to stop. But I believe the state Labor government led by Premier Steve Bracks has lacked integrity and acted dishonourably in its dealings with the loggers. (McLure 2002, 17)

Similarly, Norman Endacott had a negative view of the protestors. He writes, without specifically naming OREN, that information produced by the "green movement" was "spin" and "propaganda":

The spin doctors of the green movement have been continually telling us that the government receives only 10 cents/tonne (AUD) for woodchips from public forest . . . I forsee [sic] the new Greens ploy. After a decent interval, when it is decided that the public has probably forgotten past propaganda, the spin doctors will be announcing woodchips are so lucrative that the Department of Natural Resources and Environment is eager to trash the forests for the sake of a woodchip bonanza. (Endacott 2002,24),

A letter to the *Herald Sun* by Peter Dynes, a spokesperson for the Gellibrand River Timber Communities, also describes the forest protesters in oppositional terms. In this letter, he refers to them as "urban based conservationists" and an "urban elite" who seek to restrict the very activities that lead to their comfortable lives. "They do not understand that rural Victoria is more than just a park for them to visit: it produces the basics of life, the food and raw materials to keep them in the comfort of their urban existence" (Peter Dynes, "Elites Attack Country," in *Herald Sun*, April 24, 2002, 19). However OREN accused Timber Communities Australia as a "public relations front group paid for by woodchip companies" (Timber Communities Austral 2002).

For McLure, Endacott and Dynes, organisations such as OREN caused deep resentment and suspicion. Endacott implies that they are undermining the role of the state. McLure implies that the protesters are "ferals" and are hurting honest, hard-working people who operate within the law. Dyne implies that the protestors are urban hypocrites who know little about the rural forest areas for which they claim authority to speak. The dichotomies constructed in these views reflect opposing and adversarial categories. Despite these complexities, and while taking advantage of every pragmatic opportunity to progress the agenda in the short term, OREN's Simon Birrell was prepared to stop clearfell logging even if it took "decades".

OREN's website also sheds light on how OREN constructed meanings and how their texts intersected with individual subjectivities. In particular, one page on the website is devoted to an expose of contested understandings of logging issues. This page appears to be designed to undermine the dominant reading position put forward by the logging industry and empower readers to undertake a critical negotiated reading of commentary produced by the logging industry. Titled "Clearfell Logging—Logging Industry Propaganda," the page lists ten statements issued by the logging industry that OREN challenges (Otway Ranges Environment Network, Inc. 2002. It is evident from this quotation that OREN paid a high level of attention to the multiple interpretations that the reader would encounter of particular words such as "harvest":

- The word "harvest" is a substitute for the word "clearfell logged" because it sounds better.
- The word "harvest" implies that a complex forest ecosystem can be managed by humans in the same way as a mono-culture crop of wheat or sugar-cane is farmed. The word harvest implies forests were created by humans to exploit when in fact they evolved over millions of years. The Otways forests exists [sic] in its [sic] own right without human intervention.
- A more accurate description of the concept "harvest" would be *"the natural forests are being cut down and replaced with a modified crop*

of trees similar to a plantation that will be harvested in 60 to 80 year rotations." ("Clearfell Logging—Logging Industry Propaganda," italics in original)

OREN's website also claims that Forestry Victoria suppressed key information for subjects. A web page lists documents the state department supplied to the public that OREN claims are misleading such as incorrect maps and hydrology research (Otway Ranges Environment Network Inc. 2012). The text producers posting this information on OREN's website demonstrates the extent to which they were prepared to interrogate and challenge competing values and assumptions to produce a counter-hegemonic reading position and discourse on forestry issues.

In 1999, OREN produced and published a report that refuted arguments put forward by the Department of Natural Resources and Environment (DNRE) and logging industry. Birrell said that "the department," (now Department of Sustainable Energy), responded to OREN's claims about hydrology research by disseminating it in the Geelong-based mass media:

> The department for instance, when the hydrology research was completed, produced their own version of the findings. They mass produced it and distributed it through newspapers right across the region, but of course, we had our own media campaign. We ran ads in the *Geelong Independent* and radio ads on K-Rock and Bay FM, talking about the impacts of the research, so, there was that sort of competition between us, but a lot of the competition was actually coming from the bureaucracy, from the department, and it was tax payers money being paid to actually try and counteract our campaign. (Birrell 2003)

This extract is taken from an OREN research report and contains another example where readers were positioned by the group to challenge the preferred reading position (Chandler 2002, 192–196) of the state and industry organisations:

> Myth that native forests "regenerate" after clearfell logging. The concept that forests regenerate after logging, is widely used by industry spokes people. The use of the word regenerate, imply the forests return to their original state after logging is finished. This has the effect of deceiving the public into believing nothing is being lost. The fact is that the timber industry is clear felling on a 50 to 80 year cycle, while some areas what it is logging is over 250 years old. A eucalypt forest has a life cycle of around 400 years. In human terms we will be logging forest when they are only 13 to 20 years of age and never allowing them to even reach their 21st birthday let alone middle or even old age.
>
>   ("Timber Industry Double Talk")

With this level of informed debate and in the context of Melbourne's unsettling dry weather and shrinking water storages, OREN successfully established scientific *bona fides*, which resulted in the Melbourne media referring to them as an authority to describe logging practices in the Otways:

> Water is already a critical regional issue, with Geelong on restrictions since January last year. The warning is contained in a report by the Otways Ranges Environment Network. It is based on a five-year study by the Cooperative Research Centre for Catchment Hydrology, which found that run-off into dam catchments declines when trees are young, then progressively increases, levelling off after 240 years (Miller 1999)

The state and the timber industries continued to produce vast amounts of dense and technical information about the logging of the Otway native forests. Birrell said that the public had been easily confused by the technical and scientific detail of the issues. He said that the inaccessibility of knowledge advantaged the native forest timber industry in that they maintained their status as the authoritative source and kept public scrutiny at bay. This activity by the timber industry suggests that techno-scientific orders of discourse were being invoked to position readers and funnel thought back into the positivist and bureaucratic frameworks which had been dominant to this point (Foucault 1972, 26; Chandler 2002, 80).

Another of OREN's strategic decisions in relation to the logging industry was not to react to the advertisements like "Treetalk," the advertising campaign by Midway[9] running weekly in the Geelong Advertiser. Birrell thought that the approach was misguided and was ultimately counter-productive:

> Midways had booked an ad that they were running every week in the *Geelong Addy*,[10] "Treetalk". We'd keep an eye on those ads, but generally my opinion was that they kind of missed the mark. They tended to try and boil down issues to such simplistic arguments that they were almost offensive to the general public's intelligence, and I think they were actually counter-productive in hindsight. Occasionally there was something that they might have said that had a little bit of merit, but most of it was just scare mongering and I suppose history shows that they didn't really didn't have any impact. They were just a waste of money. (Birrell 2003)

Instead of reacting to the campaign, OREN put their time and effort into campaigns like the consumer boycott of Kimberly-Clark and the water campaign that were designed to set the agenda over the long term.

The OREN campaign is especially interesting because the group shifted its focus from fighting with the native forest logging industry and focused on the forestry department or what is now called the Department of Sustainable Development (DSE). For OREN, meanings were created for subjects by the department's refusal to acknowledge and consider new ideas, especially within the different political administrations such as ALP or Coalition state governments. This extract demonstrates how OREN ultimately understood the role of the state in the relations of power:

> The Department Sustainable Environment, the forestry bureaucrats, is what we like to call them, were intransigent. They just would not budge, and today our opinion is, they still won't budge. They will not give us any ground at all. They still want to have it all, the whole lot, and in a way this whole battle really has been, to some extent, a battle between us and the bureaucracy, more so than the woodchipping businesses and the saw millers and the logging contractors. Because ultimately the bureaucracy is supposed to be there to serve the public, but our opinion is, they serve themselves. The money and the resources of the forests are directed to nothing more than perpetuating the forestry bureaucracy. There is no real benefit for the Australian public and the sooner that that forestry department is abolished, the better. (Birrell 2003)

With sustained low rainfall, with no end in sight, and another state government election looming, in November 2002 and, Premier Steve Bracks announced that, if a Labor state government were returned, logging in the Otway native forests would stop within six years. The *Herald Sun* (2002) reported that "The Premier unveiled a $50 million plan to buy back all timber licences in the Otways and create a national park from Anglesea to Cape Otway in Victoria's southwest. Mr Bracks denied that the promise was a move to win Greens preferences. . . . We have listened to the community and we will now act of [sic] behalf of future generations to save the Otways. If re-elected, we will make the Otways one of the world's great national parks" (Bracks in OREN 2004). While OREN welcomed the ALP forest policy outcome, Birrell explains that, because the Bracks State Government did not define the term "saw logging," benchmarks to limit woodchipping could not be applied, and that, therefore, more work was needed.

> We also realised that the department, under government policy, is supposed to be sawlog driven, but there isn't actually a definition of what sawlogging means. It's a great vacuum. And one of the things that we asked for and still ask for, is that the state government, legislate a definition of what sawlog driven means. Interestingly enough and ironically enough, the Federal Liberal Government has a definition. They had to develop one as a part of the renewable energy biomass—burning biomass for electricity legislation. They didn't want to necessarily limit what was eligible for burning—biomass burning—from forests to stop; just the wholesale clearing of vegetation burning in a furnace to make electricity. So what they said was that 50% by value of any logging

operation on public land or private, has to be for sawlogs, or for high value added purpose, and woodchips were not regarded as high value added purpose by the Federal Government legislation. Now I'm not saying that we agreed to that, but, we worked out that if that benchmark at the Federal Government level was applied to the Otways, 60% of the land mass would be unavailable for any form of logging. So that's why the State Government doesn't have a definition. So the government, the Bracks Government still has a long way to go. (Birrell 2003)

The absence of a name, or definition for "sawlogging" shows that generating the movement of meaning to construct an identifiable object is central to an understanding of activism and its relationship with public relations, which seeks to thwart such action.

CONCLUSION

The three case studies demonstrate the social, economic, political and communicative consequences when two ideologies, linked to risk and scarcity society, collide. With deepening drought conditions a constant reminder of ecological fragility, the activists achieved legitimacy and depth of understanding of the issues at hand. In turn, this enabled rational critical debate within the community on their different issues and led to the opening of a social space, in which the activists were conferred the authoritative speaking position.

WRTAD's campaign in 1995 commenced at the same time as consistently low rainfall pattern in Victoria was becoming evident. Thematically, it focused on the wasteful culture of industry, and the blindness of government to the impact of this on communities and the way they wanted to live. It was also characterised by a widespread social recognition that industry and government cannot simply bury hazardous waste without understanding the consequences. That it was not acceptable to just move the problem to somewhere else. Becoming more environmentally knowledgeable—people were joining together to make these connections, and not just in terms of waste. Connections were made between the ideas of: communities, toxins and waste; communities, toxins, waste, and water tables; communities, toxins, waste, water tables and the worsening drought conditions, and changing climate, and so on and so forth.

In the BAGAG campaign, in 2001, the rising temperatures contributed to a surge in electricity demand arising from a increasing number of air conditioners used to deal with increased the more extreme and variable climate. The drain on electricity grid highlighted not only the lack of preparedness by government in dealing with this situation, but lack of attention and lack of policy, in making homes, suburbs and cities sustainable. The response of government and industry to 'fix the problem' by introducing obsolete technology displayed the same outmoded logic. Perhaps living with the perennially brown landscape and the hotness inclined people to mobilise in groups to question if government was providing the right response to their real concerns about the future.

The OREN case study straddles the entire period from 1995 to 2003. Over this time, concerned individuals and groups joined together to focus other people's attention what was going on in the Otway forests and its water catchments. In the early stages, the Kennett state government was dismissive of these concerns but as Victoria entered one of the most severe and longest periods of drought, these issues gathered greater resonance. Momentum was gained as the activists and their ideas developed credibility through the ethical conduct, energy and inventiveness of their communication campaign. With stamina and political maturity, there was a broad view that these activists had something valuable to say, and deserved to be heard.

All three activist groups developed legitimacy and authority as sub-political voices but in many instances public relations was used to deny. Far from Bernays' conception of "herds," the activists demonstrate that the new publics of risk society can outmanoeuvre public relations and effected change in meaningful and sustained ways. Significantly, the case studies each show that "Enabling self-criticism in all its forms is not some sort of danger, but probably the only way that the mistakes that would sooner or later destroy our world can be detected in advance" (Beck 1992, 234).

6 Not Public Relations
Sustainable Communication

The Fire Eaters

In the swirling new day
Ashen soft, words drift
Like snow
Over the wasteland
And settle, quietly
Covering
Its big heart
Stopped, on the road
One, followed by one,

Its whiteness,
Blinding you

This chapter constructs the political object of public communication, as an alternative organisational communicative mode to public relations. It also looks to the future and explores some of the social and cultural realities arising from risk society together with the massive uptake of digital technologies—taking the view that when activism has changed direction, so has public relations.

This book challenges the claim of public relations to theorise and speak for the unity of organisational communicantion in part because it is ideologically invested to include some sectors and exclude others, in particular, activism. It is also challenged because public relations as a form of social relations, and as characterised in twentieth-century, not only can fail to deliver the result that businesses and organisations expect in a risk society but can also work to society's detriment by stifling important social change that seeks to address issues such as the damaging effects of carbon pollution. Thus after interrogating the unity of public relations, it is argued that legitimately another grouping can be formed, that of "public communication." While Beck's ideas have been used to provide an innovative framework to develop this new unity, the ethical values of communicative activities are not central to his analysis. Adopting a citizenship focus has added to the development of this unity to define and delineate the types of communication that contribute to, or weaken, a democratic society and to analyse if this affects political participation in the public sphere and the production of public opinion (Habermas 1995, 236–250); and furthermore, whether it is of wider "holistic" community value (Breit 2007, 346, Christians 1997). Public communication is a discursive practice within the contexts of risk society and reflexive modernisation that avoids the deep contradictions and flawed coherences of essentialist public relations. It can be used by those in business and by activists and represents an important reorientation towards sustainability and ethics in the communicative fields.

If the role of theory is to develop an unbiased, clear and generalised understanding of social complexities that guides practice, then public relations theory—arising from teleological liberal pluralism and with a historical animosity to activism—fails to provide intellectual leadership in relation to activism, and particularly in the communication activities between groups within the social conditions of a risk society. Moreover, public relations theory is limited in its ability to understand in socially complex and interdisciplinary ways the Internet, social media, and communicative relations in the wake of cultural and technological developments. This failure strengthens the case for disarticulating communicative practice from institutional sites like public relations and considering alternatives. Therefore, in the second part of this chapter I show how these developments have impacted on activism and public relations in ways that have led to a form of hybridisation. These are explored from the point of view of "publics" within the setting of a risk society. In particular, I show how these elements meet to produce a range of distinct dispositions in individuals and groups that present new challenges for those seeking to reform manipulative communicative practice and its relationship to extrinsic and intrinsic forms of public relations. Lastly, I consider possible futures for public relations and activism, while flagging some emergent new directions.

Not only does this chapter set out a new communicative approach, it also sets out an agenda for reform in public relations. This is spurred by the view that in a "low-carbon world", there remains the exciting possibility of a polity that embraces, rather than stifles, dissent and has a greater expectation of a divergence of views from a wider range of people, who in turn have the ability to accept the divergent views of others.

PUBLIC COMMUNICATION: POSSIBILITIES AND LIMITS

As an approach to organisational communication, the research of the three case studies of WRATD, BAGAG and OREN at the cusp of the new millennium finds an alternative set of social relations to public relations which I call "public communication." It is important to give this alternative a new name because of the weaknesses and the outdated and politically offensive ways in which public relations has been used. Equally, a description of public relations was necessary to map out this alternative, because it is through an interdiscursive contrast that public communication can be understood in its complexity. Public communication is a mode of communicative activity that represents more than just a name change. It is a dynamically interacting values-based and holistic approach that asks what each separate organisation communicative practice adds up to, from a socio-political perspective; and how are "truth" and "self-interest" defined and acted on.

Evidently, the merits of these case studies are coherent within a model of risk society, but not within a liberal pluralist model as is public relations (Smith 1993, 27). In a liberal pluralist society, knowledge and ways to investigate and validate public relations are defined largely in economic terms which simplify complex relations of power and over-estimate the agency of individuals and groups to deal with its negative consequences (Grunig and Hunt 1984, 320; Ryan, 1991,12). There are new forms of social relations that are not public relations. Nor are these new forms of social relations characterised by simple adversarial communication activist approaches based on ideas of Marxist theory that were typical of early modernity and scarcity society (McLellan 1984, 246; Demetrious 2004, 20; Burgmann 1993, 6; Beck 1992, 19).

The campaigns mounted by the three grassroots activists groups were sustained and value-based, provided rigorous challenges to the legal and scientific institutions, and dealt adroitly with the complex and critical power positions occupied by the media. The success of these groups in achieving their stated objectives suggests that their understanding of the issues—at this time—was greater than the organisations and institutions they opposed. The groups showed a form of organisational communication that was effective and distinct from public relations, but undescribed in the literature.

The following guidelines, distilled from the WRATD, BAGAG and OREN case studies, provide an alternative approach to organisational communication:

- Public communication is open to possibility and permeated by ideas. This outward orientation exposes practice to alternative strategies that are capable of leading to new discursive formations in which values and problems are redefined, so that different relationships and boundaries emerge between groups, and lead to different choices within "the new *paradigm of risk society*" (Beck 1992, 19 italics in original; Foucault 1972, 38).

    This is evident in the activities of WRATD, BAGAG and OREN. The groups, rather than bury toxic waste, burn fossil fuels and destroy biomass, promoted waste minimisation, energy demand reduction and conservation to achieve sustainable energy, waste, and water and forest policy. In doing so, they demonstrated a willingness to accept an infusion of ideas which opened up novel possibilities to prevent, minimise or solve, and communicate the risks produced as by-products of the social production of wealth (Beck 1992, 19).

- Public communication is holistic and reaches out widely. Statements are not isolated but are related to a "domain of objects" and should be regarded as "an element in a field of coexistence" (Foucault 1972, 108–109), in order to open up new subject positions and encourage a long-term commitment to issues and groups which will develop the "themes of the future" (Beck 2000, 19).

  WRATD, BAGAG and OREN opened up numerous new subject positions through the definition of "the distribution and growth of risk" (Beck 1992, 23). For example, WRATD found new and related subject positions with the CSR shareholders and local business people who, in earlier periods of modernity, may have been unconcerned about, or disconnected to, the toxic dump's risk-producing effects. BAGAG built on existing subject positions for people in the industrial city of Geelong who had concerns about pollution in the region and reinforced this. OREN opened up social risk positions through the politicisation of logging in water catchments and its implications for drought-affected areas. The groups also encouraged long-term commitment among politically diverse participants. In this approach, WRATD, BAGAG and OREN expected active members (who had a strong commitment) to uphold citizen rights and responsibilities. The grassroots activist groups therefore acted intergenerationally, as an "eternal You" (Christians and Traber 1997, 9) and demonstrate theories of active citizenship or bearers of responsibility rather than rights (Kane 2000, 223–4); and differential citizenship or non-traditional membership (Hudson 2000, 17) through new particularism, such as grassroots activism, that acted for the common good.

- Public communication is ethically connected and respectful of existing normative social systems. It therefore interacts with intra-organisational public spheres, is goal-oriented within the prevailing social governance systems and develops meaningful exchanges between social and state organisations and institutions. It pursues the ideal that it is possible to dilute the antagonism between social groups and promote mutual satisfaction and to produce critical public opinion (Habermas 1995, 248).

  WRATD, BAGAG and OREN campaigns demonstrated a high level of Habermasian critical public opinion by integrating alternative strategies within goal-oriented prevailing systems. Examples are: WRATD's participation in state environmental authority panel hearings, BAGAG's participation in the state government disputed planning process and OREN's participation in government and timber industry long-term planning process, despite the fact that there were major concerns in all three groups about the fairness of these processes. By participating in these intra-organisational systems, the activist groups were able to avoid the antagonism that may have been caused by confining themselves to an attack on a break in logic between social spectrums, and promote mutual satisfaction. By demonstrating a willingness to participate in the state processes and its institutions, the activist groups were able to promote new coherences that linked to alternative policy and logic, such as waste minimisation, energy demand reduction and sustainable water and forest management, with authority and legitimacy that garnered credibility and social traction.

- Public communication aims to build enduring and dynamic inter-relationships between groups. It encourages, not just people's participation in intraorganisational spheres in different social settings and spaces but advocates for relations that promote feedback, discussion and debate (Habermas 1995, 248–249).

  The communication of WRATD, BAGAG and OREN had distinct features such as broad feedback, facilitated in part by the Internet and by other modes such as face-to-face discussion and community debate. Their overall interactions with society can also be judged by the successful long-term integration of their arguments into public policy. For example, in the case of WRATD, the Bracks Labor government announced a policy to abandon the practice of placing hazardous waste in landfill (Strangio 2001, 184). In the case of BAGAG, the Bracks government reversed policy to locate a 500-megawatt power station at Stonehaven and made statements promoting more energy-efficient practices (Johnstone, "Government Backflip on Stonehaven Power Station We don't need it", 5). In the case of OREN, the Bracks ALP state government established a new 103,000-hectare National Park focused around environmentally sustainable principles (Bracks in OREN 2004). Integration of activist arguments into public policy may take time. Nonetheless, when apparent, their prescience, efforts and advocacy skills should be given due credit.

- Public communication works to build people's capacities in order to facilitate rational, critical debate and opinion. It is an inclusive approach encourages political participation and draws on a "thick conception of community" rather than communication practices that exclude individuals or groups or seek to neutralise political dispositions (Kane 2000, 223–224).

  WRATD, BAGAG and OREN inclusive approach, that is, not merely promoting and identifying their cause with a particular type of person belonging to a particular social space, encouraged more general citizen participation. This was facilitated, in part, by the group eschewing dichotomies such as left and right, young and old, urban and rural, that has worked, in the past, to silo groups and therefore segregate potential support bases. This inclusiveness built capacities in people to understand the issues and break down stereotypes which, in turn, opened up new subject positions at many levels. Capacities in subjects were created in WRATD's campaign by a set of guiding principles that helped it define an ethical and effective style of communication; OREN achieved inclusiveness through a commitment to non-violent principles in their direct-action protest.

- Public communication works to develop diversity of discussion in the public sphere and to "address" and explain choices to the public as citizens not consumers (Habermas 1995, 195).

  WRATD, BAGAG and OREN developed depth of discussion in the public sphere and critical debate. All three campaigns rendered visible the public relations practices that were being deployed to counter their arguments. Through a range of discursive practices, they produced and distributed communication for subjects to promote understandings that assisted them to think and act independently on the debates and to form considered judgements. Communication throughout the campaigns was characterised by a consistent, rational and regular approach that sought to educate subjects, rather than to persuade, in order to shed light on the complex relationships between the state, business and civil sectors and the consequences for public policy.

- Public communication builds and maintains support at a grassroots level "as in the wake of subpolitization, there are growing opportunities to have a voice and a share in the arrangement of society for groups hitherto uninvolved" (Beck 2000, 23).

  WRATD, BAGAG and OREN built and maintained local support within their communities. This was demonstrated in petitions, public meetings, letter-writing campaigns, submissions and boycotts, amongst others. The groups developed strong local networks with individuals and groups and delivered information in a variety of modes such as print, group interaction, face to face and the Internet.

- Public communication emphasises lifeworld concepts such as sacred, mythic and spiritual or the "sensual-aesthetic" in response to the unfettered growth of instrumental reason (Habermas 1989, 394).

  WRATD, BAGAG and OREN defined "knowledge" and "value" in terms of lifeworld concepts such as compassion, self-sacrifice and "quality of life, equal rights, individual self-realization, participation, and human rights" (Habermas 1989, 392). For example, they produced texts that emphasised the value of air, trees, water and the future and promoted the individual's participation in community networks to achieve social cohesiveness and personal fulfilment.

- Public communication demonstrates ethical certainty through an interrelationship between communication, rationality and morals by practising to uphold human dignity, truth-telling and a commitment to living together peacefully (Christians 1997, 12–15).

WRATD, BAGAG and OREN adopted ethical principles of dignity, non-violence and truth-telling. Dignity and truth-telling were evidenced by how the groups went about explaining the rhetoric of public relations to subjects, rather than attacking the individuals within the organisations they opposed. They communicated with individuals and groups to provide an understanding of process, media and discourse in order to counter the disempowering effects of public relations. The principles of living together peacefully are evidenced by the fact that all the groups participated in intra-organisational government processes rather than continuing the Marxist activist tradition of working from outside the dominant state and business system, despite the fact that in the OREN case study there was pressure from within activist ranks to do so. However, the civil disobedience demonstrated by the case studies presents a problematic relationship to the principle of living together harmoniously. For example, OREN members trespassed and blockaded the logging coupes, WRATD members held up traffic on the Princes Highway with a car cavalcade, and some BAGAG members participated in a community picket line to block access to the proposed power station site. It is, therefore, critical to analyse what civil disobedience means in relationship to Christians' (1997, 14) principle of "nonviolence" as "a commitment to living together peacefully". Durkheim (1957) sheds light on this question. He argues that members of society submit to laws not because they are laws but because they are good; and he asserts of laws that are not accepted: "what my will has done, my will can undo" (Durkheim 1957, 107). For Durkheim, it is also important to take part in the formation of those laws and public life. Durkheim's views and the civil disobedience demonstrated in the case studies are consistent with the Clifford Christians' ideal because the protest was peaceful and reflected the inter-relation between the individual and democracy and a desire for the common good. Therefore, within these conditions civil disobedience is a legitimate form of public communication.
- Public communication strives to maintain a critical distance from its subjectivities to achieve political maturity and to avoid "irrationalism, extremism, or fanaticism" in the wake of anxieties in risk society (Beck 1992, 49).

The activists groups kept distance from their subjectivities and aimed to uphold the ideals of truth and objectivity: The policies of non-violence helped the groups to behave ethically and with restraint, maturity and rationality within the sometimes volatile social and political contexts.

Restraint and political maturity was very evident in the OREN case study when, during 1999 and 2000, the Commonwealth of Australia and the State Governments were jointly developing Regional Forest Agreements

136   *Public Relations, Activisim, and Social Change*

(RFAs) to control future hardwood woodchip exporting for the next twenty years. The Agreements were intended as a strategy for long-term forest management to balance environmental, social and economic interests. During this time, however, outbreaks of violence between the loggers and conservationists in the forests escalated. For example Michelle Pountney ("Unions Picket Protest Camp," *Herald Sun*, January 27, 1999, 21) describes such an occasion when timber workers formed a "picket line" around protesters trying to stop clearfell logging in the coupe:

> Timber workers formed an official union picket line around a group of 12 conservationists on Monday, refusing to let them in or out of their camp at SSP track, about 12km north of Apollo Bay. The members of the Otway Ranges Environment Network accused the loggers of denying them food and water . . . OREN spokesman Adrian Whitehead said the timber workers' blockade went against normal picket-line practice and protesters were being held against their will. (Pountney, "Unions Picket Protest Camp," 21)

Miller ("Seeing the Trees for the Wood," *The Age*, January 30, 1999, 10) also describes this situation and claims that the siege lasted for five days:

> Timber workers have lifted their blockade of conservationalists who were attempting to stop the clearfelling of a patch of forest in the Otways Ranges. After a siege lasting five days, in which more than 50 loggers prevented any conservationists entering or leaving their camp beside the forest access track, the protesters were allowed to leave yesterday morning. The loggers originally demanded an assurance there would be no more direct action taken against logging in the Otways before they would lift the blockade, but the area's peak green group, the Otway Ranges Environment Network, did not agree (Miller, "Seeing the Trees for the Wood," 10)

As a result, OREN achieved stability, legitimacy and depth of understanding that enabled rational critical debate on logging issues and eventually adopted an authoritative speaking position; despite journalistic and editorial predilections to engineer an anti-logging/pro-logging dichotomy; despite its members being embroiled in violent incidents with the logging industry; despite the distraction of timber industry-generated public relations; and despite the bureaucratic intransigence and the barriers to understanding it created through the technologisation and demonopolisation of discourse (Foucault 1972; Christians 1997; Hudson 2000; Habermas 1995; Beck 2000).

In summary the defining characteristics of public communication are openness to ideas; a commitment to truthfulness; the development of depth of discussion in public debate; the tendency to explain choices facing the public, rather than engage in persuasion or derision; the encouragement of a broad culture of participation; a long-term commitment to the group's objectives and the ability to maintain a critical distance from their subjectivities. Public communication practised by groups such as WRATD, BAGAG and OREN showed depth of understanding of communication and community, inventiveness, courage and tenacity and a commitment to their core values. It also demonstrates that even within the pressured and aggressive contexts, a strong ethical approach, political maturity and stamina can be maintained in powerful and productive ways.

Activism and/or fringe social movements in the new risk society, characterised by their very lack of legitimacy, could play an increasingly important role in developing and exercising knowledge independent of commercial interest that could challenge the existing status quo. In the latter years of the WRATD, BAGAG and OREN campaigns, the Internet assisted by providing an increasingly decentralised media and the resulting access to sophisticated information technologies. The digital information technologies enabled the activist groups to produce and distribute existing and new social symbolisms to describe the cultural impacts and effects of the power station, toxic dump and the logging activity. This culturally saturated form of science as "the public discursivity of experience" (Beck 2000, 30–1) undermined the dominance of laboratory science oriented to system rationality that the state and business sectors produced. These activist groups and their public critiques of laboratory science demonstrated tenacious and interrogative responses to corporate and state sectors that, in these examples, continued to behave in entrenched ways typical of scarcity society (Beck 1992; 2000). The activists developed effective scientific arguments around the concept of over-production and the long-term uncertainty that these risks, produced by the power station, toxic dump and logging activity in the Otways, pose for the "publics" that consume them.

This book has argued that the conditions of risk society create new interpretations of activist groups, such as WRATD, BAGAG and OREN. It has argued that, as a result, the accumulation of resources such as campaign experience, knowledge of state processes, infrastructure and social networks and their ethical approaches to communication, continued beyond the immediate campaign period. The Internet and their organisational websites helped the groups develop legitimacy and an authority on highly specialised areas of system rationality. This perspective challenges the pessimism associated with the Habermasian view that the public sphere is inevitably subject to cultural impoverishment through the growth and standing of specialised and "expert" knowledge in modern society.

This book also describes relations between two distinct discursive groups—public communication and public relations—through an analysis of WRATD, BAGAG and OREN and their relationship with the state and business sectors. A key defining characteristic of the grassroots activist groups' public communication was that, unlike public relations, it did not attempt to asphyxiate *extrinsic* statements outside its discursive formation in order to restore a hidden unity that serves its own organisational self-interest (Foucault 1972, 149–153). Nor did public communication attempt to harmonise surface or *intrinsic* contradictions within its discursive formation to create cohesion through symbolism and discourse resulting in the "spin" and "fluff" of public relations.

Public communication, rather than seeking to bring an extrinsic contradiction into harmony by suppressing statements, was open to and permeated by ideas and proposed alternative strategies that opened up the possibility of new discursive formations. Drawing on their social networks, the grassroots activists used public communication as a means to adjust the existing social institutions and structures to harmonise their self-chosen lives (Beck 2004, 73–5).

The permeation of ideas in public communication is vitally important to distinguish it from public relations, which as discussed in Chapter One is an organisational social practice within the normative conditions of the twentieth century drawing on functionalist notion of "harmony" to justify the control of *contradictions* between and through public and private discourses in order to maintain a dominant position of privilege and influence. In the public communication used by the grassroots activist groups, statements developed to support the objects sought—not to limit thought within the boundaries set by the group—but to open up the movement of meaning outside its own discursive formation. This is not to say thought was then led back within the dominant discourse—but that thought and form found points of intersection with it and from this position opened up new subjective positions outside the dominant discursive formation. In this sense, public communication is not penetrated by authority and the public remains independent in its decision making.

Moreover, public communication is consistent with Habermas' notion of public opinion mediated by critical publicity (1995, 247–250). Evidence of this sociologically is the definition of new objects and the opening up of subject positions in ways that brought diverse groups of people together. None of the activists in the WRATD, BAGAG and OREN case studies had an equivalent term by which to call their own communication. The *absence* of any term to describe their own communication is consistent in each of the case studies. Therefore, while the object of public relations is apparent, the object of public communication is not. Hence, rather than concentrating on the failings of public relations as do critics Beder (1997), Nelson (1989), Stauber and Rampton (1995), this chapter sets out an approach that has worked under specific conditions, but that could be explored in other social settings, times and places.

This new approach has important ramifications for the teaching and practice of public relations, and hence for activism, government and business.

Public relations education, generally, has overemphasized technical expertise. Demetrious argues that this manifests in "the creation of PR plans and communication audits over the development of how these objects are created in the first place, and who, or what, they serve". She says the ideas of Lloyd Kornelsen, (2006, p.79) shed light on this: "He argues that there are "two forms of Aristotelian knowledge, *techne* and *phronesis*. Techne is knowledge possessed by a maker and suggests sovereignty over; phronesis is knowledge that is personal and suggests communal engagement with." In relation to these, Michael McGee (2001, p.5) argues "Phronesis presents an aspect of wisdom that is missing in techne . . . we do not describe technical mastery as wisdom, for it consists of habituated familiarity of a technology" . . . Thus, public relations education can be viewed as having an embedded bias towards techne and the production of useful tools or artefacts. Moreover, deficient in phronesis, it fails to give context to the broader purpose of the way in which these artefacts interact with society." (Demetrious 2012, 257)

An important starting point is to develop differentiated understandings of public relations and to be clear that there are alternative communicative practices and relations that are sustainable, effective, viable and ethical within the uncertain and transforming social conditions of the twenty-first century. From an educational point of view, it is crucial for teachers of media and communication to present students with opportunities to learn how communication processes are both structured and ideologically invested and can be used by organisations as a powerful instrument to further self-interest and in doing so can work to society's detriment or betterment.

PUBLIC COMMUNICATION APPLICATION

Within the conditions of reflexive modernity and a risk society, I argue that public communication could be applied in other circumstances that may have positive flow-on effects for society (Beck 1992; 2000). This application could have significant consequences for the polity defined as institutions, such as the state government, the water authorities and the local councils discussed in my case studies which determine relations of power in society (Abercrombie, Hill and Turner 1994, 319). In particular, grassroots activists could, through the use of public communication, make important contributions to social debates. As a result, less concentration of decision-making in state and business sectors could occur in a more democratic distribution of resources and a shift in the polity itself to include the civil sector to a greater extent. This could produce greater diversity of ideas and more tolerance through communicative deliberation (Durkheim 1957, Habermas 1995). For example, grassroots activists have a unique ability, through their sub-political status, to present arguments about how the common good will be served, considered from a range of unusual perspectives, including the lifeworld (Habermas 1989). As a result, citizens acting within sub-political groups could describe and identify issues that the polity, linked to system rationality, may have overlooked (Giddens 1991; 1995). In turn, civil society could gain greater legitimacy to participate in political life (Hudson 2000, Kane 2000). By the same measure, for business sectors, gaining legitimacy may be harder. For example, the constant onus on activists to prove "why not" (a toxic dump or polluting power station or clearfell logging) may shift to business and industry having to prove "why."

Overall, holistic and integrated public communication, within the conditions of reflexive modernity and a risk society, may produce more diversity in public debates, which in turn can benefit the individuals involved who are exposed to greater political processes. This may well give rise to new discursive practices and the reproduction of shared understandings that facilitate further empowerment towards goals (Fairclough 1999). If this occurred, the level of debate and understanding about issues relating to the polity might be raised in communities and more rigorous and ethical decisions could be made (Hudson and Kane 2000; Christians 1997). As discussed, an outcome could be that the polity could embrace dissent and have greater expectations of a divergence of views because it has high levels of media literacy through an understanding of how discourses shape and influence meaning making. Communities of people and groups engaging in political life, using public communication, may pay attention to fairness, participation and honesty in ways that result in fewer hidden power relations by vested interests and more transparency, and in particular less junking of the collective public sphere (Breit 2007; Habermas 1995).

Significantly, within a risk society, the public communication guidelines distilled could be important to steer politically volatile, sub-political expressions to maintain their focus and longevity in the face of a range of social and economic pressures. By encouraging the values of active and differential citizenship, ethical public communication approaches could affect a greater sphere of influence than the social issue itself. The guidelines of public communication, characterised by the permeation of ideas, could help avoid the limitations and relativism of public relations. As a result, the absence and/or negativity in public relations discourse about the use of communication by grassroots activists would be addressed. Public relations' authority, for example, to describe organisational communication in a way that marginalises activism could be exposed and undermined in the future. Furthermore, the objectification and critical analysis of public relations by an increasingly knowledgeable public suggests that the area may transform to a transparent, ethical, rigorous and inclusive approach, such as public communication. Their greater exposure to political processes and interaction through active and differential citizenship could lead to new concepts and thematic choices that become culturally embedded as institutions (Hudson 2000, Kane 2000). Therefore, the movement of grassroots activism, through the mainstreaming of public communication, into a more central political and social space could result in its greater inclusion in decision making, education and practice (Habermas 1995). This is significant firstly because it is a break with the logic of modernity where business and the state dominate thinking and action and, secondly, because new ways of thinking, nurtured and expressed in public communication, could lead to creative and unusual coherences in civil, state and business sectors that are vital to deal with the imminent ecological threat and hazard that lies within a risk society in reflexive modernity (Beck 1992, 2000).

In summary, constraints in thinking around public relations have led to serious problems for the profession and for society. In unpacking public relations and its relationship to activism this book has ventured into cultural and sociological studies drawing on key thinkers like Jürgen Habermas, Ulrich Beck and Michel Foucault. It has outlined public relations failures and presents a compelling argument for real paradigmatic change in communicative approaches in civil, state and business sectors. These include:

- New approaches to pedagogy and the teaching of public relations that places critical engagement with ethics (social movements and social context) at the centre rather than the margins of curriculum development;
- New research agendas that aim to provide socially inter-related understandings of forms of public relations and their discursive effects. For example "spin" as the management of intrinsic contradictions—which in turn provide greater delineation between approaches;
- New taxonomies, for example intrinsic and extrinsic public relations, to assist in the regulation and enforcement of communicative ethics and a genuine engagement with alternative and differentiated modes and with critical values.

This book has mapped and documented key developments in activism and set out guidelines that underpin a more ethical form of social relations than public relations called "public communication." Public communication is an approach to communicative activity distilled from the observations of activist practice and supported by an analysis that draws on a broad ranging mix of social, political, communicative and discourse theories. The research findings indicate that the particular communicative approach identified in the activist campaigns is likely to occur elsewhere where risk producing industries collide with sub-political expressions of reflexive modernisation.

FUTURES AND LIMITS

I have argued that grassroots activism should not be dismissed as isolated and minor. Rather, it is significant for the redefinition of institutions and power relations in society; and it opens up a range of new positions for subjects. Furthermore, public communication is a means by which grassroots activism can become more effective and move from a fringe activity into a mainstream activity that is bound up within the state and business sectors. A positive consequence of its closer alliance with state and business sectors could be a greater emphasis on sustainable development and the redefinition of value around social, cultural and environmental issues (Andriof et al. 2002; Lyons 2001; Greenwood 2001; McIntosh et al. 1998; Birch 2001). These consequences link to Durkheim's (1957) ideal about the role of secondary groups in large-scale society in the creation of a deliberative democracy. Furthermore, these changed relations between civil, state and business sectors could address the failure by the state to protect the individual from crises, such as effects of carbon pollution (Beck 1992; Beck 2000; Giddens 1991; 1995).

Equally, there could be negative consequences of the movement of grassroots activists into a more central social space that need to be considered. One paradoxical consequence could be that their new found authority and legitimacy to describe objects such as the toxic dump, power station and the damaged native forest, is compromised. In other words, the unaligned sub-political status of grassroots activists could be undermined by their close proximity to these centres of power—as they become a part of the institutions they seek to critique. Hence, activists' claim to be an important secondary tier in a deliberative democracy could become diluted and meaningless. If this occurred, the argument that the public sphere has been reinvented with renewed integrity by sub-political groups is negated.

The research around WRATD, BAGAG and OREN distils guidelines of "public communication" that could be of benefit to society, but similarly there may also be unforeseen problems associated with this within the dynamic turbulence of social life. Activist groups, by applying this ethical framework to guide their communication, could build capacities in individuals and groups in ways that encourage participation and involvement in political debates. These new approaches to communication and diversity of subject positions in public participation are important for a society in which large corporations and governments can influence public opinion to the extent that some people feel they cannot contribute to discussion. However, what happens when everyone wants to have a say in everything, when there is an over-abundance of participating voices? What happens to the idea of leadership and how is an alternative view constructed and progressed? Bauman (1997) offers an important critical perspective that claims that the elevation of micro-style democracy could obscure the groups and individuals that offer vision and viable solutions to society's problems in the clutter of competing voices and views:

> There is no certainty—not even a high probability—that in the universe populated by communities no room will be left for the pariah. What seems more plausible, however, is that the parvenu's route of escape from the pariah status will be closed. Mixophilia may well be replaced with mixophobia; tolerance of difference may well be wedded to the flat refusal of solidarity; monologic discourse, rather than giving way to a dialogic, will split into a series of soliloquies, with the speakers no

more insisting on being heard, but refusing to listen into the bargain. These are real prospects, real enough to give pause to the joyful chorus of sociologists welcoming the new soft world of communities (Bauman 1997, 81).

If Bauman's predictions are accurate, then it remains to be seen whether the culture of tolerating differences, which is demonstrated in these case studies, may ironically create instead a splintered form of self-interest, which undercuts the unity of communities and the restructuring of modern society. The next section explores the possibility of an overabundance of voices or "soliloquies" in a digital world, and some of the consequences for activism and public relations.

RADICALISED COMMUNICATION IN THE NEW CENTURY

In a scarcity society, isolated and inarticulate publics had been restricted by both their own socioeconomic circumstances and by cultural and economic barriers surrounding centralised media industries in sending a message to reach a mass audience. Coupled with the rise of the Internet, however, risk society showed how the unpolitical had become political, leading to a "reorganization of power and authority" (Beck 1992, 24). In the twenty-first century, information and digital technologies are deeply entwined in social, economic and cultural relationships, and continue to transform the communicative landscape. More recently, since 2004 "social media" has exploded in popularity and has centrally positioned participative media in highly personal ways.

There is no doubt that the Internet has been culturally transformative. However, the claim that the Internet has facilitated enduring social, political and economic change as well as greater agency, after consideration of undesirable effects, is contestable. One line of debate is that the dominance of numeric Internet cultures facilitates merely the transmission of information, not knowledge. Another is that, rather than achieve complex social change in relation to entrenched issues of equity and fairness, the Internet simply rearranges social conditions which favour, and will continue to favour, those who have power today (Castells 2001, 265–266). Arguably then, these same technological developments which, on the one hand, open new possibilities for the agency of individuals and groups have, on the other, the potential to facilitate a form of hegemonic control that bestows new legitimacy on advanced capitalism or neoliberalism. So, while digital technologies do reorganise relationships—spatially and temporally—these need to be contextualised within the diversity and dynamism of globalisation and globalism in late capitalism. In unpacking this argument it is important to note that globalism is distinct from but sometimes conflated with the broader notion globalisation. "Globalism involves the idea of the world market, of the virtues of neoliberal capitalist growth, and of the need to move capital, products, and people across a relatively borderless world.... Globalisation.... is a much more multidimensional process of change that has irreversibly changed the very nature of the social world and of the place of states within that world (Urry in Beck and Willms 2004, 7)." Other attributes like: multiculturalism, the rise of NGOs, and transnational cultures, global protest movements, and cosmopolitan interdependence are also factors in these developments (Urry in Beck and Willms 2004, 7–8).

For Beck, this fusion of neoliberal discourses woven within globalisation and techno-economic changes brings the threat of a new authoritarianism: "We have to realise that, while the economy has taken a large bite out of the authority of the nation-state, it has also placed before it, in the form of information technology, the tools of a far more thoroughgoing control. It's not hard to imagine ways this technology could be used to short-circuit the power of public opinion" (Beck 2004, 60). Demetrious (2011, 127) writes that "Media Monitoring on sites like Second Life, Facebook and Twitter has refocused surveillance as a core function of public relations and provided it with news ways that it can operate out of view." As a corollary, she discusses the emergence of not-for-profit groups like TOR which "challenges the notion that 'transparency is good' and asks more pertinently 'who is it good for and is there really transparency'" (2011, 129). Thus the role of technology in society has general significance not only for the status and positioning of "publics," but for reducing the capacity of the individual to make decisions and choices, in turn inducing predispositions which provide potential new avenues for public relations. In particular, the confluence of purposes that form social media create ideal conditions for hidden relations of self-interest within a powerful discursive forum characterised by a culture of distraction and self-gratification. Veiled authorship, exposed so ruthlessly by activists in the twentieth century, is essential for the success of public relations and now has a new setting. Idealism of the Internet as a digital democracy should be contextualised with the social reality as a forum for discursive control which signals the return of concealed public relations and provides for new exploitative practices.

INDIVIDUALISATION

The growth of Internet-led cultures and the flow-on effects for communicative practices like public relations and public communication can be understood in part by individualisation, a concept of the individual in large-scale late-modern Western society. Beck argues that, in the conditions of late modernity, individuals design a life from a range of options around gender, marriage, sexuality, family and work, not by choice or in a voluntary sense, as the name may suggest, but as a result a mix of social and economic conditions that applies pressure for them to do so. He says that "the individuals must produce, stage and cobble together their biographies themselves" under the social conditions "of the welfare state in developed industrial labour society" (2000, 13). He also says that for a person to be a beneficiary of the welfare state it is necessary to be an active and mobile participant in work and education, and operate as an "individual." In contrast, a person who adheres to the limited social chains of "traditional ways of life and interaction" is denied access to the benefits of modern society (Beck 2000, 16). Therefore, despite an individual's desire to reject elements of late modernity, such as the Internet, mobile phones or credit cards and to opt out, it is simply not feasible to do so if a person wants to be educated or employable.

Activists advocating for marriage equality and gay and lesbian rights demonstrate the fluidity of once stable categories and broad political characteristics of late modernity. Categories around gender, work and the animal/human relationships are being reconceptualised and renegotiated through legal and cultural processes. In the past, however, there were established and predictable conceptualisations of men, women, work and parenting. Beck explains how class-based industrial society "presumes the nuclear family, which presumes sex roles, which presume the division of labour between men and women, which presumes marriage" (2000, 13). He argues that in early modernity individualism is "not based on a free decision of individuals" rather "people are condemned to individualisation" (14). Contemporary fashion is a good example of a social practice that is embedded and articulates to the social superstructure. For example, an individual's compulsion to dress differently, to stand out or be seen as innovative and creative, somewhat paradoxically is conformist because the overall social conditions are "more ambiguous and multifaceted, in keeping with the highly fragmented nature of contemporary post-industrial societies" (Crane 2000, 6). Individualisation in late modernity differs also results in people who pursue their self-interest, in ways redefined by the uncertainty of risk society. Beck argues that the rapid, techno-economic development of industrialised society is leading to a process of disembedding the known and understood ways of behaving in the social environment and only over time re-embedding new ways of behaving (2000, 13). This upheaval creates social disintegration where norms of behaviour are constantly questioned and challenged and significantly, the individual is released from the dominating and restrictive cultural patterns of the past with "the compulsion to find and invent new certainties" (Beck 2000, 14). Individualisation, disembedded within the social conditions of risk society, creates people with the confidence and knowledge to review traditional relationships and understandings in unusual and innovative ways. "Individualization does not remain private; it becomes political in a definite, new sense" (Beck 2000, 16). This also results in the deinstitutionalisation of "left" and "right" politics and sets the groundwork for politics from the grassroots or what Beck refers to as "sub-political" activity (Beck 2000, 13).

By showing how individuals and groups are unbound from tradition and driven to create new certainties, Beck's theory of individualisation helps explain the emergence of activist groups, and their lateral and tenacious approach to communication. Activists question hegemonic meanings, and in this process think differently, often cutting through established constructed objects and reconstructing new objects. This explains their innovation and originality. A consistent theme of Beck's individualisation theory is that there exists a multiplicity of entry points into political debates and a dilution of the concept of left and right politics (1992, 190; 2000, 21, Beck and Willms 2004, 96). As a result, Beck argues that individualised society will see "new centres of action" developing (Beck and Willms 2004, 97). Arguably then, the politically open grassroots activist campaigns of WRATD, BAGAG and OREN that attracted a diversity of participants, represent "new centres of action" unbound by normative conditions of the past. However, Beck's ideas suggest that these new cultures are always in opposition to "the culture of aggressive capitalism that is now widely known as neoliberalism. It may be in the future that people will think of this as the most important opposition: freedom vs. neoliberalism"[1] (Beck and Willms 2004, 87). In particular, within these social conditions two types of individuals emerge: "self entrepreneurs" and "social entrepreneurs" (73–76).

The self entrepreneur is a conception of an individual who is linked to the "neoliberal project" (Beck and Willms 2004, 73). Beck argues that these individuals act as if they are a corporation, overestimating their agency and deluding themselves that they have autonomy. "[T]hey live in the idea that each is a little Hercules, a mini-global player who exists in a societal vacuum. Each really believes he is a monad; each lives in an illusion of total independence" (74).

Social entrepreneurs are described as the "tinkers-inventors" of the world who are living self-chosen lives, in respect to marriage, sexuality and gender roles (Beck and Willms 2004, 75). Unlike the self entrepreneurs, they are aware of social conditions surrounding them and of the social conditions of individualisation. Social entrepreneurs, to harmonise their self-chosen lives, work to adjust existing social institutions and structures in a continual process, drawing on their social networks (Beck and Willms 2004, 73–75).

These concepts of the individual have relevance to sites of grassroots activism as politicised "new centres of action" that provide forums for ideas should be considered in relation to a counter ideal. Thus the social media site also presents as one of these oppositional "new centres of action" that, on face value, contains the characteristics Beck described in his individualisation thesis. Social media, such as Facebook and Twitter, are neither "left" nor "right," attract a diversity of participants, break with norms and provide many avenues for individuals to engage and organise life. Moreover, these are social spaces which preach freedom, and in which categories such as "friend" and "community" are hybridised with commercial discourses, appearing innovative and different. These notions work within the discursive space to fill a void, and create the conviction that helps individuals to feel stable and surefooted in a rapidly moving world. Yet, despite this, the purpose of social media is not a public space that promotes the good of its members, nor is it a not-for-profit organisation with volunteers that is democratically controlled. It is a self-serving business. In the main, profit-making is achieved by mining and on selling the "data" gleaned from the private conversations, photographs and activity of consumers. In this sense, social media sites can be seen as the neoliberal project in action because, rather than "freedom," this is shaping a range of dispositions and a climate of control. Participants are subject to the legal constraints and the discursive structures and norms of the social space and arguably undergo an acculturation process through which they are shaped as "self entrepreneurs" who assume a capitalist role linked to the neoliberal project. As such commercial social media sites may be in opposition to "new centres of action," such as the grassroots activism in individualised society.

Running parallel to these notions are ideas about new forms of self-identity. Giddens (1991, 214) presents contemporary politics as a dichotomy between "emancipatory" and "life politics." He defines "emancipatory politics" as the traditional practice of mobilising action around the achievement of better life conditions and/or redistributing power relations within a hierarchical structure (1991, 214). He defines life politics as existing once inequality has been reduced and tradition disembedded, arguing that "while emancipatory politics is a politics of life chances, life politics is 'the politics of lifestyle'" (Giddens 1991, 214). Once dismissed as banal and inconsequential, life politics, for Giddens, is a social phenomenon now regarded as a legitimate political arena in which public policy can be reflected on and rebellion can be seeded; hence, the expression "the personal is political." An example is political activism that promotes a vegan lifestyle and which challenges human domination of animals. Thus in individualised cultures in risk society there are many characteristics emerging: new centres of action, new certainties, new social spaces, new categories of identity and politics working with and in opposition to neoliberalism, that position publics in new ways towards both public relations and activism.

CITIZENS OF THE BRIGHT PLANET

Drawing on these ideas, and the case studies of WRATD, BAGAG and OREN, this section develops a framework to understand the reception of texts by different segments of society in late modern society. In the main, it maps out broad sociological terrain using the idea of a "risk society" as one in which thinking and action are re-defined in relation to the hazards and threats produced by industrialisation processes (and the desire to find new certainties) within the related conditions of life politics and individualisation. In addition, it overlays the Habermasian idea of the "public sphere" as discussed a conceptual space where citizens engage in dialogue and debate focused around issues for the common good. The theories have been selected not only to explain the emergence of new political and social groupings and their relationship to socio-political and cultural contexts, but to provide context to view their dynamic intersections to public relations and activism in the twenty-first century.

While the idea of a risk society is the overarching framework, it is also overlayed with a reworking of the public relations concept of "publics." The functionalist and liberal pluralist idea of "publics" was seeded in Bernays' 1928 book *Propaganda* that was discussed in detail in Chapter 1. In referring to ways in which groups disseminate influence in other groups, Bernays (2005, 44) writes: "This invisible, intertwining structure of groups and associations is the mechanism by which democracy has organized its group mind and simplified its mass thinking. To deplore the existence of such a mechanism is to ask for a society such as never was and never will be. To admit that it exists, but expect that it shall not be used, is unreasonable." As discussed in Chapter 4, it is a notion that gained traction in a succession of public relations texts. In particular, Grunig and Hunt (1984, 148) explain that the idea of "Situational Theory" to identify variables that affect publics: "The theory states that communication behaviors of publics can be best understood by measuring how members of publics perceive situations in which they are affected by such organizational consequences as pollution, quality of products, hiring practices, or plant closing."

Therefore "publics" are more than receivers or transmitters of messages; they are targeted and constructed categories for social control. Coupled with this are connotations about the essentialist "nature" of these social categories and the problems with which they are associated and to which they react. Accordingly, the public relations idea of "publics" has a particular meaning, which is important to draw out and expose for its conceptual confusion and under-development. Therefore, while I construct four subdivisions or "publics", it is important to note that they should not be regarded as complete, essentialist or indeed stable, but rather as representing core constitutive elements that are interrelated and in turn dynamically interact to influence how meanings are constructed and represented in the twenty-first century. For example, using this ensemble of ideas, it is quite possible, as a "public," to remain in a scarcity society mindset, within risk society, in much the same way as Bernays described. Invoking the concept of "publics' is not an attempt to reconcile a flawed concept but to understand how the flawed concept may be applied to new social realities of a risk society.

By setting out various characteristics of "publics" within risk society, the framework shows how different social elements of late modern society create a range of dispositions towards public relations practice and activism.

It is hoped that reworking of "publics" and combining it with sociological concepts will provide greater access to these ideas and help the reformation of public relations practices. This book, through the utilisation of Beck's theories, sheds light and helps reposition the concept. Indeed, this seemingly contradictory alliance between social theory and public relations is demonstrative of one of the defining characteristics of risk society: the repositioning of boundaries around "ambivalences" (Beck 2000, 29).

In the twenty-first century public relations, activism and publics are a dynamic intersection of the following:

1. Marginalised publics. Occupying social risk positions and primarily concerned with emancipatory politics, these publics are disempowered by eco-discourses. They have low access to technology, and the economic and sociocultural resources required for political participation in the public sphere. They lack media literacy and/or vigilance and therefore have potential for malleability in the reception of intrinsic and extrinsic public relations. They are highly indisposed to lifestyle activism while predisposed to emancipatory activism.
2. Scarcity society publics. These publics may or may not occupy social risk positions, but are primarily concerned with emancipatory politics and are averse to eco-discourses. They have a mixed access to technology, and the economic and sociocultural resources required for political participation in the public sphere. They lack media literacy and/or vigilance and therefore have potential for malleability in the reception of intrinsic and extrinsic by public relations. They are indisposed to lifestyle activism while predisposed to emancipatory activism.
3. Reflexive publics. These publics are highly individualised lifestyle "social-entrepreneurs" who may or may not occupy social risk positions. They are empowered by eco-discourses and have high access to technology, and the economic and sociocultural resources required for political participation in the public sphere. With high levels of media literacy they are vigilant and less tolerant in the reception of intrinsic and extrinsic public relations. They are predisposed to lifestyle activism.
4. Digital publics. These publics are highly individualised, lifestyle "self entrepreneurs" that are less likely to occupy social risk positions. They are not intolerant of eco-discourses but are empowered by digital cultures of narcissism celebrity/voyeurism. They have high access to technology, and to the economic and sociocultural resources required for political participation in the public sphere. As co-producers of self-promotion, they have a high tolerance for the reception of intrinsic public relations and lack vigilance for extrinsic public relations, and have potential malleability. They are less predisposed to lifestyle activism.

SOCIAL RELATIONS IN RISK SOCIETY: MOLTEN AND TRANSMUTING

"Marginalised publics" economically disadvantaged by the decline of early industrial activity are sometimes faced with a bleak prospect of unemployment and lack of opportunity, and often resist eco-discourses of risk society. In the latter stages of the OREN campaign, grassroots activists appeared to be gaining social traction and support by locals, government and media for conservationism. Contextualised thus, pro-logging groups were involved in outbreaks of violence in the Otways. This quotation from OREN's newsletter describes an unlawful incident at the Apollo Bay music festival:

> March 26, 2000: all power supply to Apollo Bay was cut off in an act of terrorism against the Apollo Bay community. Two electricity poles that supply the town with power were cut down with a chainsaw during the Apollo Bay music festival, a major event which drew 50,000 visitors to the town. Graffiti was sprayed on the power poles—"OREN war". Police investigations have failed to find those responsible (Otway Ranges Environment Network [OREN 2002,1])

Following this, loggers and conservationists clashed again. Newspaper reports promoted the dichotomy and polarisation. Edmonds and Kelly said that "Greenies injured at a logging site confrontation have ignored a noon deadline to get out of the Otways" (Edmonds and Kelly 2000, 2). While Claire Miller (2000, 4) reported that "anti-logging campaigners yesterday blamed the Government for the weekend's violence in the Otways, saying it provoked the confrontation by sending a logging crew into Geelong's water catchment last week to begin clearfelling." These examples demonstrate that communicative relations are working with and through the narratives of marginalised publics to construct a sense of empowerment through confrontation and violence, within conditions of disadvantage and powerlessness. In risk society, the deindustrialisation process has the potential to create isolated and disengaged sub-groups. Within these depressed social conditions, and the changed logic of modernity, groups and individuals left behind may be targeted for exploitation by public relations particularly, when, in a globalised world, so many socio-economic and cultural activities are linked to markets and capital.

"Scarcity publics" think and act and create frameworks based on ideas in earlier stages of modernity such as the once stable categories of gender, sexuality work and class. Despite the changes that have been brought about in the latter stages of modernity, and the fluidity affecting these categories, there are many scarcity society publics that are functional within risk society. For example, in the BAGAG case study, "John" wrote a letter to the editor opposing the grassroots activists' stance and demonstrating a passive political position that is typical of early modernity (Kane 2000, 224). He regarded campaign against the power station as frivolous and had a view that the protestors should accept the by-products of modernisation, even if they were unhealthy:

> I used to live in that area and, you know, we had the same sort of arguments; environmentalists, you know, wanted to have impact statements and studies on the effect to the environment and all of this, and you know, they really go over the top because we've had power stations in the world for, you know, well over a hundred years and, and you know, we all know what power stations do, they put out a bit of fumes and, you know, they have big high smoke stacks. And you know, it does cause a problem with the environment and it's just part of life, so get on with it (John in Rehame Transcript, January 4, 2002, 13).

John's views suggest that he accepts that "risk" is a necessary by-product of the techno-economic development process, and shows that he adopts the logic of early modernity and the organising principle of a society based on lack (Beck 1992, 19). Moreover, "John" was just the sort of target public expected by the corporation proposing the power station, AES. In a letter to residents, AES argued that:

> There has been a degree of negative reporting of the AES Golden Plains power station and AES itself recently through the local media. This has been based upon the misconception of some key facts, and regrettably, in some cases the result of misleading information propagated by people opposing the development. As we move closer to the power station's imminent construction phase, I am pleased to report AES will considerably step up communication with key stakeholders, including the local Golden Plains and Greater Geelong communities in order to ensure the station's smooth integration. First and foremost, AES is concerned to encourage a full understanding of the project—particularly to clarify present misconceptions regarding environmental impacts. (Graham Dowers, Letter, October 4, 2001)

Dowers' letter is an attempt to achieve legitimacy in the changing conditions of risk society to establish the inevitability of the AES project. In particular, metaphors convey the systemic notion of steps and sequencing in an order to achieve a goal. Examples are, "as we move closer", "imminent construction phase," "step up communication" "in order to ensure the station's smooth integration". Dowers, in this approach, develops the idea of a teleological path to create the hegemonic state of "common sense" that positions the reader in a positivist framework in which "investigating the social and cultural world is no different in principle to investigating the natural world and that the same basic procedures apply to both" (Deacon et al. 1999, 4). The positivist belief that instrumental methods of investigation and objectification lead to progress are applied in this social context because the view is promoted that economic expansion through technological development is of benefit to society through the social production of wealth, but not risk and locates the thinking within the logic of early modernity (Beck 1992, 19). These views demonstrate that competing frameworks of thought existed at this time and place in particular, about the role of activist groups and their legitimacy and mandate to communicate and contribute to policy and decision-making. Therefore, marginalised and scarcity publics do not see the grassroots activists as virtuous citizens of a risk society. Lifestyle politics may also threaten internalised concepts of gender, work, class and sexuality by destabilising a sense of identity; while loss of status through joblessness, inequality, and ongoing social disadvantage sets the groundwork for exploitative communicative practices.

Beck argues that it is the patterns and routines of work that provide individuals with the means to internalise structures of power. As such, he says labour "is the central engine of social control" (Beck and Willms 2004, 158). However in the event that the deindustrialisation of scarcity society takes place, as argued in this book, then what alternative will replace it? Beck explores this question:

> If this system is beginning to dissolve, and if, in many ways, we want it to dissolve, then how can we create an alternative milieu in which individuals who have been fragmented and atomized can be socialized. Where they can experience something like society and internalize the values of society? (Beck and Willms 2004, 158)

Therefore, despite grassroots activists' success in communicating their causes, and the evidence of a deep self-criticism in risk society, disturbing social effects remain for those marginal and scarcity publics that are disempowered by these events.

By the turn of millennium, the dynamic convergence of text, image, audio and interactivity had redefined the traditional communication tools in powerful new ways. This development enhanced the way individuals and groups formed, defined, and communicated issues in risk society as it provided new ways in which they could counter the claims of offending organisations. Thus "reflexive publics" could target companies wishing to expand their activities and, for example, expose those companies' poor track records in industrial disputation and breaches of licence or other inconsistencies.

The WRATD, BAGAG and OREN campaigns were evidence of a risk society. Their campaigns were characterised by reflexive publics that question science, challenge authority and re-define value and relationships. Moreover, the campaigns demonstrated how groups reposition boundaries and create "possible ambivalences" or contradictory allegiances and to form consensus, based on a redefinition of societal self-interest (Beck

2000, 29). As such, investors in a company might be supposed to be on side with the entity that the activists opposed. However, the WRATD campaign shows a contradictory repositioning of boundaries, typical of early modernity, that occurred between the grassroots activist group and CSR's shareholders. For example WRATD produced a flyer entitled "Stockbrokers and Shareholders: 5 Reasons Why You Should Not Trade in CSR Shares" (c. 1998); and a "Submission to CSR Directors and Shareholders" (1998) in which CSR's owners were asked to consider how the social interest of the environment and community linked to their economic interests.

These alliances between WRATD and CSR shareholders were unusual because they showed that a grassroots activist group was capable of complex consensus building between community, business and professional sectors. Their leadership in this matter undermined the Kennett government's total authority to represent an economic rationalist position. This case study demonstrates Beck's theories of risk society in a period of reflexive modernity. Significantly, it shows how in a hazardous, risk-producing society seemingly opposing sectors and groups can join together and form a consensus based on their merging social/economic mutual self-interest (2000, 29–31).

Reflexive, activist publics also engage with the Internet and can be characterised as social entrepreneurs who find ways to promote social causes of life politics by mounting highly networked campaigns for conservation and environment, as well as other causes. The WRATD, BAGAG and OREN websites established new relations with other groups and individuals which gained the groups further credibility from their fringe position. To facilitate this, the grassroots activists produced texts for the websites that did not assume that readers would passively accept anything they were told, indeed anticipating that it may be challenged. This cautious interpretation of the subject position by the activist groups determined a rigorous and ethical approach to their communication. Generally, statements on the websites relied significantly less on persuasion and more on objective information that encouraged the reader to act and think independently. Most claims made by the groups were backed up with evidence. This was often facilitated by hypertext in ways that led the subject to a broader understanding of the historicity of texts. The activist websites therefore contribute to the sociological theory of public opinion that Habermas (1995, 239–247) says is tied to principles of social rights, critical rational discussion and democracy.

Importantly, the websites provided points of coherence for different subject positions to critique these examples of system rationality in a way that was free of the commercial and political interference that is sometimes present in the bourgeois public sphere. The websites' fusion of information, interpretation, symbolism and interactivity is a good example of Beck (2000, 30–31) "the public discursivity of experience" and associated with a critique of expertise and the political shift of activist groups in late modernity. As new enunciative modalities, the websites also had potential to affect the agency of people to participate in the political life of their communities and became a dynamic social forum for the activist groups to be "*producers, and distributors, or cultural codes*" (Castells 2000, 362; italics in original). The activist websites thereby restored the integrity of the weakened public sphere as a vehicle for critical rational discussion.

In establishing new sets of relations or modalities, the Internet countered cultural uniformity and augmented the politics of self-identity by facilitating the construction of active and differential citizenship (Giddens 1991, 214; Hudson 2000, 15–25). The websites, through the fusion of statements and other textual forms such as graphics and photographs, also helped to build the identity of the grassroots activists and to promote and distribute their ethic of participation, inclusiveness and rational debate. For example, people who accessed websites were exposed to numerous symbolic visual elements in ways that ordered the experience and information into a coherent paradigmatic whole. Therefore, noting the social and economic conditions that may limit Internet access (Castells 2001, 247–270), the WRATD, BAGAG and OREN websites, if they are without hidden commercial or political self-interest, represent an expansion of the public sphere, and a point of coherence for subjects to construct the sub-political identities of the grassroots activist groups, and thus are an example of public communication.

"Digital publics" have been most apparent in the second wave of internet usage. Web 2.0 gained prominence in 2004 with the rise of "social media" and enabled ordinary web users to build "words, pictures, sounds and video" into web sites (Brown 2009, 1). According to Tim O'Reilly, it was important to delineate a new era of Internet usage after the collapse of the Internet market in 2001 (O'Reilly 2012). The "next generation" of the Internet delivered the promises that seemed to have floundered at the turn of the century. The usability gives an individual not only the ability to control content, but also the opportunity to design and configure components in powerful new participative modalities such as social networking sites, blogs and wikis. Digital publics in these contexts are characterised as individualised self entrepreneurs who have key communicative tools of corporations in their promotion of self, including the gaze of audience and the ability to gather what may pass for public opinion. "Friends", "fans" and "followers" are invested by the idea of the celebrity management of their personal sites which are infused with cultural codes and symbols linked to discourses that normatively legitimise voyeurism, self-aggrandizement, and amusement.

An extensive study by Buffardi and Campbell (2008, 1304) found that social media such as Facebook is especially "fertile ground" for narcissism, a personality trait that involves a "self-inflated self-concept linked to intelligence, power and physical attractiveness and entitlement." Moreover, "[t]he results of the study demonstrate that narcissists act, portray themselves, and are perceived on social networking sites in a manner similar to how they behave in real, offline life" (2008, 1312). The Internet publishes texts, but it is a dynamic discursive forum in which conditions determining the reception of those texts can change ways in which meaning is inter-related and interpreted. However, the promotion of self, coupled with the hybridisation of news, entertainment, public relations and advertising in social media, has consequences for both public relations and activism. Thus in one of the most significant changes to the communicative landscape, digital publics have become co-producers of "spin" and have become more tolerant of intrinsic, or surface, public relations practices. The pre-occupation with "self" and lack of criticality and tolerance of promotional cultures could also flag the social conditions that give rise to new forms of authoritarianism and characteristic "herd" like obedience in publics identified as far back as 1928.

It is worth pausing here to explain some overlap evident between digital and reflexive publics. In the twenty-first century, activist campaigns are often embedded in commercial social media sites such as Facebook and Twitter, weakening the claim that activist campaigns are expanding the public sphere. This fusion of civil and commercial discourses has been described as "activist public relations", an emerging mode, which "draws on public relations principles, strategies and tactics, such as promotion, to form public opinion and thus strengthen cases put to the state and business sectors and to the citizenry" (Demetrious 2011b). Evidence of the extent of the hybridisation of public relations and activism is that industry magazine *PRWeek* featured the anti capitalist Occupy Movement in one of the "Top 5 PR Picks" for 2012 ("Top 5 PR Picks 2012). The feature story analysed the success of the worldwide protest phenomenon as one of "members' favourite campaigns from last year". Some contemporary activism also has exclusive online activity. Many online activists have achieved worthy ends and reached vast numbers of people who perhaps would not have been otherwise engaged with the political issues about which the activists have been campaigning. Nonetheless, it is noted that with this mode there is a tendency to adopt some of the tactics used in traditional public relations, such as gimmicks, sensationalised and/or simplistic narrative structures, the setting up of basic dichotomies, imposing teleological limits on action, and overrating the role of the individual in achieving outcomes. For this reason, some online activism becomes almost transactional, engaging with a "thin" liberal individualism conception of community rather than with the "thick" civil communitarian conception that builds inclusion and political participation (Kane, 2000, 223–224), and that was so evident in the public communication activities of WRATD, BAGAG and OREN. The colonisation of the commercial discourse of public relations into civic social spaces such as activism, is fast gaining status as hegemonic "common sense". This is invisible public relations at work yet again. It illustrates the deepening of the contradictions discussed in this book and strengthens the case for unbinding the study of communicative practices from institutional sites and focusing more on variations in practices and social settings.

New digital publics inured in promotional and celebrity cultures are less critical of persuasion because they engage willingly to promote themselves. This suggests that cultural discourses are embedded hegemonically, and that digital publics are less likely to notice or be concerned about the political activities of public relations. The object of panoptical public relations is transforming once again. While some of the more extreme, extrinsic practices that were evident in the twentieth century are now less obvious, at least in the public gaze, such as the issuing of Strategic Lawsuits Against Public Participation (SLAPPS), paying people to infiltrate activists groups, framing active citizens as extremists, in general intrinsic 'PR" practices are proliferating contextualised by social tolerance and co-production of public relations, in ways that create unprecedented forms of acceptance and legitimacy.

CONCLUSION

This chapter has discussed two ideas. The first is the possibility of a communicative mode distilled from grassroots activist campaigns at the cusp of the millennium that can be used in political circumstances and applied more widely that I have called public communication; and secondly, new risks for communicative relations in society apparent in developments in public relations and activism since the rise of social media. The four subdivisions of "publics" as marginal, scarcity, reflexive and digital that have been discussed in this chapter aim to provide some conceptual clarity to relations between public relations and activism and assist in developing theoretical cohesion. In the main, I have drawn on parts of Beck's thesis of risk society and reflexive modernisation, which I have found relevant to a discussion of public relations, activism and social change. Beck's theories (1992. 2000, 2004) explain why new social movements such as WRATD, BAGAG and OREN, in late modernity, have courage, freshness and energy. They explain that this growth in activism is more than re-invention of community for its own sake and that it is an important social response to an unfolding ecological global crisis which interlinks state, business and civil sectors. However, these theories do not show what happens to these new social movements when forces such as unethical public relations are directed against them. They do not show how the forces of public relations within the unfolding ecological global crisis can affect the stamina of the activist groups to maintain their arguments, integrity, inventiveness and their level of expertise. There are new complications to understanding both activism and public relations as people rapidly adopt new digital technology and with it new forms of community, and new relations as co-producers of "spin" defined as the management of intrinsic contradictions. I explore some of the questions arising from these developments in this book.

It is hoped that this study of communication between interdiscursive groups develops a deeper understanding of activism and its relationship to public relations in the uncertain new terrain of risk society and in the period of reflexive modernisation. In acknowledging and describing organisational communication that reveals—not only different positions, but objects, strategies and their consequences—the intention was to bring to light a mode that is ethical and effective and yet overlooked by activists and public relations. The notions of risk society and reflexive modernisation have opened up new cultural fields in mapping objects. By describing this discursive formation more precisely, a new unity of organisational communication emerges that could contribute to a more ethically grounded and creative approach.

Other scholars are also working to provide a greater level of clarity in public relations as an underdeveloped concept. Recognising the importance of reform in public relations, is a movement of critical scholars within the discipline who are similarly researching to eliminate grey areas of conceptual confusion. Some of these are: Christine Daymon, Rhonda Breit, Kay Weaver, Judy Motion, Juliet Roper, Shirley Leitch, Anne Surma, Caroline Hodges, Kate Fitch, David McKie, Jacquie L'Etang, Lee Edwards, Tim Coombs and Sherry Holladay, Magda Pieczka, Steve Mackey, Magnus Fredriksson, Paul Elmer, Johanna Fawkes and Kevin Moloney. In reviewing basic concepts in public relations that are applied to activists, I hope this work has value in furthering the conversation.

I have canvassed some recent cultural and technological developments in relation to the advent of Web 2.0 in 2004 which impact on both public relations and activism, and hence the agency of groups to effect social change, showing how activism and public relations are merging in very different ways from the past (around the 1970s and 1980s) and from the time of the case studies of WRATD, BAGAG and OREN (around the 1990s and early 2000s); and I show how these developments have consequences for the wider social and cultural communicative role. However, more work is needed: to understand how public relations will transect with publics and position them to assume certain values in the coming years; to understand if the vulnerabilities of marginalised and scarcity publics, caught between two changing worlds, will be subject to persuasion and exploited for political ends; and to understand if digital publics inured in social media cultures represent a regressive criticality that affects the processes of self-interpretation in ways that herald a new era of arrogant, unethical, manipulative communicative cultures. Therefore, the challenge to scholars of communication is to understand how in risk society meanings and discursive relations are created, distributed and inter-relate. Identifying the discourses of public relations and activism and understanding the relationship between them opens up the "discontinuities, ruptures, gaps, entirely new forms of positivity, and of sudden distributions" (Foucault 1972, 169). As the planet gets hotter, and collectively we face the social realities and effects of carbon pollution (Climate Commission Secretariat 2011), vigorous debate must be heard. This approach, together with an analysis of the transforming power of public relations in the normative conditions of late modernity, will assist in building robust knowledge in the communicative relations between different groups acting for change in this new political and social space.

Notes

NOTES TO CHAPTER 4

1. Modernisation refers to the process of change for society and its institutions towards modernity (Abercrombie, Hill & Turner 1994, 270).
2. For Beck (1992, 50), later periods in modernity are associated with "changes of lifestyle and forms of love, change in the structure of power and influence, in the forms of political repression and participation, in view of reality and in norms of knowledge".
3. Evan Jones' 2005/6 blog "Alert and Alarmed' is now inactive. Original printed downloads in possession of author.

NOTES TO CHAPTER 5

1. Originally Colonial Sugar Refinery, now referred to as CSR.
2. The public EES process is to facilitate orderly growth in planning and to assess "the potential impacts of the proposal on the environment" (<http://www.dse.vic.gov.au/dse/index.htm> accessed 29/5/2006. "Once the EES is prepared, the DSE checks its adequacy for public exhibition. The EES is exhibited, for a period of between one and two months, and public submissions are invited" (<http://www.dse.vic.gov.au/dse/index.htm> accessed 29/5/2006).
3. Peter Kirby was CSR's Chief Executive.
4. The letter PDF file is sourced from the Internet and has no direct addressee.
5. Victorian Civil and Administrative Tribunal (VCAT) was created by an Act in 1998 to deal with disputes between people and government (state/local) in areas such as planning and environment, amongst others. (http://www.vcat.vic.gov.au/-Accessed19/12/2006).
6. Community Picket Line's website is now inactive. Original printed downloads in possession of author.
7. NEMMCO has "responsibility under the National Electricity Rules for ensuring that the power system is operated in a safe, secure and reliable manner." (NEMMCO, accessed January 17, 2007, http://www.nemmcol.com/ancillary_services/ancillaryservices.htm).
8. Forest Commission Victoria.
9. Midway Pty Ltd is a Geelong based wood chip company that during the OREN campaign sourced and harvested timber for this purpose in the Otways.
10. Geelong Advertiser.

NOTES TO CHAPTER 6

1. Neoliberalism is the nation-state's declining importance together with the development of global trading markets (Urry 2004, 7).

References

ABC Radio National Background Briefing, Global Resistance: http://www.abc.net.au/radionational/programs/backgroundbriefing/global-resistance/3482018#transcript. Broadcast: Sunday 18 February 2001 9:00AM. Accessed 24/10/2012.
Abercrombie, Nicholas, Stephen Hill, and Bryan S. Turner. *Penguin Dictionary of Sociology*. London: Penguin Books, 1994.
Achbar, Michael, and Jennifer Abbott. *The Corporation*. Directed by Michael Achbar. Saskatchewan, Canada, Big Picture Media Corporation in association with TV Ontario, Vision TV, Knowledge Network, Saskatchewan Communications Network and ACCESS: The Education Station, Saskatchewan, Canada, 2003.
AESPO Pty. Ltd., 9/7/01, *AES Generation Licence Application*.
Alford, John, and Deirdre O'Neill. (eds) 1994, *The Contract State Public Management and the Kennett Government*, Deakin University Press, Geelong
Alinsky, Saul D. *Rules for Radicals: A Practical Primer for Realistic Radicals*. New York: Vintage Books 1971.
Andersen, Robin. "Women, Welfare and the United States Media." In *Communication Ethics and Universal Values*, edited by Clifford G. Christians and Michael Traber. London: Sage, 1997.
Anderson, Leslie M. Letter to D. K. MacFarlane, James Hardie Asbestos Limited. Eric White & Associates 1978.
Andriof, Jörg, and Sandra Waddock. "Unfolding Stakeholder Engagement " In *Unfolding Stakeholder Thinking, Theory, Responsibility and Engagement*, edited by Jörg Andriof, Sandra Waddock, Bryan Husted and Sandra Sutherland Rahman, 19–42. Sheffield Green Leaf Publishing Limited, 2002.
Andriof, Jörg, and Malcolm McIntosh, eds. *Prespective on Corporate Citizenship*. Sheffield, UK: Greenleaf Publishing, 2001.
Australian Asbestos Network. "ADS WA," 2011. Accessed August 9, 2012, http://www.australianasbestosnetwork.org.au/Asbestos+History/The+Battles/The+campaigners/ADS+WA/default.aspx.
Australian Government National Health and Medical Research Council. "Asbestos Related Diseases," 2012. Accessed August 9, 2012, http://www.nhmrc.gov.au/your-health/asbestos-related-diseases.
Baird, Oliver. "Power to the People," *The Geelong Times*, August 22, 2001, 13.
Batesford Action Group Steering Committee, 7/8/2001, *Re: Generation License Application by AES for power station Stonehaven*, Melbourne.
Baudrillard, Jean. *Revenge of the Crystal*. Leichhardt, NSW: Pluto Press Australia Ltd in association with the Power Institute of Fine Arts, University of Sydney, 1990.
Bauman, Zygmunt. *Postmodernity and Its Discontents*. Cambridge: Polity Press, 1997.

Beck, Ulrich. "The Reinvention of Politics: Towards a Theory of Reflexive Modernization." In *Reflexive Modernization: Politics, Tradition and Aesthetics in the Modern Social Order*, Ulrich Beck, Anthony Giddens and Scott Lash, 1–55. Cambridge: Polity Press, [1994] 2000.

Beck, Ulrich. *Risk Society: Towards a New Modernity*. London: Sage, 1992.

Beck, Ulrich, Anthony Giddens, and Scott Lash, eds. *Reflexive Modernization: Politics, Tradition and Aesthetics in the Modern Social Order*. Cambridge: Polity Press, [1994] 2000.

Beck, Ulrich, and Johannes Willms. *Conversations with Ulrich Beck*. Cambridge: Polity Press, 2004.

Beder, Sharon. *Global Spin: The Corporate Assault on Environmentalism*. Melbourne: Scribe Publications, 1997.

Bernays, Edward. *Crystallizing Public Opinion*. New York: Liveright Publishing Corporation, [1923] 1961.

Bernays, Edward. *Propaganda*. Brooklyn, New York: IG Publishing 2005.

Birch, David. "Corporate Citizenship: Rethinking Business Beyond Corporate Social Responsibility." in *Perspectives on Corporate Citizenship*, edited by Jörg Andriof and Malcolm McIntosh, 53–65. Sheffield: Greenleaf Publishing, 2001.

Birrell, Simon. Interview with the author, Geelong, July 8 2003.

Bliss, Tamara J. "Citizen advocacy groups: corporate friend or foe?" In *Unfolding Stakeholder Thinking, Theory, Responsibility and Engagement*, edited by Jörg Andriof, Sandra Waddock, Bryan Husted and Sandra Sutherland Rahman, 251–266. Sheffield: Green Leaf Publishing Limited, 2002.

Bloomfield, Jude, and Franco Bianchini. "Cultural Citizenship and Urban Governance in Western Europe." In *Culture and Citizenship*, edited by Nick Stevenson, 99–123. London; Thousand Oaks, California: Sage, 2001.

Bottomore, Tom. "Citizenship and Social Class, Forty Years On." in *Citizenship and Social Class*, T. H.Marshall and Tom Bottomore, 55–93. London: Pluto Press, [1992] 1996.

Box, Gavin. "Anniversary for Power Station Opponents Picketers Fight On."*Geelong Advertiser*, December 13, 2002, 14.

Breit, Rhonda. *Law and Ethics for Professional Communicators*. Chatswood, N.S.W.: LexisNexis Butterworths, 2007.

Breit, Rhonda, and Kristin Demetrious. "Professionalisation and Public Relations: An Ethical Mismatch." *Ethical Space: The International Journal of Communication Ethics* 7, no. 4 (2010): 20–29.

Brown, Rob. *Public Relations and the Social Web How to Use Social Media and Web 2.0 in Communications*. London; Philadelphia: Kogan Page, 2009.

Buffardi, Laura E., and W. Keith Campbell. "Narcissism and Social Networking Web Sites." *Personality and Social Psychology Bulletin* 34, no. 10 (2008): 1303–1314.

Burgmann, Verity. *Power and Protest: Movements for Change in Australian Society*. St Leonards: Allen & Unwin, 1993.

Burson-Marsteller: "Non-Governmental Organizations Seek More Candor in Corporate Social Responsibility Reports NGOs Find Less than Half of All Corporate Responsibility Reports Are 'Believable'." 2012. Accessed October 29, 2012. http://www.prnewswire.com/news-releases/non-governmental-organizations-seek-more-candor-in-corporate-social-responsibility-reports-73013562.html

"Campaigns: Kleenex Boycott". Otway Ranges Environment Network Inc. 2006. Accessed June 23, 2006, http://www.oren.org.au/archives/otkleenex.htm.

Carson, Rachel. *Silent Spring*. Harmondsworth: Penguin, [1962] 1971.

Carter, April. *The Political Theory of Global Citizenship*. London, Routledge, 2001.

Castells, Manuel. *The Information Age: Economy, Society and Culture: The Power of Identity*. Malden, MA: Blackwell Publishers Inc, 1997.
Castells, Manuel. *The Information Age: Economy, Society and Culture: The Power of Identity*. Malden, MA: Blackwell, 2000.
Castells, Manuel. *The Internet Galaxy*. Oxford: Oxford University Press, 2001.
Cerrell Associates, Inc. "Political Difficulties Facing Waste-to-Energy Conversion Plant Siting." Los Angeles: Cerrell Associates, Inc. for the California Waste Management Board 1–60, 1984.
Chandler, Daniel. *Semiotics: The Basics*. London: Routledge, 2002.
Cheney, George, and Lars T. Christiansen. "Public Relations as Contested Terrain: A Critical Response" In *Handbook of Public Relations*, edited by Robert L. Heath, 167–182. Thousand Oaks, CA: Sage, 2001.
Christians, Clifford G. "The Ethics of Being in a Communications Context." In *Communication Ethics and Universal Values*, edited by Clifford G. Christians and Michael Traber, 3–23. London: Sage, 1997.
Christians, Clifford G., and Michael Traber, eds. *Communication Ethics and Universal Values*. London: Sage, 1997.
Climate Commission Secretariat (Department of Climate Change and Energy Efficiency). "The Critical Decade: Climate Science, Risks and Responses." 2011. http://climatecommission.gov.au/report/the-critical-decade.
Cobb, Chris. "Driving Public Relations: Chrysler Moves PR under the HR Umbrella, Spurs Debate about Where PR Reports " *The Stategist* (2008). Accessed August 9, 2008, http://www.prsa.org/Intelligence/TheStrategist/Articles/view/7532/102/Driving_public_relations_Chrysler_moves_PR_under_t.
Cohen, Anthony. *The Symbolic Construction of Community*. Chichester: Ellis Horwood Limited and Tavistock Publications, 1985.
"Community Picket Line," 2002. Accessed, March 15, 2002, http://www.Chalicedreams. (Link no longer available.)
Coombs, W. Timothy, and Sherry J. Holladay. "Fringe Public Relations: How Activism Moves Critical PR toward the Mainstream." *Public Relations Review*, DOI: 10.1016/j.pubrev.2012.02.008 (2012).
Coombs, W. Timothy, and Sherry J. Holladay. *It's Not Just PR: Public Relations in Society*. Malden, MA: Blackwell, 2007.
Crane, Diana. *Fashion and Its Social Agendas: Class, Gender, and Identity in Clothing*. Chicago: University of Chicago Press, 2000.
Cunningham, William P., Barbara Woodworth Saigo, and Mary Ann Cunningham. *Environmental Science: A Global Concern*. 8th ed. Boston: McGraw-Hill Higher Education, 2005.
Cutlip, Scott M., Allen H. Center, and Glen M. Broom. *Effective Public Relations*. Upper Saddle River, NJ: Prentice Hall, 2000.
Dann, Christine. "The Environmental Movement." In *New Zealand Government and Politics* edited by Raymond Miller, 368–377. South Melbourne, Victoria: Oxford University Press, 2003.
Daymon, Christine, and Immy Holloway. *Qualitative Research Methods in Public Relations and Marketing Communications*. Abingdon: Routledge 2011.
Deacon, David, Michael Pickering, Peter Golding, and Graham Murdock. *Researching Communications: A Practical Guide to Methods in Media and Cultural Analysis*. London: Oxford University Press, 1999.
Deegan, Denise. *Managing Activism: A Guide to Dealing with Activists and Pressure Groups*. London: Kogan Page, 2001.
Demetrious, Kristin. "Bubble Wrap: Social Media, Public Relations, Culture and Society." In *Public Relations, Society & Culture: Theoretical and Empirical Explorations*, edited by Lee Edwards and Caroline E. M. Hodges, 118–132. New York: Routledge, 2011.

Demetrious, Kristin. "Media Effects: E-Simulations and Authentic 'Blended' Learning." In *Professional Education Using E-Simulations: Benefits of Blended Learning Design*, edited by Dale Holt, Stephen Segrave and Jacob L. Cybluski, 255–270. IGI Global, Hershey Pa, 2012.

Demetrious, Kristin. "The Object of Public Relations and Its Ethical Implications for Late Modern Society—a Foucauldian Analysis." *Ethical Space: The International Journal of Communicaiton Ethics*, 5, no. 4 (2008): 22–31.

Demetrious, Kristin. "What's the Point of Corporate Responsibility." *The Corporate Citizen*, 4, Melbourne: Deakin University (2004): 20–21.

Demetrious, Kristin. "Activist Public Relations." In *International Encyclopedia of Communication*, 1–2. Malden, MA: Blackwell. 2011.

Demetrious, Kristin, and Patrick Hughes. "'Publics' or 'Stakeholders'? Performing Social Responsiblity through Stakeholder Software." *Asia Pacific Public Relations Journal* 5, no. 2 (2004): 1–12.

Dent, Sarah. "Dump Plan Switch Fury," *Herald Sun*, May 9, 1998, 12.

Dowers, Graham. 4/10/2001, AES Golden Plains, Brisbane.

Doyle, Timothy. *Green Power, the Environment Movement in Australia*. Sydney: UNSW Press, 2001.

Dozier, David M., and Martha M. Lauzen. "Liberating the Intellectual Domain from the Practice: Public Relations, Activism, and the Role of the Scholar." *Journal of Public Relations Research* 12, no. 1 (2000): 3–22.

Durkheim, Émile. *Professional Ethics and Civic Morals*. London: Routledge and Kegan Paul Ltd., 1957.

Dutta, Mohan J. *Communicating Social Change: Structure, Culture, and Agency*. New York: Routledge, 2011.

Dynes, Peter. "Elites Attack Country." *Herald Sun*, April 24, 2002, 19.

Edmonds, Mike, and Jen Kelly. "Greens Hurt in Logging Clash," *Herald Sun*, April 3, 2000, 2.

Edwards, Lee. "Defining the 'Object' of Public Relations Research: A New Starting Point." *Public Relations Inquiry* 1, no. 1 (2011): 7–30.

Endacott, Norman. "Green 'Spin Doctors' Fight the Woodchip War," *Geelong Advertiser*, June 26, 2002, 24.

Environmental Research Foundation. "Al Gore Takes on the Wti Incinerator." Environmental Research Foundation, http://www.ejnet.org/rachel/rhwn315.htm. December 9, 1992. Accessed 30 October 2012. Eric White & Associates. "Public Relations Action Plan for James Hardie Asbestos."

Eric White & Associates, September 1978, Reid Collection, State Library of NSW.

Erickson, Brad, ed. *Call to Action: Handbook for Ecology, Peace and Justice*. San Francisco: Sierra Club Books, 1990.

Esteva, Gustavo, and Madhu S. Prakash, eds. *Grassroots Post-Modernism, Remaking the Soil of Cultures*. London and New York: Zed Books, 1998.

Facey, George A. *Otway Timber Mills and Pioneering Days*: Angelsea: GA Facey, 1979.

Fairclough, Norman. *Discourse and Social Change*. Cambridge: Polity Press, 1999.

Foucault, Michel. *The Archaeology of Knowledge*. London and New York: Routledge, 2005.

Foucault, Michel. *The Archaeology of Knowledge*. London: Tavistock, 1972.

Foucault, Michel (translated by Josué V. Harari). "What Is an Author?" Lecture presented to the Societé Francais de Philosophie on February 22, 1969. https://wiki.brown.edu/confluence/download/attachments/74858352/FoucaultWhatIsAnAuthor.pdf?version=1&modificationDate=1296272754000. Accessed August 6, 2012.

Freeman, R. Edward. *Strategic Management: A Stakeholder Approach*. Boston: Pitman, 1984.

Galston, William A. *The Practice of Liberal Pluralism*. Cambridge: Cambridge University Press, 2005.
Gardner, Ashley. "Parties Trade Blows over Power Crisis." *Herald Sun*, January 3, 2002, 13.
Giddens, Anthony, and Philip W. Sutton. *Sociology: Revised and Updated with Philip W. Sutton*. Cambridge: Polity, 2009.
Giddens, Anthony. *The Consequences of Modernity*. Cambridge UK: Polity Press, 1995.
Giddens, Anthony. *Modernity and Self-Identity, Self and Society in the Late Modern Age*. Stanford, CA: Stanford University Press, 1991.
Golden Plains Shire 28/6/2001, *Council Meeting Minutes*: 9–34.
Gore, Al. Press statement from U.S. Senator Al Gore dated December 7, 1992. Available by fax from the senator's office at (202) 224-4944.
Greenberg, Morris. "Biological Effects of Asbestos: New York Academy of Sciences 1964." *American Journal of Industrial Medicine* 43 (2003): 543–552.
Greenwood, Michelle R. *Community as a Stakeholder in Corporate Social and Environmental Reporting*. Caufield: Monash University, 2001.
Grunig, James E. "Collectivism, Collaboration, and Societal Corporatism as Core Professional Values in Public Relations." *Journal of Public Relations Research* 12, no. 1 (2000): 23–48.
Grunig, James E., ed. *Excellence in Public Relations and Communication Management*. Hillsdale, NJ: Lawrence Erlbaum Associates, 1992.
Grunig, James E., and Todd Hunt. *Managing Public Relations*. New York: Holt, Rinehart and Winston, 1984.
Grunig, Larissa A. "Activism: How It Limits the Effectiveness of Organizations and How Excellent Public Relations Departments Respond." In *Excellence in Public Relations and Communication Management*, edited by James E. Grunig, 503–30. Hillsdale NJ, and London: Lawrence Erlbaum Associates, 1992.
Habermas, Jürgen. *The Structural Transformation of the Public Sphere: An Inquiry into the Category of Bourgeois Society*. Cambridge, MA: The MIT Press, 1995.
Habermas, Jürgen. *The Theory of Communicative Action: The Critique of Functionalist Reason, Volume Two*. Cambridge: Polity Press, 1989.
Habermas, Jürgen. *The Theory of Communicative Action: Reason and the Rationalization of Society, Volume One*. Boston: Beacon Press, 1984.
Hager, Nicky, and Bob Burton. *Secrets and Lies*. Munroe, ME: Common Courage Press, 1999.
Haigh, Gideon. *Asbestos House: The Secret History of James Hardie Industries*. Carlton North, Victoria Australia: Scribe Publications Pty Ltd, 2006.
Hamilton, Peter. "Editor's Foreword." In *The Symbolic Construction of Community*, Anthony P. Cohen, 7–9, Chichester: E. Horwood; London; New York: Tavistock Publications, 1985.
Harrison, John. "Conflicts of Duty and the Virtues of Aristotle in Public Relations Ethics: Continuing the Conversation Commenced by Monica Walle". *PRism* 2 (2004), accessed October 29, 2012. http://www.prismjournal.org/fileadmin/Praxis/Files/Journal_Files/Issue2/Harrison.pdf
Heath, Robert L. *Strategic Issues Management : Organizations and Public Policy Challenges*. Thousand Oaks, CA: Sage, 1997.
Heath, Robert L., and Richard A. Nelson. *Issues Management: Corporate Public Policymaking in an Information Society*. Newbury Park, CA: Sage, 1986.
Hendrix, Jerry A. *Public Relations Cases*. Belmont USA: Wadsworth Thompson Learning, 2001.
Herald Sun. "Promises, Promises." *Herald Sun*, November 7, 2002, 1.

Heywood, Andrew. *Political Ideologies: An Introduction*. Hampshire: Palgrave Macmillian, 2007.
Hills, Ben. *Blue Murder Two Thousand Doomed to Die—the Shocking Truth About Wittenoom's Deadly Dust*. Crows Nest 2065: The Macmillan Company of Australia Pty Ltd, 1989.
Hindess, Barry. "Representative Government and Participatory Democracy." In *Citizenship and Democracy in a Global Era*, edited by Andrew Vandenberg, 33–50. London: Macmillan, 2000.
Hodgson, Shelley. "Outrage over Power Plant," *Sunday Herald Sun*, August 12 2001, 39.
Holmes, Paul 2011. "Global Rankings 2011: Industry Up 8 Percent To Around $8.8 Billion." The Holmes Report. Accessed December 3, 2012, http://www.holmesreport.com/news-info/10894/showdetailspage.aspx?type=news-info&id=10894&url=Industry-Up-8-Percent-In-2010-To-Around-88-Billion.
Holtzhausen, Derina R., and Rosina Voto. "Resistance from the Margins: The Postmodern Public Relations Practitioner as Organizational Activist." *Journal of Public Relations Research* 14, no. 1 (2002): 57–84.
Horton, James L. "What Is PR Today?" 2007. Accessed August 9, 2012, http://www.online-pr.com/Holding/What_is_PR_Today.pdf.
Hosking, Patrick. "Accident Fuels Opposition to Werribee Dump." *The Age*, November 1, 1996, 4.
Hudson, Wayne. "Differential Citizenship." In *Rethinking Australian Citizenship*, edited by Wayne Hudson and John Kane, 15–25. Cambridge: Cambridge University Press, 2000.
Hudson, Wayne, and John Kane, eds. *Rethinking Australian Citizenship*. Cambridge: Cambridge University Press, 2000a.
Hudson, Wayne, and John Kane. "Rethinking Australian Citizenship." In *Rethinking Australian Citizenship*, edited by Wayne Hudson and John Kane, 1–11. Cambridge: Cambridge University Press, 2000b.
Ihlen, Øyvind, Magnus Fredrikson, and Betteke van Ruler, eds. *Public Relations and Social Theory*. New York: Routledge/Taylor and Francis Group, 2009.
James Hardie, Ltd. Pamphlet, 1979. In the possession of the author.
John (talkback caller, surname not cited), 5.37 pm 4/1/2002, in '*Interview with Srechko Kontelj, City of Greater Geelong Mayor; Talkback Callers Comments*', Rehame Transcript, 15.
John, Steve, and Stuart Thomson. *New Activism and the Corporate Response*. Houndmills, Basingstoke, Hampshire; New York: Palgrave Macmillan, 2003.
Johnstone, Kate. "Power Protest Marks 200-Day Milestone," *Geelong Advertiser*, June 26, 2002a, 5.
Johnstone, Kate, "Government Backflip on Stonehaven Power Station, We don't need it," *Geelong Advertiser*, March 22, 2002b, 5.
Jones, Evan. "Corporate Social Non-Responsiblity." In *Alert and Alarmed*, Blogspot, 20/5/2006 http://alertandalaramed.blogspot.com/2006/05corporate-social-non . . .
Kane, John. "Communitarianism and Citizenship." In *Rethinking Australian Citizenship*, edited by Wayne Hudson and John Kane, 215–230. Cambridge: Cambridge University Press, 2000.
Kitchen, Philip J. *Public Relations Principles and Practice*. London: Thompson Learning, 2000.
Kontelj, Stretch., 7.44 am 7/1/2002, in 'Interview with Stretch Kontelj, City of Greater Geelong', Rehame Transcript, 1–8.
Kronelsen, Lloyd. "Teaching with Presence." *New Directions for Adult and Continuing Education* 111(Autumn), (2006) 73–82.
Lane, Terry. "Conspiring Against All Common Sense." *The Sunday Age*, February 9, 1995, 16.

L'Etang, Jacquie. *Public Relations Concepts, Practice and Critique*. London: Sage, 2008.
Lapierre, Dominique, and Javier Moro. *Five Past Midnight in Bhopal*. New York: Warner Books, 2002.
Leaked Memo. "Guide to the Seattle Meltdown." March 10, 2000. Accessed October 23, 2010, http://www.commondreams.org/headlines/031000-03.htm 2012.
Lees, Rue. Interview with the author, Geelong, July 8 2003.
Leitch, Shirley, and Judy Motion. "Publics and Public Relations: Effecting Change." In *The Sage Handbook of Public Relations*. edited by Robert L. Heath, 99–110. Thousand Oaks, CA: Sage, 2010.
Lindlof, Thomas R., and Bryan C. Taylor. *Qualitative Communication Research Methods*. London: Sage, 2002.
Lippmann, Walter. *Public Opinion*. Blacksburg, Virginia: Wilder Publications Inc., 2010.
Lorimer, Graeme S. *Pollution Impact of the Proposed Stonehaven Power Station: Report to VCAT*. October 31, 2001.
Lupton, Deborah, ed. *Risk and Sociocultural Theory New Directions and Perspectives*. Cambridge University Press: Cambridge, 1999.
Lygo, Ian. Interview with the author, Geelong, July 10 2003.
Lyons, Mark. *Third Sector: The Contribution of Nonprofit and Cooperative Enterprise in Australia*. Crows Nest, N.S.W.: Allen & Unwin, 2001.
Macdonell, Diane. *Theories of Discourse: An Introduction*. Oxford: Basil Blackwell, 1986.
Macnamara, Jim R., and Robert Crawford. "Reconceptualising Public Relations in Australia: A Historical and Social Re-Analysis." *Asia Pacific Public Relations Journal* 11, no. 2 (2010): 17–34.
Magee, Kate, and John Owens. "Top 5 PR Picks." *PR Week*, no. 30 March (2012): 21–23.
Marks, Deborah. "Disability and Cultural Citizenship: Exclusion, 'Integration' and Resistance " In Culture & Citizenship, edited by Nick Stevenson, 167–80. London: Sage, 2001.
Marshall, T. H., and Tom Bottomore. *Citizenship and Social Class*. London: Pluto Press, 1996.
Mayne, Nicole. "AES Pull the Plug Power Station Site on Market", *Geelong Advertiser*, February 21, 2003, 5.
Mayne, Nicole "Power Fears Realised," *Geelong Advertiser*, April 19, 2002, 7.
McCallum, Stuart. Interview with the author, Geelong, July 10 2003.
McCann, Karen. "This is Life on the Line," *Geelong News*, February 12, 2002, 1.
McCann, Karen. "Power Struggle into New Phase," *Geelong News*, November 27, 2001a, 7.
McCann, Karen. "Power Fight to Continue," *Geelong News*, December 18, 2001b, 5.
McCulloch, Jock. *Asbestos Its Human Cost*. St Lucia Qld: University of Queensland Press, 1986.
McElreath, Mark P. *Managing Systematic and Ethical Public Relations Campaigns*. Madison, WI: Brown and Benchmark Publishers, 1997.
McGee, Michael, Calvin (2001) Phronesis in the Habermas vs. Gadamer debate. Accessed December 12, 2012, http://mcgeefragments.net/OLD/Phronesis.in.the.Habermas.vs.Gadamer.Debate.htm
McIntosh, Malcolm, Deborah Leipziger, Keith Jones, and Gail Coleman, eds. *Corporate Citizenship Successful Strategies for Responsible Companies*. London: Financial Times Pitman Publishing, 1998.
McKie, David, and Debashish Munshi. *Reconfiguring Public Relations: Ecology, Equity, and Enterprise*. London: Routledge, 2007.

McLure, Daryl. "Workers Make a Point with Style," *Geelong Advertiser*, November 25, 2002, 17.
McLellan, D., ed. *Karl Marx Selected Writings*. London: Oxford University Press, 1984.
Meadows, Donella H., Dennis L. Meadows, and Jørgen Randers. *Limits to Growth: The 30-Year Update*. [Rev. ed.] London: Earthscan, 2005.
Miller, Claire. "Move to Quell Violence in State Forests," *The Age*, April 4, 2000, 4.
Miller, Claire. "Water 'at Risk' from Logging," *The Age*, June 24, 1999, 9.
Miller, Mark C. "Introduction." In *Propaganda, by Edward Bernays*, 9–33. IG Publishing: Brooklyn, New York, 2005.
Moloney, Kevin. *Rethinking Public Relations: PR Propaganda and Democracy*. London: Routledge, 2006.
Moss, Danny, Dejan Verčič, and Gary Warnaby, eds. *Perspectives on Public Relations Research*. London and New York: Routledge, Taylor and Francis Group, 2000.
Motion, Judy, and Shirley Leitch. "On Foucault: A Toolbox for Public Relations." In *Public Relations and Social Theory* edited by Øyvind Ihlen, Betteke Van Ruler and Magnus Fredriksson, 83–102. New York: Routledge, 2009.
Murphy, Noel. "Critics Claim Victory as Station Stalls," *Geelong Advertiser*, March 16, 2002, 3.
National Medical Health and Medical Research Council. "Asbestos Related Diseases." Australian Government, National Health and Medical Research Council. Accessed August 7, 2012, www.nhmrc.gov.au/your-health/asbestos-related-diseases.
Neales, Sue. "A Park Would Be Their Grand Prix." *The Age*, November 26, 1994, 20.
Nelson, Joyce. *Sultans of Sleaze: Public Relations and the Media*. Toronto: Between the Lines, 1989.
Newbold, Yve. 'The Changing Language in the Boardroom', in *Visions of Ethical Business*, vol. 4, pp. 11–13, in association with PriceWaterhouseCoopers and Council for Economic Priorities, London, circa 2001.
Noble, Trevor. *Social Theory and Social Change*. New York: St. Martin's Press, 2000.
Ohio Citizen Action. "Background on WTI." Last modified December 31, 2011, http://www.ohiocitizen.org/campaigns/wti/background.html.
Oliver, Pamela, and Hank Johnston. "What a Good Idea! Frames and Ideologies in Social Movement Research." In *Frames of Protest: Social Movements and the Framing Perspective* edited by Hank Johnston and John A. Noakes. Maryland: Rowman and Littlefield, 2005.
"Oren News—What the Papers Say!" Otway Ranges Environment Network Inc. Accessed June 23, 2006, http://www.oren.org.au/archives/otwhatpaper.htm.
OREN, (2001), *Otway Ranges Environment Network Newsletter No. 8*, September 2001, 1.
OREN Timber Industry Double Talk n.d. Accessed April 8, 2012, http://www.oren.org.au/archives/inf_2tlk.
O'Reilly, Tim. *What Is Web 2.0 Design Patterns and Business Models for the Next Generation of Software*. 09/30/2005. Accessed October 24, 2012. http://oreilly.com/web2/archive/what-is-web-20.html
Otway Ranges Environment Network, Inc. "Forestry Victoria research and information suppression," n.d.(a). Accessed November 29, 2004, http://www.oren.org.au/logging/who/FVsupress.htm.
Otway Ranges Environment Network, Inc. "Otway Native Forests 'Woodchip Free' since 2008" n.d.(b). Accessed August 8 2012, http://www.oren.org.au.

Otway Ranges Environment Network, Inc. "What Is Clearfell Logging?," 2002. Accessed November 29, 2004, http://www.oren.org.au/logging/clearfell.htm/
Pakulski, Jan. *Social Movements the Politics of Moral Protest*. Melbourne: Longman Cheshire, 1991.
Parker, Ian. *Discourse Dynamics: Critical Analysis for Social and Individual Psychology*. London: Routledge, 1992.
Peacock, Matt, and Australian Broadcasting Corporation. *Killer Company : [James Hardie Exposed]*. Sydney; New York: ABC Books/HarperCollins Publishers, 2009.
Pescott, Trevor. *The Otway Ranges*. Belmont: Yaugher Print, 1998.
Philogène, Gina. "From Race to Culture: The Emergence of African American." In *Representations of the Social*, edited by Kay Deaux and Gina Philogène, 113–128. Oxford: Blackwell, 2001.
Pieczka, Magda, and Jacquie L'Etang. "Public Relations and the Question of Professionalism." In *Public Relations Critical Debates and Contemporary Practice* edited by Jacquie L'Etang and Magda Pieczka, 265–78. Mahwah, NJ: Lawrence Erlbaum Associates, 2006.
Pixley, Jocelyn. "Economic Citizenship." In *Rethinking Australian Citizenship*, edited by Wayne Hudson and John Kane, 121–135. Cambridge: Cambridge University Press, 2000.
Poehland, Sally. "Doubt over Power Plant Objectors Claim Company has Hit Financial Troubles," *Geelong Independent*, February 22, 2002, 7.
"Power To The People," *The Age* November 22, 1998, 24.
Public Relations Institute of Australia. "Half Day Workshop: ACTIVISTS: How to Beat Them at Their Own Game." South Melbourne, Victoria: Public Relations Institute of Australia, 2005.
Public Relations Society of America. "Industry Facts & Figures: Industry Size and Growth, " n.d. Accessed August 6, 2012, http://media.prsa.org/prsa+overview/industry+facts+figures/.
Rakow, Lana, and Diana Nastasia. "On Feminist Theory of Public Relations: An Example from Dorothy E. Smith." In *Public Relations and Social Theory*, edited by Øyvind Ihlen, Betteke Van Ruler and Magnus Fredriksson, 252–277. New York: Routledge 2009.
Rattray Taylor, Gordon. *The Doomsday Book* London: Thames and Hudson, 1970.
Rawls, John. *Political Liberalism*. New York: Columbia University Press, 1993.
Rembert, Tracey C. "Terri Swearingen, the Long War with WTI." In *E/The Environmental Magazine*. 1997. Accessed August 8, 2012, http://www.ohiocitizen.org/campaigns/wti/1197conversations.html
Roche, Michael, "Vale Lindsay Poole (1908–2008)." In *Australian Forest History Society Inc.*, Newsletter No. 48 January 2008, 3.
Roper, Juliet. "Government, Corporate or Social Power? The Internet as a Tool in the Struggle for Dominance in Public Policy." *Journal of Public Affairs* 2, no. 3 (2002): 113–124.
Ruiz, Carmelo. *Burson-Marsteller: PR for the New World Order*. Accessed October 29, 2012. http://home.intekom.com/tm_info/ge_bm.htm
Ryan, Charlotte. *Prime Time Activism Media Strategies for Grassroots Organizing*. Boston: South End Press, 1991.
Salmon, Charles T., ed. *Information Campaigns: Balancing Social Values and Social Change*. Newbury Park, CA: Sage, 1989.
Schudson, Michael and C. W. Anderson. "Objectivity, Professionalism and Truth Seeking in Journalism." In *The Handbook of Journalism Studies*, edited by Karin Wahl-Jorgensen and Thomas Hanitzsch, 88–101. New York and London, Routledge: 2009.
Seitel, Fraser P. *The Practice of Public Relations*. New Jersey: Prentice Hall, 1998.

Shevory, Thomas. *Toxic Burn: The Grassroots Struggle against the WTI Incinerator* Minneapolis: University of Minnesota Press, 2007.

Siry, Darryl, August 10, 2010, (11:44 AM) Guest Post, "What's Wrong with Public Relations?" *VB*. Accessed August 6, 2012.

Smith, Martin J. *Pressure Power and Policy, State Autonomy and Policy Networks in Britain and the United States*. Pittsburgh, PA: University of Pittsburgh Press, 1993.

Smith, Michael F. and Denise P. Ferguson. "Activism." In *Handbook of Public Relations*, edited by Robert L. Heath, 291–300. Thousand Oaks, CA: Sage, 2001.

Stauber, John C. and Sheldon Rampton. *Toxic Sludge is Good for You: Lies, Damn Lies, and the Public Relations Industry*. Monroe, ME: Common Courage Press, 1995.

Strangio, Paul. *No Toxic Dump! A Triumph for Grassroots Democracy and Environmental Justice*. Annandale NSW: Pluto Press Australia Limited, 2001.

Strong, Geoff. "The Gentle Art of Defeating a Giant," *The Age*, November 21, 1998, 10.

Surma, Anne. "Challenging Unreliable Narrators: Writing and Public Relations." In *Public Relations Critical Debates and Contemporary Practice*, edited by Jacquie L'Etang and Magda Pieczka, 41–60. Mahwah, NJ: Lawrence Erlbaum Associates, 2006.

Tarbell, Ida M. "The History of the Standard Oil Company: The Oil War of 1872." In *The Muckrakers: The Era in Journalism That Moved America to Reform: The Most Significant Magazine Articles of 1902–1912.*, edited by Arthur M. Weinberg and Lila Weinberg, 22–39. New York: Capricorn Books, [1961] 2001.

Tench, Ralph, and Liz Yeomans. *Exploring Public Relations*. 2nd ed. Harlow: FT Prentice Hall, 2009.

Thomas, Terry and Bill Eyers. "Why an Ethical Business is not an Altruistic Business." *Visions of Ethical Business*. vol. 1 (1998): 10–13. London: Financial Times Managementin association with PriceWaterhouseCoopers and Council for Economic Priorities.

Threadgold, Terry. *Halliday's Language as a Social Semiotic: Forgotten Issues and Necessary Directions*. Geelong: Deakin University, 1993.

Thwaites, John., 8.05 am 2/1/2002, *Interview with Acting Premier John Thwaites Talkback Caller Comments,* in Rehame Transcript, 9.

Tilson, Donn James, and Emmanuel C. Alozie. 2004. *Toward the Common Good: Perspectives in International Public Relations*. Boston: Pearson, 2004.

Timber Communities Australia. "Timber Communities Australia Exposed," 2002. Accessed September 28, 2012, http://www.oren.org.au/logging/who/tca.htm 17/05/2007.

"Top 5 PR Picks." *PR Week*, March 30, 2012, p. 23.

Turner, Bryan S. "Outline of a Theory of Human Rights." In *Citizenship and Social Theory*, edited by Bryan S. Turner, 162–190. London: Sage, 1994a.

Turner, Bryan S., ed. *Citizenship and Social Theory*. London: Sage, 1994b.

Tweedale, Geoffrey, and Jock McCulloch. "Fighting Back: Victims' Action Groups and the Ban Asbestos Movement." Review written for the International Ban Asbestos Secretariat. Available at <http://www.ibasecretariat.org/gt-jmc-fighting-back-action-groups-ban-asbestos-movement.pdf> 7, 2011. Accessed 30 October 2012.

Urry, John. "Introduction." In *Conversations with Ulrich Beck*, edited by Ulrich Beck and Johannes Willms, 1–10, 2004.

van Moorst, Harry. The Proposed Werribee Toxic Dump and the failure of government, in Shaw, Kate. (ed.), *Planning Practice 1998, The Best And Worst Examples of City Planning and Development*, People's Committee for Melbourne, North Melbourne, 1998, 26–34.

van Moorst, Harry. Interview with the author, Geelong. November 18 2004.
Vandenberg, Andrew. "Contesting Citizenship and Democracy in a Global Era." In *Citizenship and Democracy in a Global Era*, edited by Andrew Vandenberg, 3–17. London: Macmillan, 2000.
Verrall, Derek. "Russia: Withdrawal to the Private Sphere." In *Citizenship and Democracy in a Global Era*, edited by Andrew Vandenberg, 188–201. London: Macmillan 2000.
Watson, Ian. *Fighting over the Forests*. Sydney Allen & Unwin, 1990.
Weaver, Kay, Judy Motion, and Juliet Roper. "From Propaganda to Discourse (and Back Again): Truth, Power, the Public Interest and Public Relations." In *Public Relations: Critical Debates and Contemporary Practice*, edited by Jacquie L'Etang and Magda Pieczka, 7–22. Mahwah, NJ: Lawrence Erlbaum Associates, 2006.
Weinberg, Arthur M., and Lila Weinberg, eds. *The Muckrakers: The Era in Journalism That Moved America to Reform—The Most Significant Magazine Articles of 1902–1912*. New York: Capricorn Books, [1961] 2001.
Wilcox, Dennis L., Phillip H. Ault, Warren Kendall Agee, and Glen T. Cameron. *Public Relations Strategies and Tactics*. New York: Longman, 2000.
World Trade Organization. "The WTO . . . . . . In Brief." 2012. Accessed October 29, 2012. http://www.wto.org/english/thewto_e/whatis_e/inbrief_e/inbr00_e.htm.
Wragg, George. *The Asbestos Time Bomb*. Annadale: Catalyst Press 1995.
Yeatman, Anna. *Activism and the Policy Process*. St. Leonards, NSW: Allen & Unwin, 1998.

Index

2,4,5-T herbicide 38
2,4-D herbicide 38

A
AA1000 Assurance Standard 97
Abbott, Jennifer 9, 161
Abercrombie, Nicholas 42, 97, 139, 161
Aboriginal land rights 47
abortion groups (anti) 35
abortion groups (pro) 35
AccountAbility 1000 Framework 97
Achbar, Michael 9, 161
activism
  and CSR 98–99
  as discourse 4, 6, 29, 157
  environmental 37–40, 62, 64, 68–76, 86, 87, 103–127, 151
  forms of 34–36
  general 2, 4, 7, 8, 20, 22–26, 30, 32–54, 78, 79, 84, 87, 94, 95, 98–100, 129, 137–142, 155
  grassroots 2, 6, 41, 42, 78, 79, 100, 102–128, 130–138, 142, 146, 147
  green 36–40
  guerrilla 39
  interest-based 35
  issue-based 35, 36
  media's social representation of 50–53; see also: social movements 33–36
  political 147
  relationship to public relations 1, 5–7, 15, 21, 22, 24–26, 36, 42, 45–48, 55–77, 87, 89, 102, 128–130, 140, 147–149, 155–157
  relationship to social change 7
  social 7
  and information technology 40, 41

  universalist form of 36
activists 1, 2, 4–6, 8, 10, 15, 17–19, 21–26, 30–35, 37–47, 49–56, 58, 60–65
advertising 9, 13, 17, 28, 31, 106, 107, 125, 155
AES Power One (AESPO) 110–117, 161
Agee, Warren Kendall 170
agency 5, 8, 14, 15, 28, 30, 33, 41, 43, 19, 53, 99, 101, 143, 146, 154, 157
Alford John, & Deirdre O'Neill, 105
Alinsky Saul 38, 39, 161
Alozie, Emmanuel C. 26, 170
American Cancer Society 74
American Textiles Institute 59
Amnesty International 36
Andersen, Robin 16, 161
Anderson, Leslie 72, 161
Andriof, Jörg 94, 142, 161
animal liberationists 36
anti-nuclear 40
  groups 40
Asbestos Disease Society of Western Australia 60
Asbestos Information Committee 72
Asbestos International Association 57
asbestosis 58
astroturfing 70
audience 10, 11, 15, 24, 27, 95, 143, 154
Ault, Phillip H. 171
Australian Asbestos Network 60
Australian Labor Party 37, 103, 109, 114, 122, 126, 133
authenticity 3

B
Baird, Oliver 110, 111, 161

174 Index

Batesford Action Group Steering Committee 111, 161
Batesford and Geelong Action Group (BAGAG) 102, 103, 109–117, 127, 130–138, 142, 146, 147, 150, 152–157
Battle for Seattle 75
Baudrillard, Jean 21, 161
Bauman, Zygmunt 142, 143, 161
Beck, Ulrich 4, 24, 30, 44, 47, 76, 77, 79–87, 90, 100, 102, 128, 129, 131, 132, 134–139, 141–146, 149, 151–153, 156, 162, 170
Beder, Sharon 30, 74, 138, 162
Bernays, Edward 10, 20, 27, 70, 71, 79, 128, 148, 162
Bhopal, India 85
Bianchini, Franco 91, 93, 162
Birch, David 94, 142, 162
Birrell, Simon ix, 117, 118, 121–127, 162
Bliss, Tamara J. 97, 98, 162
Bloomfield, Jude 162
boilermakerstatements 51
boomerangeffect 85
Bottomore, Tom 4, 50, 90, 91, 162, 167
boundary riders (public relations practitioners as) 29, 30
Box, Gavin 116, 162
Boycott Woodchipping Campaign Victoria 121
Bracks, Steve 109, 111, 122, 126, 127
Breit, Rhonda ix, 8, 26, 28, 89, 130, 140, 157, 162
Broom, Glen M. 20, 21, 26, 163
Brown, Kevin 68
Brown, Rob 154, 162
Buffardi, Laura E. 154, 162
Burgmann, Verity 34–36, 43, 46, 47, 131, 162
Burson-Marsteller (BM) 74, 75, 78, 87, 162, 169
Burton, Bob 67–70, 165

C

Cameron, Glen T. 171
Campbell, Keith W. 154, 162
Cape Asbestos 57
Carson, Rachel 37, 38, 81, 162
Carter, April 79, 89–91, 93, 94, 100, 162
Castells, Manuel 35, 39–41, 143, 154, 163

Center, Allen H. 20–22, 26, 163
Cerrell Associates, Inc. 62, 63, 65, 72, 163
Chandler, Daniel. 30, 124, 125, 163
chemical industry 37, 38
Cheney, George 26, 163
Chomsky, Noam 9–11
Christians, Clifford G. 5, 89, 90, 100, 130, 132, 134–136, 161, 163
Christiansen, Lars T. 163
Chrysler Corporation 25, 163
citizen initiative groups 84
citizenship 4, 27, 42, 89–92, 130
    active 10, 92, 93, 132, 140, 154, 156
    corporate 46, 78, 96
    differential 93, 94, 140, 154
    global 86
    passive 10, 27, 92, 93
    theory 4, 5, 79, 98, 100
civil disobedience 39, 50, 135
civil society (sectors), 10, 15, 25, 33, 34, 140, 141
Clamshell Alliance 22
clearfell logging 119, 136
Climate Commission Secretariat 3, 158 163
Coalition government, Australia (federal) 37
Cobb, Chris 25, 163
Cohen, Anthony 163, 165
Coleman Gail 167
communist nation states 84
communitarianism, 92, 95
community (thick) 92, 93, 133, 155
communities (thin) 92, 93, 155
Community Picket Line (CPL) 115, 116
consumer awareness campaigns 121, 122
Coombs, W. Timothy 7, 11, 12, 15, 20, 21, 26, 27, 31, 157, 163
co-optation 20, 77
Corporate social responsibility (CSR) 42, 43, 44, 94–98
countervailing groups 21
Crane, Diana 145, 163
Crawford, Robert 11, 167
CSR (originally Colonial Sugar Refinery) 103–109, 132, 153
cultural impoverishment 137
Cunningham, Mary Ann 163
Cunningham, William P. 163
Cutlip, Scott M. 20–22, 26, 163

D

Dalton, Alan 60
Dann, Christine 67, 163
Daymon, Christine ix, 11, 25, 27, 157, 163
DDT 38
Deacon, David 10, 11, 29, 151, 163
Deaux, Kay 168
Deegan, Denise 24, 26, 41, 80, 87, 163
Deep Ecology 39
deliberative democracy 100, 117, 142
Demetrious, Kristin 8, 28, 31, 42, 131, 139, 144, 155, 162–164
demographic profile 63
Dent, Sarah 106–108, 164
discourse 4, 8, 21, 28–31, 51, 52, 61, 96, 124, 125, 135, 136, 138, 140–142, 155
  definitions of 29
Dowers, Graeme 113, 151, 164
Doyle, Timothy 37, 39, 40, 164
Dozier, David M. 26, 164
Durkheim, Émile 33, 43, 47–50, 53, 135, 139, 142, 164
Dutta, Mohan J. 8, 20, 77, 164
Dynes, Peter 123

E

Earth First! 39
East Europe 84
East Liverpool, Ohio 56, 62, 63, 66
ecotage 39
Edmonds, Mike 150, 164
Edwards, Lee 26, 31, 157, 163, 164
Endacott, Norman 122, 123, 164
Engels, Friedrich 33, 43–48, 82, 86
ENRON 116
Environment Protection Authority Victoria (EPA) 110, 111, 113, 114
Eric White Associates (EWA) 72
Erickson, Brad 33, 164
Esteva, Gustavo 41, 164
Eyers, Bill 98, 170

F

Facebook 154, 155
Facey, George A. 118, 164
Fairclough, Norman 4, 28–30, 51, 53, 140, 164
Ferguson, Denise P. 26, 170
Fitch, Kate 157
Foucault, Michel 3, 4, 29–32, 34, 52, 125, 131, 132, 136, 138, 141, 158, 164

framing 50, 52, 53
Fredriksson, Magnus 31, 157, 166, 169
Freeman, R. Edward 43, 95, 96, 98, 164
functionalism 10, 15, 21, 26, 31, 94

G

Galston, William A. 21, 165
Gandhi, Mahatma 90
Gardner, Ashley 110, 165
gatekeeper (media) 23, 40
gay rights 47
Geelong Environment Council 119
Giddens, Anthony 4, 35, 44, 85, 86, 90, 91, 100, 140, 142, 147, 154, 162, 165
Global Alliance 8
Global Compact 97
Global Project 41
globalisation, 44, 143, 144
globalism 143, 144
Golding, Peter 163
Gore, Al 66, 164, 165
grasstops communication 74
Greenpeace 36
greenwashing 42, 65, 69, 73, 106
Greenwood, Michelle R. 43, 94–98, 142, 165
Grunig, James E. 15, 22, 23, 26, 27, 30, 70, 78–80, 92, 96, 131, 148, 165
Grunig, Larissa A. 24, 165
Grunigian paradigm 12
Guide to Seattle Meltdown 75

H

Habermas, Jürgen 16–18, 20, 26, 27, 31, 40, 50–52, 79, 88–90, 100, 130, 132–134, 136–141, 153–165
Hager, Nicky 56, 67–70, 165
Haigh, Gideon 57, 165
Hamilton, Peter 41, 165
Harrison, John 70, 165
Heath, Robert L. 24–26, 163, 165
hegemony
  and activism 146
  and "common sense" 151, 155
  counter-hegemonic 124
  and cultural discourses 156
  hegemonic acceptance 65
  hegemonic control 20
  and philanthropy 20
  and power of the PR industry 73
  and social obligation of workers 91

and "truths" 53
Hendrix, Jerry A. 20–22, 26, 165
Heywood, Andrew 39, 166
Hill & Knowlton 72, 73
Hill, Stephen 42, 97, 139, 161
Hills, Ben 57, 58, 60, 166
Hindess, Barry 91, 165
Hodges, Caroline 157, 163
Hodgson, Shelley 111, 166
Holladay, Sherry 7, 11, 12, 15, 20, 21, 26, 27, 31, 157, 163
Holloway, Immy 11, 25, 27, 163
Holtzhausen, Derina R. 26, 166
Hooker Chemical 73
Horton, James L. 22, 166
Hosking, Patrick 104, 166
Howard, John 37
Hudson, Wayne 4, 79, 91, 93, 94, 100, 132, 136, 140, 154, 166, 169
Hughes, Patrick ix, 8, 164
Hunt, Todd 15, 22, 23, 30, 70, 80, 131, 148, 165

I
ideology 51, 53
Ihlen, Øyvind 31, 166, 169
Independent Media Centre 74
individualisation 144–149
individualism *in genre* 48
Indymedia 42
intertexuality 51
Irvine, Ross 25

J
James Hardie 55–62, 71, 72, 77, 161, 164–166, 169
John, Steve 166
Johns Manville Corporation 57, 72
Johnston, Hank 51, 168
Johnstone, Kate 116, 117, 133, 166
Jones, Evan 97, 98, 166
Jones, Keith 167
journalism 9, 20, 23, 24

K
Kane, John 4, 10, 79, 91–94, 100, 132, 133, 140, 150, 155, 166
Kelly, Jen 150, 164
Kelly-Turner, Sue 115
Kennett, Jeff 105, 106, 108–110, 115, 116, 128, 153
key messages 51, 68
Kimberly-Clark 119–121, 125
King, Martin Luther 90
Kitchen, Philip J. 26, 166
Kleenex 120, 121, 162
Kontelj, Stretch 114, 116, 166

L
L' Etang, Jacquie 8, 26, 28, 31, 157, 167, 169–171
Labor government, Australia (*See* Australian Labor Party) 37
Labor Party, Australia (*See* Australian Labor Party) 103
laboratory science 83, 137
Lane, Terry 105, 166
Lapierre, Dominique 85, 167
Lash, Scott 162
Lauzen Martha M. 26, 164
Lee, Ivy 18
Lees, Rue ix, 119–121, 167
left and right politics 84, 145, 146
Leipziger, Deborah 97, 98, 167
Leitch, Shirley 26, 31, 157, 167, 168
Liberal and national party coalition state government (coalition) 102, 103, 105, 109, 110, 126
Liberal Party, Australia 105, 114, 116, 126
lifeworld 18, 27, 40, 65, 88, 134, 139
Lindlof, Thomas R. 11, 167
Lippmann, Walter 10, 13, 14, 167
Lorimer, Graeme 113, 114, 167
Love Canal 73
Lupton, Deborah 85, 86, 167
Lygo, Iain ix, 112–114, 167
Lyons, Mark 10, 37, 92, 94, 95, 142, 167

M
Macdonell, Diane 29, 167
MacFarlane, D. K. 72, 161
Macnamara, Jim R. 11, 167
Magee, Kate 155, 167
Maltby, David 103, 104
Marks, Deborah 91, 93, 167
Marshall, T. H. 4, 79, 90, 91, 94, 100, 162
Marx, Karl 33, 43–48, 52, 53, 82, 86, 131, 135
mass mobilisation 36
materialism/materialistic backgrounds 38
Mayne, Nicole 114, 116, 117, 167
McCallum, Stuart ix, 111, 113–115, 167
McCann, Karen 115, 116, 167

McCulloch, Jock 55, 59–61, 167
McElreath, Mark P. 15, 20, 79, 80, 87, 89, 167
McIntosh, Malcolm 43, 94, 96, 98, 142, 161
McKie, David 11, 157, 167
McLellan, D. 43–46, 131, 168
McLure, Daryl 122, 123, 168
Meadows, Dennis L. 39, 168
Meadows, Donella H. 39, 168
Médecins Sans Frontieres (MSF) 36
media 1, 2, 3, 7, 8, 9, 10, 11, 16, 17, 18, 20, 25, 31, 34, 39, 50, 51, 52, 53, 54, 56, 59, 60, 69, 71, 72, 73, 75, 78, 79, 83, 84, 85, 88, 89, 99, 105, 106, 109, 113, 117, 124, 125, 131, 135, 137, 139, 143, 144, 150, 151, 155
  culture 6
  images 18
  literacy 12, 149
  power of 23, 40
  social 3, 130, 143, 144, 146, 147, 154, 155, 156, 157
  studies 4
media monitoring 69, 144
Miller, Claire 125, 136, 150, 168
Miller, Mark C. 13, 14, 168
Miller, Raymond. 163
Moloney, Kevin 11, 12, 26, 157, 168
Moro, Javier 85, 167
Moss, Danny 26, 168
Motion, Judy 10, 11, 26, 31, 157, 168, 171
Muckrakers 19, 20, 171
Mulder, Terry 114
Munshi Debashish 11, 167
Murdock, Graham 163
Murphy, Noel 116, 168

N

Nastasia, Diana 26, 31, 169
National Forest Action Committee (NFAC) 67
National Party (Australia) 102, 105
National Union of Students (NUS) 119
Neales, Sue 105, 168
Nelson, Joyce 30, 73, 138, 168
Nelson, Richard A. 24, 25, 165
neoliberalism
  and capitalism 146
  definition of 159
  discourses within globalisation and techno-economic changes 144
  and freedom 146
  and identity 147
  and relationship between public relations and activism 74
  and social media 147
Nestle 73
new social movements (NSM) 35 ff
New Zealand Forest Service (NZFS) 67
Newbold, Yve 98, 168
NIMBY (not-in-my-backyard) 61, 64, 105
Noakes, John A. 168
Noble, Trevor 43, 168
Non-governmental organisations (NGOs) 25, 36, 37, 87, 89, 100, 144

O

O'Brien, Jerry 115
O'Reilly, Tim 154, 168
Occupy Movement 155
Ogilvy & Mather Public Relations 73, 74
Ohio 62
Ohio Citizen Action 56, 64, 65, 168
Oliver, Pamela 51, 168
Otway Ranges Environment Network, Inc. (OREN) 103, 117–138, 142, 146, 147, 150, 152–157, 162, 168, 170
Owens, John 167
Oxfam 36

P

Pakulski, Jan 36, 43, 169
panopticon public relations, *see* public relations, panopticon
Parker, Ian 29, 169
peace movements 36
Peacock, Matt ix, 60–62, 71, 169
Peckham, Gardner G. 75, 76
people power 34
Pescott, Trevor 118, 119, 169
philanthropy 20
Philogène, Gina 52, 53, 169
Pickering, Michael 163
Pieczka, Magda 8, 26, 157, 169–171
Pixley, Jocelyn 50, 169
pluralism 12, 95, 99, 130, 131, 148, 165
  defined, 21
  and environmentalism, 37
  liberal 26, 95, 130, 164

and media power, 23
relationship to public relations,
    21–24, 26, 31, 44
Poehland, Sally 116, 169
population 38, 39
positivism, 10, 14, 151
Prakash, Madhu S. 41, 164
protonorms 90
public communication 5, 6, 129–158
public information 23
public opinion 4, 13, 15–17, 20, 27,
    31, 34, 38, 47–49, 51–53, 70,
    89, 90, 107, 130, 132, 138, 142,
    144, 153
public relations
  activist 155
  aim 2, 88, 95, 129
  and contradictions 15, 31, 130, 138
    intrinsic contradictions 29, 30, 76,
      130, 138, 141, 149, 155–157
    extrinsic contradictions 29–31,
      130, 138, 149, 156
    reflexive definition of public relations 31
  as discourse 4, 5
  education 138, 139, 141
  general 2–4, 7–32, 34, 36, 38–40,
    42, 43, 45–49, 51–77,
    78–82, 86–89, 93, 94, 98, 100
  and grassroots activism 1, 2,
    102–128
  panopticon 70–74, 156
  and possible obsolescence 83
  as propaganda, 12, 14
  as a quasi-intelligence unit 69
  relationship to activism 1, 5–7, 15,
    21, 22, 26, 36, 42, 43, 45,
    46, 49, 55–77, 86, 89, 102,
    129, 130, 140, 143, 147–149,
    155–157
  as "spin" 7, 9, 30, 42, 98, 112, 122,
    138, 141, 157
  and sustainable communication
    129–158
Public Relations Institute of Australia
  (PRIA) 8, 25, 26, 169
Public Relations Institute of New Zealand (PRINZ) 8, 70
Public Relations Society of America
  (PRSA) 22, 25, 163, 169
public sphere 16, 31, 50, 52, 69,
    88–90, 130, 132, 134, 137, 140,
    142, 148, 149, 153, 154, 155,
    165

publics
  active 92
  aware 27, 92
  digital 149
  environmental 22
  gendered 14
  latent 92
  marginalised 149
  reflexive 149
  scarcity society 149

R
Rakow, Lana 26, 31, 169
Rampton. Sheldon 30, 38, 138, 170
Randers, Jørgen 168
rationality 17, 18, 27, 82, 83, 86, 89,
    134, 135
  action 17, 27
  communicative 27
  system 17, 18, 27, 137, 140, 153
Rattray Taylor, Gordon 38, 169
Rawls, John 14, 169
reflexive modernisation 79, 82, 83, 88,
    99, 100, 102, 130, 131, 139,
    141, 156, 157, 162
Regional Forests Agreements (RFAs)
  136
Reid, Bob 106–108
Reid, Jock 57
relativism 90
Rembert, Tracey C. 64, 66, 169
risk communications 24, 34, 80
Roche, Michael 67, 169
Rockefeller John D., Senior 18–20
Roper, Juliet 10, 11, 26, 74, 75, 157,
    169, 171
Ruiz, Carmelo 78, 169
Ryan, Charlotte 23, 50, 75, 169

S
Salmon, Charles 35, 169
Save Albert Park (SAP) 105
Save Our Country 64, 66
Save the Otways 117, 119
Second Life 144
secondary groups, 47, 49
Seitel, Fraser P. 26, 169
Selikoff, Irving 59
Shandwick, international 74
Shandwick, New Zealand 67–70, 74
Shevory, Thomas ix, 62, 64–67, 170
Sierra Club 22
silent majority 30
Silent Spring, see Carson, Rachel

Siry, Darryl 9, 170
situation management 88
Situational Theory to Identify Publics 79, 80, 87, 148
Smith, Martin J. 21, 23, 95, 131, 170
Smith, Michael F. 26, 170
Social and environmental reporting (SER) 96, 97
social movements 33, 34, 36, 40, 41, 50, 76, 82–84, 86, 98, 99, 137, 156
  defined 34
  shape of 35
social change
  and civil disobedience 50
  contrast with co-optation 20
  and early industrialisation 44
  effecting/bringing about 6, 157
  individuals' capacity for agency in 49
  movement of 29
  notions of "truth" in relation to 52
  relationship to activism and activist groups 7, 15, 31, 33, 34, 36, 42, 43, 46, 47, 53, 84, 156
  relationship to discourse 28, 51
  relationship to intertextuality 51
  relationship to MSM (mass social movements) 36
  relationship to political action 47
  relationship to public relations 1, 2, 7, 15, 43, 46, 47, 55, 76, 87, 129, 156
  relationship with public, and public agency 2, 84, 157
  and technology 84, 90, 143
  understanding of 1
Social movements: mass social movements (MSMs) 36
  new social movements (NSMs) 35
  old social movements 35
social risk positions 85
society, risk 79–89, 91, 99, 100, 102, 128–131, 135, 137, 139–141, 143, 145, 147-153, 156, 157, 162
specieism 52
species extinction 38
stakeholder theory 95, 96, 97
Stauber, John C. 30, 38, 73, 138
Stevenson, Nick 162
stimulus-response models, 10, 11
Strangio, Paul 103, 106, 108–110, 133, 170

Strategic Lawsuit Against Public Participation (SLAPP) 66, 69, 156
Strong, Geoff 107, 170
Student Environmental Confederation 38
Students for a Better Environment 38
sub-political activity 84
Surma, Anne 26, 157, 170
surveillance 144
Sutherland Rahman, Sandra 161
sustainable capitalism 96
sustainable communication (*see* public communication)
Sutton, Philip W. 165
Swearingen, Terri 64, 66, 169
systems theory 84

T
Tait, Nancy 60
Tarbell, Ida M. 19, 20, 170
target publics 15, 95, 97, 151
Tench, Ralph 13, 170
Thomas, Terry 98, 170
Thomson, Stuart 34, 166
Threadgold, Terry 30, 170
Thwaites, John 111, 115, 116, 170
Tilson, Donn James 26, 170
Timberlands West Coast Ltd 56, 67–70, 77
Traber, Michael 132, 161, 163
trade unions 35, 45, 46, 61, 136
transmission (model of) communication 10, 11, 41, 143
Tri-State Environmental Council 64
truth, notions of 2, 3, 38, 42, 43, 50–54, 71, 90, 107, 131, 134–136
Turner & Newell 57
Turner, Bryan S. 4, 42, 50, 79, 91, 92, 94, 97, 100, 139, 161, 170
Turner, Janine 25
Tweedale, Geoffrey 59, 60, 170
Twitter 155

U
Union Carbide 85
United Steelworkers Union 62
universal ethical framework 90
Urry, John 159, 170
utilitarianism 93

V
van Moorst, Harry ix, 103–109, 170
Van Ruler, Betteke 31, 166, 168, 169

Vandenberg, Andrew 91, 166, 171
veganism 147
Velsicol Chemical Corporation 38
Verčič, Dejan 26, 168
Verrall, Derek 10, 171
Victoria University Environment Group (VEG) 69
vocal minority 30
Vojakovic, Robert 60
Von Roll America, Inc. 64, 65, 66
Voto, Rosina 26, 166

W

Waddock, Sandra 94, 161, 162
Warnaby, Gary 26, 168
Waste Technology Industries Inc 62–67, 77
Waste-to-Energy 63, 65, 72
Watson, Ian 39, 171
Weaver, Kay ix, 10, 11, 26, 157, 171
Web 2.0 154, 157
Weinberg, Arthur M. 19, 20, 170, 171
Weinberg, Lila 19, 20, 170, 171
Whitehead, Adrian 136
Wilcox, Dennis L. 20–22, 26, 171
Willms, Johannes 4, 90, 144, 146, 152, 162, 170
Wittenoom, Western Australia 58, 60
Workers' rights 35, 87
World Assembly of Public Relations 21, 22
World Trade Organisation (WTO) 74, 75, 171
world views (religious-metaphysical) 18
World War II 38
World Wildlife Fund (WWF) 37
Wragg, George 61, 171
WRATD (Werribee Residents Against Toxic Dump) 102–109, 127, 130–138, 142, 146, 147, 152–157

Y

Yeatman, Anna 34, 171
Yeomans, Liz 13, 170
youth culture 38, 39, 40

Printed in Great Britain
by Amazon